THE HAMPTON ROADS CONFERENCE

∞§ THE LOCHLAINN SEABROOK COLLECTION §∞

AMERICAN CIVIL WAR
Abraham Lincoln Was a Liberal, Jefferson Davis Was a Conservative: The Missing Key to Understanding the American Civil War
Confederacy 101: Amazing Facts You Never Knew About America's Oldest Political Tradition
Confederate Blood and Treasure: An Interview With Lochlainn Seabrook
Everything You Were Taught About African-Americans and the Civil War is Wrong, Ask a Southerner!
Everything You Were Taught About the Civil War is Wrong, Ask a Southerner!
Give This Book to a Yankee! A Southern Guide to the Civil War For Northerners
Heroes of the Southern Confederacy: The Illustrated Book of Confederate Officials, Soldiers, and Civilians
Lincoln's War: The Real Cause, the Real Winner, the Real Loser
Seabrook's Complete Battle Book: War Between the States, 1861-1865
The Great Yankee Coverup: What the North Doesn't Want You to Know About Lincoln's War!
The Hampton Roads Conference: The Southern View
The Ultimate Civil War Quiz Book: How Much Do You Really Know About America's Most Misunderstood Conflict?
Women in Gray: A Tribute to the Ladies Who Supported the Southern Confederacy

CONFEDERATE MONUMENTS
Confederate Monuments: Why Every American Should Honor Confederate Soldiers and Their Memorials

CONFEDERATE FLAG
Confederate Flag Facts: What Every American Should Know About Dixie's Southern Cross
What the Confederate Flag Means to Me: Americans Speak Out in Defense of Southern Honor, Heritage, and History

SECESSION
All We Ask Is To Be Let Alone: The Southern Secession Fact Book

RECONSTRUCTION
Twelve Years in Hell: Victorian Southerners Debunk the Myth of Reconstruction, 1865-1877

SLAVERY
Everything You Were Taught About American Slavery is Wrong, Ask a Southerner!
Slavery 101: Amazing Facts You Never Knew About America's "Peculiar Institution"
The Bittersweet Bond: Race Relations in the Old South as Described by White and Black Southerners

NATHAN BEDFORD FORREST
A Rebel Born: A Defense of Nathan Bedford Forrest - Confederate General, American Legend (winner of the 2011 Jefferson Davis Historical Gold Medal)
A Rebel Born: The Screenplay (film about N. B. Forrest)
Forrest! 99 Reasons to Love Nathan Bedford Forrest
Give 'Em Hell Boys! The Complete Military Correspondence of Nathan Bedford Forrest
I Rode With Forrest! Confederate Soldiers Who Served With the World's Greatest Cavalry Leader
Nathan Bedford Forrest and African-Americans: Yankee Myth, Confederate Fact
Nathan Bedford Forrest and the Battle of Fort Pillow: Yankee Myth, Confederate Fact
Nathan Bedford Forrest and the Ku Klux Klan: Yankee Myth, Confederate Fact
Nathan Bedford Forrest: Southern Hero, American Patriot - Honoring a Confederate Icon and the Old South
Saddle, Sword, and Gun: A Biography of Nathan Bedford Forrest For Teens
The God of War: Nathan Bedford Forrest As He Was Seen By His Contemporaries
The Quotable Nathan Bedford Forrest: Selections From the Writings and Speeches of the Confederacy's Most Brilliant Cavalryman

QUOTABLE SERIES
The Alexander H. Stephens Reader: Excerpts From the Works of a Confederate Founding Father
The Quotable Alexander H. Stephens: Selections From the Writings and Speeches of the Confederacy's First Vice President
The Quotable Jefferson Davis: Selections From the Writings and Speeches of the Confederacy's First President
The Quotable Nathan Bedford Forrest: Selections From the Writings and Speeches of the Confederacy's Most Brilliant Cavalryman
The Quotable Robert E. Lee: Selections From the Writings and Speeches of the South's Most Beloved Civil War General
The Quotable Stonewall Jackson: Selections From the Writings and Speeches of the South's Most Famous General
The Unquotable Abraham Lincoln: The President's Quotes They Don't Want You To Know!

CIVIL WAR BATTLES
Encyclopedia of the Battle of Franklin - A Comprehensive Guide to the Conflict that Changed the Civil War
Nathan Bedford Forrest and the Battle of Fort Pillow: Yankee Myth, Confederate Fact
Seabrook's Complete Battle Book: War Between the States, 1861-1865
The Battle of Franklin: Recollections of Confederate and Union Soldiers
The Battle of Nashville: Recollections of Confederate and Union Soldiers
The Battle of Spring Hill: Recollections of Confederate and Union Soldiers

CONSTITUTIONAL HISTORY
America's Three Constitutions: Complete Texts of the Articles of Confederation, Constitution of the United States of America, and Constitution of the Confederate States of America
The Articles of Confederation Explained: A Clause-by-Clause Study of America's First Constitution
The Constitution of the Confederate States of America Explained: A Clause-by-Clause Study of the South's Magna Carta

CHILDREN
Honest Jeff and Dishonest Abe: A Southern Children's Guide to the Civil War
Saddle, Sword, and Gun: A Biography of Nathan Bedford Forrest For Teens

VICTORIAN CONFEDERATE LITERATURE
I, Confederate: Why Dixie Seceded and Fought in the Words of Southern Soldiers
Rise Up and Call Them Blessed: Victorian Tributes to the Confederate Soldier, 1861-1901
Support Your Local Confederate: Wit and Humor in the Southern Confederacy
The Bittersweet Bond: Race Relations in the Old South as Described by White and Black Southerners
The God of War: Nathan Bedford Forrest As He Was Seen By His Contemporaries
The Old Rebel: Robert E. Lee As He Was Seen By His Contemporaries
Victorian Confederate Poetry: The Southern Cause in Verse, 1861-1901

ABRAHAM LINCOLN
Abraham Lincoln: The Southern View - Demythologizing America's Sixteenth President
Lincolnology: The Real Abraham Lincoln Revealed in His Own Words - A Study of Lincoln's Suppressed, Misinterpreted, and Forgotten Writings and Speeches
Lincoln's War: The Real Cause, the Real Winner, the Real Loser
The Great Impersonator! 99 Reasons to Dislike Abraham Lincoln
The Unholy Crusade: Lincoln's Legacy of Destruction in the American South
The Unquotable Abraham Lincoln: The President's Quotes They Don't Want You To Know!

NATURAL HISTORY
North America's Amazing Mammals: An Encyclopedia for the Whole Family
The Concise Book of Owls: A Guide to Nature's Most Mysterious Birds
The Concise Book of Tigers: A Guide to Nature's Most Remarkable Cats

PARANORMAL
Carnton Plantation Ghost Stories: True Tales of the Unexplained from Tennessee's Most Haunted Civil War House!
UFOs and Aliens: The Complete Guidebook

FAMILY HISTORIES
The Blakeneys: An Etymological, Ethnological, and Genealogical Study - Uncovering the Mysterious Origins of the Blakeney Family and Name
The Caudills: An Etymological, Ethnological, and Genealogical Study - Exploring the Name and National Origins of a European-American Family
The McGavocks of Carnton Plantation: A Southern History - Celebrating One of Dixie's Most Noble Confederate Families and Their Tennessee Home

MIND, BODY, SPIRIT
Autobiography of a Non-Yogi: A Scientist's Journey From Hinduism to Christianity (Dr. Amitava Dasgupta, with Lochlainn Seabrook)
Britannia Rules: Goddess-Worship in Ancient Anglo-Celtic Society - An Academic Look at the United Kingdom's Matricentric Spiritual Past
Christ Is All and In All: Rediscovering Your Divine Nature and the Kingdom Within
Christmas Before Christianity: How the Birthday of the "Sun" Became the Birthday of the "Son"
Jesus and the Gospel of Q: Christ's Pre-Christian Teachings As Recorded in the New Testament
Jesus and the Law of Attraction: The Bible-Based Guide to Creating Perfect Health, Wealth, and Happiness Following Christ's Simple Formula
Seabrook's Bible Dictionary of Traditional and Mystical Christian Doctrines
Sea Raven Press Blank Page Journal: For Reflections, Notes, and Sketches
Secrets of Celebrity Surnames: An Onomastic Dictionary of Famous People
The Bible and the Law of Attraction: 99 Teachings of Jesus, the Apostles, and the Prophets
The Book of Kelle: An Introduction to Goddess-Worship and the Great Celtic Mother-Goddess Kelle, Original Blessed Lady of Ireland
The Goddess Dictionary of Words and Phrases: Introducing a New Core Vocabulary for the Women's Spirituality Movement
The Martian Anomalies: A Photographic Search for Intelligent Life on Mars
Victorian Hernia Cures: Nonsurgical Self-Treatment of Inguinal Hernia
Vintage Southern Cookbook: 2,000 Delicious Dishes From Dixie

WOMEN
Aphrodite's Trade: The Hidden History of Prostitution Unveiled
Princess Diana: Modern Day Moon-Goddess - A Psychoanalytical and Mythological Look at Diana Spencer's Life, Marriage, and Death (with Dr. Jane Goldberg)
Women in Gray: A Tribute to the Ladies Who Supported the Southern Confederacy

REPRINTS
A Short History of the Confederate States of America (author Jefferson Davis; editor Lochlainn Seabrook)
Prison Life of Jefferson Davis (author John J. Craven; editor Lochlainn Seabrook)
Life of Beethoven (author Ludwig Nohl; editor Lochlainn Seabrook)
The New Revelation (author Arthur Conan Doyle; editor Lochlainn Seabrook)
The Rise and Fall of the Confederate Government (author Jefferson Davis; editor Lochlainn Seabrook)

Lochlainn Seabrook does not author books for fame and glory, but for the love of writing and sharing his knowledge.

SeaRavenPress.com

THE HAMPTON ROADS CONFERENCE

The Southern View

CONCEIVED, COLLECTED, EDITED, & ARRANGED, WITH AN INTRODUCTION BY THE AUTHOR, "THE VOICE OF THE TRADITIONAL SOUTH," COLONEL

LOCHLAINN SEABROOK
JEFFERSON DAVIS HISTORICAL GOLD MEDAL WINNER

Diligently Researched and Generously Illustrated by the Author for the Elucidation of the Reader

2024

Sea Raven Press, Park County, Wyoming, USA

THE HAMPTON ROADS CONFERENCE

Published by
Sea Raven Press, Cassidy Ravensdale, President
Park County, Wyoming, USA
SeaRavenPress.com

Copyright © all text and illustrations Lochlainn Seabrook 2024
in accordance with U.S. and international copyright laws and regulations, as stated and protected under the Berne Union for the Protection of Literary and Artistic Property (Berne Convention), and the Universal Copyright Convention (the UCC). All rights reserved under the Pan-American and International Copyright Conventions.

PRINTING HISTORY
1st SRP paperback edition, 1st printing, January 2024 • ISBN: 978-1-955351-34-8
1st SRP hardcover edition, 1st printing, January 2024 • ISBN: 978-1-955351-35-5

ISBN: 978-1-955351-34-8 (paperback)
Library of Congress Control Number: 2024930024

This work is the copyrighted intellectual property of Lochlainn Seabrook and has been registered with the Copyright Office at the Library of Congress in Washington, D.C., USA. No part of this work (including text, covers, drawings, photos, illustrations, maps, images, diagrams, etc.), in whole or in part, may be used, reproduced, stored in a retrieval system, or transmitted, in any form or by any means now known or hereafter invented, without written permission from the publisher. The sale, duplication, hire, lending, copying, digitalization, or reproduction of this material, in any manner or form whatsoever, is also prohibited, and is a violation of federal, civil, and digital copyright law, which provides severe civil and criminal penalties for any violations.

The Hampton Roads Conference: The Southern View, by Lochlainn Seabrook. Includes an introduction, illustrations, index, endnotes, appendices, and bibliography.

ARTWORK
Front and back cover design and art, book design, layout, font selection, and interior art by Lochlainn Seabrook
All images, image captions, graphic design, and graphic art copyright © Lochlainn Seabrook
All images selected, placed, manipulated, cleaned, colored, tinted, and/or created by Lochlainn Seabrook
Title page soldier image from Lochlainn Seabrook's book, *Heroes of the Southern Confederacy*
Cover image: Vessels at Anchor, Hampton Roads, as seen from Old Point Comfort, Virginia; lithograph, 1862

All persons who approve of the authority and principles of Colonel Lochlainn Seabrook's literary work, and realize its benefits as a means of reeducating the world about facts left out of mainstream books, are hereby requested to avidly recommend his titles to others and to vigorously cooperate in extending their reach, scope, and influence around the globe.

The views documented in this book concerning the War for Southern Independence are those of the publisher.
WRITTEN, DESIGNED, PUBLISHED, PRINTED, & MANUFACTURED IN THE UNITED STATES OF AMERICA

DEDICATION

To my patriotic Southern kinsman, American statesman Jefferson Davis, for standing firm with the Constitution while resisting the transparent trickery, dishonesty, treachery, misrepresentations, and illegalities perpetrated by tyrant Lincoln and his warmongering administration.

EPIGRAPH

Why the Hampton Roads Conference Failed

Enough has already been said to convince any unprejudiced person that the South wished peace; the North wished peace, but Abraham Lincoln wished war, for he had promised war to [Joseph] Medill and other of his constituents who voted for him and war had to be forced. Mr. Medill of the Chicago *Tribune* says:

> "In 1864 when the call for extra troops came Chicago revolted. Chicago had sent 22,000 and was drained. There were no young men to go, no aliens, except what was already bought. The citizens held a mass meeting and appointed three men of whom I (Medill) was one to go to Washington and ask [U.S. Secretary of War Edwin M.] Stanton to give Cook County a new enrollment. He refused. Then we went to President Lincoln. 'I cannot do it,' said Lincoln, 'but I will go with you to Stanton and hear the arguments on both sides.'
>
> "So we went over to the War Department together. Stanton and [U.S.] General [James B.] Fry were there and they both contended that the quota should not be changed. The argument went on for some time, and was finally referred to Lincoln who had been silently listening. When appealed to, Lincoln turned to us with a black and frowning face: 'Gentlemen,' he said, with a voice full of bitterness, 'after Boston, Chicago has been the chief instrument in bringing this war on the country. The Northwest opposed the South and New England opposed the South. It is you, Medill, who is largely responsible for making blood flow as it has. You called for war until you had it. I have given it to you. What you have asked for you have had. Now you come here begging to be left off from the call for more men, which I have made to carry on the war you demanded. You ought to be ashamed of yourselves. Go home and raise your 6,000 men.'"[1]

There is no doubt that peace could have been made at any time Mr. Lincoln had willed it, and history proves this by authenticated facts.[2]

Mildred Lewis Rutherford, 1923

CONTENTS

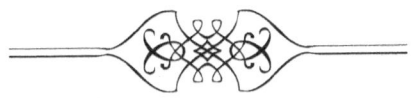

Notes to the Reader - 11
The Three Confederate States Commissioners - 19
The Two United States Commissioners - 20
The River Queen - 21
Introduction: "Our Two Countries" or "Our One Common Country"? by Lochlainn Seabrook - 23

SECTION ONE
HISTORY & BACKGROUND
1: The Hampton Roads Conference: An Overview - 37

SECTION TWO
REPORTS OF C.S. & U.S. OFFICIALS & PARTICIPANTS
2: Account of the Conference by Jefferson Davis - 79
3: Account of the Conference by John H. Reagan - 87
4: Account of the Conference by Alexander H. Stephens - 100
5: Account of the Conference by John A. Campbell - 119
6: Account of the Conference by Robert M. T. Hunter - 125
7: Account of the Conference by Abraham Lincoln - 130
8: Account of the Conference by William H. Seward - 130

SECTION THREE
MYTHS, LIES, & DEFAMATION: THE CONTROVERSY
9: Beginnings of the Legend - 139
10: The Truth About the Hampton Roads Conference - 166

SECTION FOUR
PERSONAL VIEWS & COMMENTARY

11: When Gen. Lee Lost Hope of Success - 193
12: Politics & Shenanigans - 195
13: Yankee Lies Never Cease - 199
14: Alexander H. Stephens at Liberty Hall - 199
15: That Hampton Roads Conference - 200
16: Reagan Replies to a Critic of His Speech Above - 202
17: Report of William P. Tolley - 208
18: Reagan Addresses Another Attack - 218
19: Reagan Replies to Massey Criticism - 227
20: What Happened at Hampton Roads? - 231
21: The Bitter Tide of Liberalism at Hampton Roads - 233
22: One Reason Jefferson Davis Believed the South Would Win - 235
23: The Confederacy After July 4, 1863 - 235
24: Treatment of Southern Commissioners - 240
25: The Amazing Jefferson Davis - 242
26: The Left Will Not Stop Lying About the Hampton Roads Conference - 243
27: The Truth Will Rise Again - 247
28: More Falsehoods of Northern Mythology - 248
29: The Hallucination - 250
30: The Absurdity of the Hampton Roads Myth - 251
31: The South's Sixth & Final Attempt at Peace - 251
32: Disseminating Untruth - 256

Appendix A - Additional Commentary - 259
Appendix B - Historical Data on the U.S. Steamer River Queen *- 261*
Notes - 265
Bibliography - 269
Index - 277
Meet the Author-Editor - 291
Learn More - 293

NOTES TO THE READER

"NOTHING IN THE PAST IS DEAD TO THE MAN WHO WOULD
LEARN HOW THE PRESENT CAME TO BE WHAT IT IS."
WILLIAM STUBBS, VICTORIAN ENGLISH HISTORIAN

THE TWO MAIN POLITICAL PARTIES IN 1860
☛ In any study of America's antebellum, bellum, and postbellum periods, it is vitally important to understand that in 1860 the two major political parties—the Democrats and the newly formed Republicans—were the opposite of what they are today. In other words, the Democrats of the mid 19th Century (founded by what we now call "right-wingers" or "traditionalists")[3] were Conservatives, akin to the Republican Party of today, while the Republicans of the mid 19th Century (founded by what we now call "left-wingers" or "progressives")[4] were Liberals, akin to the Democratic Party of today.[5]

Thus the Confederacy's Democratic president, Jefferson Davis, was a Conservative (with libertarian leanings); the Union's Republican president, Abraham Lincoln, was a Liberal (with socialistic leanings).[6] This is why, in the mid 1800s, the conservative wing of the Democratic Party was known as "the States' Rights Party,"[7] as opposed to the Republican Party, which was widely known to have been created in 1854 by "progressive elements."[8] Indeed, the party's first candidate was radical (that is, socialist), and later Union general, John C. Frémont. As socialist Eugene V. Debs asserted: "Lincoln would not join today's Republican Party any more than Thomas Jefferson would become a member of today's Democratic Party";[9] correctly adding: "The Republican Party was once Red."[10]

The author's cousin, Confederate Vice President and Democrat Alexander H. Stephens: a Southern Conservative.

Hence, the Democrats of the Civil War period referred to themselves as "conservatives," "confederates," "anti-centralists," or "constitutionalists" (the latter because they favored strict adherence to the original Constitution—which tacitly guaranteed states' rights—as created by the Founding Fathers). The Civil War Republicans, on the other hand, called themselves "liberals," "nationalists," "centralists," or "consolidationists" (the latter three because their goal was to nationalize the central government and consolidate political power in Washington, D.C.).[11]

More evidence comes from a common phrase used at the time, "states' rights Democrats," a term that could have only applied to Conservatives, since then, as today, Liberals are squarely against states' rights (unless, in hypocritical fashion, they find that states' rights benefit their agenda in some way).[12] This is in perfect keeping with what *Confederate Veteran* once referred to as "the Mussolini-like procedure of the Federal authorities,"[13] that is, the fascist dictatorial views and actions of the then Left-wing Republican Party.

In 1889 Right-wing Democrat President Davis himself, who referred to the 1860 Democrats as "the conservative power of the country,"[14] described the political situation at the time in the following manner:

> . . . the names adopted by political parties in the United States have not always been strictly significant of their principles. In general terms it may be said that the old Federal party [Liberal] inclined to nationalism [then a term for big government], or consolidation [that is, consolidation of power in the Federal government], and that the Whig party [liberalistic], which succeeded it, although not identical with it, was favorable, in the main, to a strong Central Government [liberalism, socialism, communism]. On the other hand, its opponent, the Republican [Conservative], afterward known as the Democratic party, was dominated by the idea of the sovereignty of the States and the federal or confederate character of the Union [Americanism, traditionalism, conservatism]. Although other elements have entered into its organization at different periods, this has been its vital, cardinal, and abiding principle.[15]

We will note here that, while Davis would not live to witness the transition, a mere six years after he penned these words, during the 1896 U.S. presidential election, the two major parties would reverse positions, the Democratic Party adopting a Left-wing platform, the Republican Party adopting a Right-wing platform—the status they hold to this day.

Since this idea is new to most of my readers, let us further demystify it by viewing it from the perspective of the American Revolutionary War. If Davis and his Conservative Southern constituents (the Democrats of 1861) had been alive in 1775, they would have sided with George Washington and his followers, the independence-loving American colonists (known as

The War for Southern Independence pitted Northern Liberals (then the Republican Party) against Southern Conservatives (then the Democratic Party).

"patriots" or "rebels")—who sought to secede from the tyrannical government of Great Britain; if Lincoln and his Liberal Northern constituents (the Republicans of 1861) had been alive at that time, they would have sided with King George III and the English monarchy, who sought to maintain the American colonies as possessions of the British Empire. It is due to this very comparison that we Southerners often refer to our secession from the U.S. as the Second Declaration of Independence, and the "Civil War" as the Second American Revolutionary War.

Without a basic understanding of these facts, the American "Civil War" will forever remain incomprehensible. For a full discussion of this all-important topic see my book, *Abraham Lincoln Was a Liberal, Jefferson Davis Was a Conservative: The Missing Key to Understanding the American Civil War*.

THE TERM "CIVIL WAR"

☛ As I heartily dislike the phrase "Civil War," its use throughout this book (as well as in my other works) is worthy of explanation.

Our entire modern literary system refers to the conflict of 1861 using the Northern term the "Civil War," whether we in the South like it or not. Of course, this is purposeful, for America's book industry, which determines everything from how books are categorized and designed to how they are marketed and sold, is almost solely controlled by Liberals, socialists, globalists, collectivists, and communists, individuals who will do anything to prevent the truth about Lincoln's War from coming out. An important aspect of this wholesale revisionism of American history is the use of the phrase "Civil War," which Yankee Liberals thrust into the public forum even as big government Left-winger Lincoln was diabolically tricking the Conservative South into firing the first shot at the First Battle of Fort Sumter in April 1861.[16]

The American "Civil War" was not a true civil war as Webster defines it: "A conflict between opposing groups of citizens of the *same* country." It was a fight between two individual countries; or to be more specific, two separate and constitutionally formed confederacies: the C.S.A. and the U.S.A.

The progressives' blatant American "Civil War" coverup continues to this day, one of the more overt results which pertains to how books are coded, indexed, and identified.[17] Thus, as all book searches by readers, libraries, and retail outlets are now performed online, and as all bookstores categorize works from or about this period under the heading "Civil War," honest book publishers and authors who deal with this particular topic have little choice but to use this deceptive term. If I were to refuse to use it, as some of my Southern colleagues have suggested, few people would ever find or read my books.

Add to this the fact that scarcely any non-Southerners have ever heard of the names we in the South use for the conflict, such as "the War for Southern Independence," "the War Against Northern Aggression," "Lincoln's War," or my personal preference, because it is the most accurate: "the War for the Constitution." It only makes sense then to use the term "Civil War" in most commercial situations, historically inaccurate though it is.

We should also bear in mind that while today educated persons, particularly educated Southerners, all share an abhorrence for the phrase "Civil War," it was not always so. Confederates who lived through and even fought in the conflict regularly used the term throughout the 1860s, and even long after. Among them were Confederate generals such as Nathan Bedford Forrest, Richard Taylor, and Joseph E. Johnston, not to mention the Confederacy's vice president, Alexander H. Stephens.

In 1895 Confederate General James Longstreet wrote about his military experiences in a work subtitled, *Memoirs of the Civil War in America*, while in 1903 Confederate General John Brown Gordon, the first commander-in-chief of the United Confederate Veterans, entitled his autobiography, *Reminiscences of the Civil War*.

Confederate General Nathan Bedford Forrest, just one of many Southern officials who referred to the conflict of 1861 as the "Civil War."

Even the Confederacy's highest leader, President Jefferson Davis, used the term "Civil War,"[18] and in one case at least, as late as 1881—the year he wrote his brilliant exposition, *The Rise and Fall of the Confederate Government* (see the Sea Raven Press reprint of this book, of which I am the editor, collector, technician, and designer).[19]

Authors writing for *Confederate Veteran* magazine sometimes used the phrase well into the early 1900s,[20] and in 1898, at the Eighth Annual Meeting and Reunion of the United Confederate Veterans (the forerunner of today's Sons of Confederate Veterans), the following resolution was proposed: that from then on the Great War of 1861 was to be designated "the Civil War Between the States."[21]

A WORD ON EARLY AMERICAN MATERIAL
☛ In order to preserve the authentic historicity of the antebellum, bellum, and postbellum periods, I have retained the original spellings, formatting, and punctuation of the early Americans I quote. These include such items as British-English spellings, long-running paragraphs, obsolete words, and various literary devices peculiar to the time. However, I have corrected misspelled names to prevent confusion, and also *where possible*, inaccurate dates and locations (the inevitable result of aging faulty memories). Bracketed words are *always* my additions and clarifications (added mainly for my new, foreign, and young readers), while italicized words are (where indicated) my emphasis.

REPETITION
☛ As each observer I have selected for this book offers his or her own comments on the *same* conference, there is an inevitable repetition of material. While I could have edited out these recapitulations, it would have weakened the work overall, for each commentator offers his or her own unique personality, voice, color, perspective, and observations, which, in my opinion, only add more detail and interest, and thus more value, to *The Hampton Roads Conference: The Southern View*. Thus I have purposefully chosen to leave in the many recapitulations and reiterations created by my Victorian contributors.

Union General August von Willich: Typically labeled a "radical" in mainstream history books, Willich was actually a card-carrying communist who led a revolutionary workers' party, studiously followed the teachings of Karl Marx, and participated in the failed European socialist revolution of 1848 — all before joining Lincoln's army in 1861.

19TH-CENTURY CODE WORDS
☛ An early American *Southern* abolitionist was someone who simply desired the end of slavery. *Northern* abolitionists, however, were something quite different altogether: they identified themselves with socialism and communism[22]—the modern forms which were developed in the 1840s by German revolutionary Karl Marx.[23] Also, as noted above, our modern political party names have different meanings than those of the mid 1800s. Hence, one must bear the following in mind when reading 19th-Century literature:

1. "Abolitionist" (Northern): A 19th-Century Left-wing euphemism for a socialist or communist.
2. "Radical" (Northern): Also a 19th-Century Left-wing euphemism for

a socialist or communist.
3. "Republican": Between 1854 and 1896 the Republicans were the major Left-wing or Liberal party of that era.
4. "Democrat": Between 1828 and 1896, the Democrats were the major Right-wing or Conservative party of that era.

For more information on items 1 and 2 above, see my introduction in my book *The Bittersweet Bond: Race Relations in the Old South As Described by White and Black Southerners*.

For more information on items 3 and 4 above, see my books *Abraham Lincoln Was a Liberal, Jefferson Davis Was a Conservative: The Missing Key to Understanding the American Civil War*, and *Lincoln's War: The Real Cause, the Real Winner, the Real Loser*.

PRESENTISM

☛ As a historian I view *presentism* (judging the past according to present day mores and customs) as the enemy of authentic history. And this is precisely why the Left employs it in its ongoing war against traditional American, conservative, and Christian values. By looking at history through the lens of modern day beliefs—and, just as heinous, fabricating obviously fake history based on emotion, opinion, and political ideology—they are able to distort, revise, and reshape the past into a false narrative that fits their ideological agenda: the liberalization *and* Northernization of America, the enlargement and further centralization of the national government, and total control of American political, economic, educational, and social power, the same plan that Lincoln championed.[24]

Judging our ancestors by our own standards is dishonest, unfair, unjust, misleading, and unethical.

This book rejects presentism and replaces it with what I call *historicalism*: judging our ancestors based on the values of their own time.

To get the most from this work the reader is invited to reject presentism as well. In this way—along with casting aside preconceived notions and the fake history churned out by our Left-wing education system—the truth in this work will be most readily ascertained and absorbed; truth that has been rigorously researched and forensically uncovered by myself using the scientific method. In 1901 Confederate

Colonel Bennett H. Young noted:

> History is valuable only as it is true. Opinions concerning acts are not history; acts themselves alone are historic.[25]

CONTINUE YOUR SOUTHERN HISTORY EDUCATION
☛ Lincoln's War on the Constitution and the American people can never be fully understood without a thorough knowledge of the South's perspective. As this book is only meant to be a brief introductory guide to these topics, one cannot hope to learn the complete story here. For those who are interested in additional material from Dixie's viewpoint, please see my comprehensive histories listed on pages 2 and 3. You are either for or against the Truth. There is not and can never be true neutrality on this subject, which is why there is no such thing as a purely "neutral" book on the War Between the States—despite the claims of many pro-North partisans. Thus in the year 1900, former Confederate General John Brown Gordon wrote:

> Neutrality has no place in masterful minds nor in heroic hearts. Neutrality has never yet developed a great character nor characterized a great people nor written one sparkling page in human history.[26]

FINAL THOUGHTS: HOW TO HONOR BOTH OUR SOUTHERN & OUR AMERICAN HERITAGE
☛ To all Americans: It is time to resurrect the South's true history. It is time to allow the authentic chronicle of past events to be told accurately and honestly. It is time to disseminate this knowledge far and wide, guilelessly and decisively. It is time to shine the Light of Truth into the dark corners of ignorance, malice, divisiveness, and deceit fomented by the gaslighting enemies of the South.[27] Then and only then do we truly honor our gallant Confederate ancestors, do justice to their names, military service, and memories, and confer upon them the respect and reverence they so richly deserve as American patriots.

LOCHLAINN SEABROOK

Keep Your Body, Mind, & Spirit Vibrating at Their Highest Level
YOU CAN DO SO BY READING THE BOOKS OF

SEA RAVEN PRESS

There is nothing that will so perfectly keep your body, mind, and spirit in a healthy condition as to think wisely and positively. Hence you should not only read this book, but also the other books that we offer. They will quicken your physical, mental, and spiritual vibrations, enabling you to maintain a position in society as a healthy erudite person.

KEEP YOURSELF WELL-INFORMED!

The well-informed person is always at the head of the procession, while the ignorant, the lazy, and the unthoughtful hang onto the rear. If you are a Spiritual man or woman, do yourself a great favor: read Sea Raven Press books and stay well posted on the Truth. It is almost criminal for one to remain in ignorance while the opportunity to gain knowledge is open to all at a nominal price.

We invite you to visit our Webstore for a wide selection of wholesome, family-friendly, well-researched, educational books for all ages. You will be glad you did!

Artisan-Crafted Books & Merch From the Rocky Mountains!

SeaRavenPress.com

LochlainnSeabrook.com
TheBestCivilWarBookEver.com
AmbianceGoneWild.com
Pond5.com/artist/LochlainnSeabrook

THE THREE CONFEDERATE STATES COMMISSIONERS AT HAMPTON ROADS

C.S. Vice President Alexander H. Stephens.

C.S. Assist. Sec. of War John A. Campbell.

C.S. Senator Robert M. T. Hunter.

THE TWO UNITED STATES COMMISSIONERS AT HAMPTON ROADS

U.S. President Abraham Lincoln.

U.S. Sec. of State William H. Seward.

The River Queen

The *River Queen*. This famous side paddlewheel steam-powered vessel was built in New Jersey in 1864, at a cost of about $150,000. She was 181 feet in length, with a beam of 28.5 feet, and a weight of 587 tons. Though used by U.S. Gen. Ulysses S. Grant, U.S. General Benjamin F. Butler, and other "Civil War" luminaries, it is most famous for hosting, in a saloon on her upper deck, the Hampton Roads Conference on February 3, 1865—the second word of the region's name, Roads, being an abbreviation of the word *roadstead*, meaning "a protected stretch of water near shore where vessels can ride at anchor"; that is, "a protected anchorage." In attendance were Confederate icons Alexander H. Stephens, John A. Campbell, and Robert. M. T. Hunter, along with U.S. officials Abraham Lincoln and William H. Seward. According to some reports, discussion began on February 1, with an unannounced Lincoln joining the other four men on February 3. This was not the last "Civil War" conference on the *River Queen*. Some eight weeks later, on March 27, 1865, Lincoln met with General Grant, U.S. General William T. Sherman, and U.S. Rear Admiral David D. Porter, to discuss final strategies for defeating the Confederate States of America. Despite this famous second assemblage aboard the *River Queen*, the War ended a mere few days later when C.S. General Robert E. Lee laid down his arms at Appomattox Court House, Virginia, on April 9, 1865. Though technically the War might have continued since Lee had surrendered only his army and not the C.S.A. itself, when news spread that the great Confederate chieftain had yielded to Grant, reluctantly the rest of the Southern military forces soon followed. Some Confederate army leaders, however, such as General Nathan Bedford Forrest, fought on. Another, Cherokee C.S. General Stand Watie, became the last Confederate general to cede, not surrendering his command until June 23, 1865 (at Doaksville, Oklahoma), some 75 days after Lee's capitulation at Appomattox.

Loyalty to the truth of Confederate history

U.D.C. MOTTO, 1921

INTRODUCTION

"Our Two Countries" or "Our One Common Country"?

THE HAMPTON ROADS CONFERENCE was the sixth and final serious meeting between the Confederate States of America and the United States of America during the War for the Constitution. Present at the conference were three Confederate officials, C.S. Vice President Alexander H. Stephens, C.S. Assistant Secretary of War John A. Campbell, and C.S. Senator Robert M. T. Hunter, and two U.S. officials, U.S. President Abraham Lincoln and U.S. Secretary of State William H. Seward. The four-hour meeting between these five men took place on February 3, 1865, on board the U.S. steamer *River Queen*, anchored in a calm U.S. controlled harbor at Hampton Roads, Virginia. The purpose? To discuss terms upon which the War might be brought to a close.

The Hampton Roads Conference was one of the most important events in American history, perhaps in world history. Yet it is all but ignored by the average historian and is barely mentioned in our history books, except to assure the public that it "it was an insignificant effort that failed, achieving nothing."

In those rare cases when it is discussed beyond a curt dismissal, mainstream historians portray Lincoln as a patriotic and benevolent world leader, who not only instigated the conference, but who made overly generous offer after overly generous offer to the Southern "insurgents" as to how they could easily end the War overnight with a mere signing of a pen.

In this, the *Northern* version of the conference, the "erring South" refused all of the lenient and humanitarian attempts at peace offered by a "frank, honest, and kind-hearted" Lincoln,[28] with Confederate President Jefferson Davis depicted as the epitome of stupidity, selfishness, guile, and arrogance; little more than a duplicitous autocrat who placed "illegal" political theory over Southern lives.

But is any of this historically accurate?

Of course not. In fact, the following well documented pages will prove, down to the last detail, that the real story behind the conference has been completely rewritten, and that the opposite is true. Before we examine the facts, let us look at *how* and *why* this occurred.

THE LEFT & HOW IT OPERATES TO REWRITE HISTORY
The main culprit behind these "Civil War" schemes is, as always, the intolerant, dictatorial, alethophobic Left; that is, liberals, socialists, and communists (in all their forms). The Left hates and fears truth so intensely that it has already thoroughly revised nearly every aspect of American history, from the early Native American and European Colonial periods up to the War Between the States, the Great Depression, World War II, the Vietnam War, and beyond. Indeed, members of the Left-wing establishment are now busily rewriting present day history as I pen these words, an attempt to prevent future generations from ever knowing, for example, the truth about Donald Trump and his presidency—even using anti-South laws, like the Fourteenth Amendment, which they created over 150 years ago, against him.

The Left's targets are not those who *lie* about American history, as any rational individual would naturally assume. It is those who tell the *truth* about American history; in other words, those who disseminate factual information the Left dislikes or disagrees with. This is just one aspect of this diabolical group's plan to divide and conquer traditional America.

The tactics liberals, socialists, and communists use to redact and reshape history specifically are numerous and nefarious. Let us look at a few of them:

- Create confusion, disorder, and doubt by changing dates and erasing facts, while simultaneously inserting alleged words and statements that were never made, as well as events that never occurred (known as gaslighting).
- Add misinformation to history books while liberally creating

disinformation to further clutter and obscure, while bewildering and upsetting the general public.
- Describe the War in elementary cut-and-dry, black-and-white terms, using a broad brush to paint vague simplistic generalities for quick and easy mass consumption. (History is *never* simple.)
- *Always* depict the opposition (in this case, the South) as the antagonist, and just as importantly, as the adversary of America, the Constitution, freedom, democracy, and even humanity itself.
- Break down factual arguments by replacing them with manufactured nonsensical counter-arguments.
- Distract, polarize, fluster, and weaken the opposition (that is, truth-tellers) by falsely accusing its members of racism, sexism, classism, fascism, etc.
- Weaponize invented falsehoods and fabrications to undermine the facts and discredit honest historians.
- Pretend you are telling the truth, while asserting that the opposition is lying.
- Accuse the opposition of the crimes against history that you, not they, have committed.
- Use ridicule, derision, ad hominem attacks, and even defamation against the opposition to divert attention away from yourself and destroy the enemy's credibility.
- Complicate historical matters by constantly denying facts and asserting falsehoods. Repeat. Then repeat again.
- Create artificial conflict if or when there is none.
- Even though it is you who is whipping up fake history, paint the opposition as the "enemy of truth."
- Present opinions as facts and facts as opinions; sow chaos, reap control.
- Though you are biased and approach history in a subjective manner, claim that it is the opposition which is "biased" and "subjective."
- Harass, demonize, ban, censor, outlaw, and suppress honest historians and their works to prevent the general public from learning true history; make up lies about them then use the lies against them.
- Fill the vacuum left from the mass purge of real history books with thousands of titles containing distorted fabricated history.
- Force schools to replace *all* genuine history books with fake ones.
- Deny all charges of deception.
- Maintain the coverup at all costs.
- Pass these methods down to the next generation in order to continually perpetuate the process of the destruction and rewriting of authentic history.

As you read the following pages you will find that the Left, that is, the mainstream, has repeatedly used, and continues to use, many of these exact strategies to whitewash American history, and in particular "Civil War" history.

THE LEFT: EXPERT LANGUAGE MANIPULATORS, THEN & TODAY

When it comes to our topic, the Hampton Roads Conference, perhaps the most overt example of Left-wing history-redaction concerns the name of the meeting itself.

Leftist writers, are, if nothing else, master manipulators of language. To this end they employ words and names that are in fact the precise opposite of reality, an effort to misdirect attention while attempting to garner public favor. Hence we have a number of absurd Left-wing words and terms in usage today, such as:

- "Democratic Party," for a group that is anything but democratic in its views and goals. (Today's Democrats are, in fact, socialists.)
- "higher education," for a mostly Left-wing run educational system that now indoctrinates more than it teaches, and whose "lessons" often promote the very discriminatory ideas it claims to be against; namely, for instance, racism, xenophobia, sexism (in particular homosexism), classism, intolerance, discrimination, ageism, antisemitism, etc.
- "elite," for a group, the so-called "Democrats," that is made up primarily of ordinary working class citizens, the opposite of the meaning of "elite." (In actuality, the word should be, not elite, but "elitist," for this is a movement of people who believe strongly in the wholly undemocratic political philosophy of elitism.)
- "woke," for a group that is very much sound asleep to reality.
- "mostly peaceful," for a group that readily employs and sanctions violence.
- "hate speech," used by one of history's most hateful and hate-filled groups for views, opinions, and beliefs they dislike or disagree with.
- "tolerant," for one of history's most prejudiced, biased, partial, and narrow-minded groups.

The Left's use, or rather misuse, of opposing terms is not new. In the mid 19th Century liberals took the oxymoronic term "anti-slavery" to label themselves, a cover for a so-called "abolitionist" movement that was seeking to enslave the entire American populace under socialistic and ultimately communistic rule.[29]

They also, following Lincoln's lead, began calling the Southern Cause (conservatism) a "revolution," when it was the Left under Lincoln (and later Liberal Republican U.S. President Ulysses S. Grant) that was fomenting a revolution[30]—in this case what the Conservative South accurately referred to as the "Bolshevik Period," that is, a communist revolution.[31] In fact, because they were attempting to overthrow the Constitution created by the Founding Generation, it was not Davis and his Right-wing Democratic followers, it was Lincoln and his Left-wing Republican followers who were the true "insurgents," the true "revolutionaries," the true "rebels."[32]

In 1854 this same progressive social group adopted the name "Republican" for their new Left-wing party, another attempt at masquerading as something they were decidedly not: a patriotic all-American party devoted to a republican style government—a government in which power is held by the people rather than its leaders. (Thankfully this term was taken back by Conservatives during the 1896 presidential election, where it remains to this day.)[33]

HOW THE LEFT HAS USED & CONTINUES TO USE THE CONFERENCE TO FURTHER ITS GOALS

As for our subject, 19th-Century Southern historians and commentators routinely and correctly referred to it as "The Hampton Roads Conference." Yet, modern mainstream historians and commentators call it "The Hampton Roads *Peace* Conference."

Why?

The Left would like the world to believe that the conference was formed for the express purpose of seeking a peaceful settlement to the War. The emphasis on "peace" is made here to ensure that the unsuspecting public views C.S. President Jefferson Davis, not Lincoln, as the villain of the conference—even though Davis was not even present, while Lincoln was. Despite this crucial fact, in order to satisfy the Left's insatiable hunger to control, influence, and misrepresent authentic history, the Confederate chief executive had to be depicted as the individual who ruined the two countries' sixth and final attempt at peace and allowed the War to continue for another two months, unnecessarily sacrificing the lives of thousands of Confederate and U.S. soldiers.

The truth? Here is what C.S. Vice President Alexander H. Stephens, who *was* present at the conference, later noted in a written report to the Confederate Congress, the gist of which was:

> [Confederate President Davis] himself, had no power to accept or reject any terms offered, and the conference was not for the purpose of making peace terms, but to ascertain terms on which peace might be procured, and, of course, the Confederate Congress had the decision in its hands. Yet Mr. Davis has been blamed for not accepting peace terms which were never offered.[34]

One of the most notable mainstream lies invented about the conference is that an empathetic Lincoln told the three Confederate commissioners that he would write "Union" at the top of a blank piece of paper, and they could then fill in whatever terms they wished to bring the War to an immediate close; simultaneously Lincoln is said to have offered the South $400,000,000 (the equivalent of $1 billion in today's currency) in compensation for its slaves, if only it would lay down its arms and rejoin the Union.

The fact of history is that these offers were never made, but were instead devilish creations of either South-haters in the North or Davis-haters in the South, designed to lure the world away from the truth. Here is what Confederate Postmaster General John H. Reagan later wrote about this tall tale:

> "[It] has been repeated by citizens of acknowledged ability and high character, and it has been said that these offers could not be acceded to because the instructions given to the Commission by President Davis prevented it. The purpose of urging these untrue statements seems to have been to induce the public to believe that Mr. Davis could have obtained peace on almost any terms desired and

$400,000,000 for the Southern slaves if he would have consented to a restoration of the Southern States to the Union; and that, because of this, he was responsible for the losses of life and property caused by the continuance of the war. . . . Undoubtedly, one of the purposes of insisting that such offers were made is to mislead the public as to the truth."³⁵

What really happened at the conference, as the reader will see, is that Lincoln weaponized the slavery issue then used it to lure the Confederacy into "immediate submission" and "unconditional surrender." This he did by stating categorically that the Emancipation Proclamation was nothing more than a "war measure" that would cease when the War ended, and that the South, after rejoining the U.S., could easily defeat the Thirteenth Amendment by "voting it down as members of the Union. The whole number of States being thirty-six, [stated Lincoln,] any ten of them could defeat this proposed amendment."

According to Vice President Stephens, during the conference Lincoln

> "went into a prolonged course of remarks about the [Emancipation] Proclamation. He said it was not his intention in the beginning to interfere with Slavery in the States; that he never would have done it, if he had not been compelled by necessity to do it, to maintain the Union; that the subject presented many difficult and perplexing questions to him; that he had hesitated for some time, and had resorted to this measure, only when driven to it by public necessity; that he had been in favor of the General Government prohibiting the extension of Slavery into the Territories, but did not think that that Government possessed power over the subject in the States, except as a war measure; and that he had always himself been in favor of emancipation, but not immediate emancipation, even by the States. Many evils attending this appeared to him."³⁶

This is not the *fake* Lincoln of mainstream history. What we are seeing here is the *real* Lincoln, a lifelong member of the racist American Colonization Society who cared little about blacks or slavery personally, but who merely wanted to prevent the distasteful institution of slavery from spreading outside the South into the newly developing Western Territories—an area he wanted set aside for "homes for free white people."³⁷ Why? Because according to Lincoln: "There is a natural disgust in the minds of nearly all white people, at the idea of an indiscriminate amalgamation of the white and black races."[38] This is the same Left-wing idol who publicly supported the idea of creating an all-black U.S. state set aside exclusively for African-Americans.[39]

Is any of this taught in our schools? Do any of these facts appear in our history books? No, and for good reason: They would reveal the truth about both Lincoln and his War on the U.S. Constitution and the American people.

WHO WAS RESPONSIBLE FOR THE FAILED CONFERENCE?
Numerous other fairy tales have been created by the nihilistic Left to overcloud the truth about the Hampton Roads Conference, perhaps none more egregious than the one claiming that if not for President Davis' stubbornness and shortsightedness concerning secession, along with his strict adherence to the cause of  Southern independence, the War would have ended two months earlier than it did.

But who was really responsible for the continuation of the War and the loss of American lives after the conference ended? Let us look more closely at the facts.

Lincoln was always fully aware that secession was legal (as it remains to this day), even once referring to it as a "most sacred right." Here, for example, is what he said on January 12, 1848, in a speech before the U.S. House of Representatives:

> "Any people anywhere, being inclined and having the power, have the right to rise up, and shake off the existing government, and form a new one that suits them better. This is a most valuable, a most sacred right—a right which, we hope and believe, is to liberate the world. Nor is this right confined to cases in which the whole people of an existing government may choose to exercise it. Any portion of such people that can may revolutionize, and make their own of so much of the territory as they inhabit."[40]

Being a Left-wing demagogue, when it was politically expedient to change his mind, Lincoln, of course, did just that. Thus, as U.S. president thirteen years later, on July 4, 1861, in his Message to Congress in Special Session, he called the new Southern Confederacy an "illegal organization," and the constitutional right of secession an "ingenious sophism," an "insidious debauching of the public mind," and a "sugar-coated invention" of the South, while those who challenged these views were labeled "traitors" and "rebels."[41]

At the Hampton Roads Conference, Lincoln continued this conspicuous charade, taking the position that because the North (U.S.) and the South (C.S.) belonged to "one common country," secession was illegal. Thus the Southern states had violated the Constitution, which prevented him from agreeing to any terms with the Confederacy except what C.S. commissioner Robert M. T. Hunter bitterly and rightly called "unconditional submission."[42]

But Lincoln, like President Davis, knew full well that 1) at that moment (February 1865) the Northern states and the Southern states were, as Davis correctly phrased it, "two [separate] countries"; that 2), there was (and is) no ban on secession in the U.S. Constitution, for that word appears nowhere in that hallowed document; and 3), despite this omission (intentionally excluded by the Founding Fathers because the right of secession was well-known and assumed by every American citizen at the time), secession is tacitly sanctioned by the Ninth and Tenth Amendments.[43]

Our mainstream history books, however, continue to blame President Davis for the failure of the Hampton Roads Conference due to his overriding belief in the so-called "unconstitutional" act of secession. Yet, due to the fact that secession was and is legal, Lincoln must be the one held responsible for the collapse of the conference, for it was he who both ignored the Ninth and Tenth Amendments of the Constitution, *and* conveniently "forgot" the 1848 speech he gave before the U.S. House of Representatives.

If only Stephens, or one of the other two Confederate commissioners at the conference, had directly confronted Lincoln about his earlier House address; the War might have had an entirely different outcome, one that actually benefitted instead of disadvantaged both countries.

Though many other Left-wing conference myths could be examined, we will only look at one more.

This one claims that it was wholly the Confederacy's fault for the failure of the conference to arrive at a mutual agreement over the War. Here, however, is what one of the three Confederate commissioners, Confederate Assistant Secretary of War John A. Campbell, later stated:

> "*Both* [parties] agreed that in the present temper of both nations that a reunion would not be profitable to either, and should not be desired by either."

We are now left with only one conclusion, as Reagan observed: The ultimate object of all these absurd mainstream fictions

> ". . . was no doubt to cast odium on the Confederate President and authorities by trying to show that they would accept no terms of peace and were responsible for the continuance of the war."

In the final analysis, which side then was the one truly responsible for the failure of the Hampton Roads Conference, unnecessarily prolonging the war, and the needless deaths of thousands of soldiers? Since there can only be one correct answer, it is obvious. In an 1864 interview with a Northern journalist, a year *before* the infamous meeting, President Davis said:

> "I tried all in my power to avert this war. I saw it coming, and for twelve years I worked night and day to prevent it, but I could not. The North was mad and blind; it would not let us govern ourselves, and so the war came, and now it must go on till the last man of this generation falls in his tracks, and his children seize his musket and fight our battle, unless you acknowledge our right to self-government. We are not fighting for slavery. We are fighting for Independence, and that, or extermination, we *will* have. . . . [Slavery] never was an essential element. It was only a means of bringing other conflicting elements to an earlier culmination. . . . There are essential differences between the North and the South, that will, however this war may end, make them two nations."[44]

SUMMATION

These are just a few examples of the countless important facts erased from our mainstream history books.

Read on and learn how Left-wingers Lincoln and Seward, with the backing of the then Liberal Republican Party, purposefully waited to meet with the Confederacy until they knew her armies were on the verge of defeat, then used the Hampton Roads Conference to disingenuously obfuscate, double-talk, trick, coerce, and humiliate Conservative Democrat Davis and the Southern states—all to make the Yankees appear as patriotic peacemakers, the Confederates as traitorous warmongers. And so has false history remembered them!

As you read, you will begin to realize that this cannot be the only "Civil War" event that the mainstream has revised. And you will be correct. As noted earlier, the entire conflict has been rewritten to fit the dogmatic, bigoted, fact-loathing narrative of the Left. My book, *The Hampton Roads Conference: The Southern View*, is one small ember that will help keep the flame of Truth alive.

Lochlainn Seabrook
Park County, Wyoming, USA
January 2024
In Nobis Regnat Christus

Hampton Roads, Virginia, around 1865, the time of the Hampton Roads Conference.

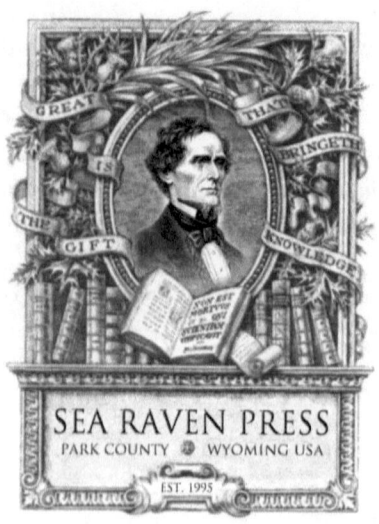

"Books invite all they constrain none."
Hartley Burr Alexander (1873-1939)

SECTION ONE

History & Background

1. THE HAMPTON ROADS CONFERENCE: AN OVERVIEW
☛ [By the end of 1864, the Blairs, one of America's oldest, most respected, and powerful families on the East Coast, was declining in influence due to a series of political defeats, troubles, and unpopular back-room machinations. But all was not lost, yet.]

The old man, [Francis Preston Blair, Sr., 1791-1876,] the father of his race [that is, family], was to strike one last blow to recover the prestige which had thus dwindled away. By making himself instrumental in bringing about a peaceful settlement between the North and South he could recoup his political fortunes and deal a death blow at the extremists and their policies. By forestalling a peace, dictated to a subjugated people, he could prevent the imposition of extreme terms of reconstruction; by anticipating a victorious conclusion to the war, he could ease the pressure which the [Left-wing] extremists were exerting upon Lincoln to compel him to adopt their war and peace policy. The time for such a movement was now, before the radicals [the socialist-communist wing of the then Liberal Republican Party] organized or were conscious of their power.

Other reasons made it logical for the older Blair to undertake such negotiations.

A long political career, an extensive family connection, and a position in the border states, had given Blair a wide acquaintance among Confederate statesmen. Jefferson Davis had been a frequent visitor at Silver Spring [MD] in the old days; Mrs. Blair in 1867 thought he [Davis] was one of the greatest men she ever knew or "that ever lived"; and hardly was the war over when Burton M. Harrison, the private secretary of Jefferson Davis, married one of her "blood relations."

Then the Blair relatives were scattered all through the Confederacy. Their connection even involved the Lees, for a third cousin of Robert E. Lee, [U.S.] Rear Admiral Samuel P. Lee, had married Elizabeth, the daughter of Francis P. Blair, Sr. Other "cousinhoods" included General Joseph O. Shelby, Major-General William B. Preston, and Brigadier General Randall L. Gibson—all of the Confederate Army; and the respective wives of [C.S.] General Albert Sidney Johnston and of [C.S. Gen.] John B. Floyd. It might well seem desirable to protect this vast family connection from the ravages of confiscation and racial amalgamation.

Southerner Francis P. Blair, Sr., the originator of the conference.

At just what time Francis P. Blair, Sr., conceived the idea of a peace mission it is impossible to say. By the end of November [1864], John Murray Forbes writes to Montgomery [Blair, son of F. P. Blair, Sr.] deprecating the talk of peace; perhaps the astute Bostonian was trying to head off such negotiations at their source. It is certain that old Blair applied in December to Lincoln for permission to undertake such a negotiation, but Lincoln postponed his permission until after the fall of Savannah. When this provision had been met, on December 28, 1864, he issued a pass to the old man. Lincoln's knowledge of the plan which his peace emissary proposed to offer the Confederates was very slight.

F. P. Blair, Sr., and [his son] Montgomery Blair then departed for the military headquarters of the Northern [U.S.] armies, whence they sent two notes to Jefferson Davis. One, which was to be used as an explanation for the public, asserted that F. P. Blair came to Richmond in search of papers which had been taken from his house at Silver Spring during the raid of [C.S.] General Jubal A. Early. The other stated that the writer, a private citizen of the

North, wholly unaccredited, requested an interview to discuss the "state of our country" with a view to repairing the ruin wrought by the war. When no reply was received to these two communications, the Blairs returned to Washington. Hither a belated but favorable answer of Jefferson Davis was forwarded and on January 7 [1865] the elder Blair left Washington at once.

A few days later he was at the Spottswood Hotel in Richmond. The departures and arrivals, North and South, of F. P. Blair, Sr., were the occasion to a buzz of comment. It was rumored that he went to sell some North Carolina stock. At another time he was seeking to recover papers taken in Early's raid. The degree of authority he possessed was a matter of great speculation. The [New York] *Times* lamented his mission; the [New York] *World* gave a prospectus of his terms which were amnesty, abolition, and the Union as it was and the constitution as it is; and an "old hand at peace negotiations" declared that hostilities would cease within ten days.

On January 12, [1865,] F. P. Blair, Sr., held a confidential interview with the President [Davis] of the Southern Confederacy. Blair began the interview with a few remarks which were prefatory to the reading of a long paper in the form of an editorial—a form native to his genius [as a newspaperman]. In these introductory words Blair [who had been born in Virginia] asserted his affection for the South which had been the home of his family; and said that he relied upon the frankness of the President to tell him if the "dreams of an old man," which he was about to submit, could be realized or not.

Then followed the reading of the plan which Blair had drawn up. Its keynote was the fear that, if the Civil War should continue any longer, the republican and democratic institutions of this country were in danger of overthrow by monarchy and tyranny. This danger had appeared in tangible form in Mexico. Here Louis Napoleon [III] had set in motion his grand design to make "the Latin race supreme in the southern section of the North American Continent." This object previously had been a dream, foreshadowed by the great Napoleon "in a letter to one of his dictations at St. Helena"; it was at present in process of realization by the subjugation of Mexico and the appointment of Maximilian

[I] to rule over its shattered liberties. Now Napoleon stands ready on the flank of our nation to march northward and to create a vast Latin colony on the shores of the Gulf of Mexico. But this disaster to free institutions will occur only if the differences between the South and North continue.

What are the bases of these differences?

There is first of all, slavery. This institution, Blair says, is condemned by all the world and its extinction is inevitable. Even the South proposes to use its slaves in order to conquer a peace. The inescapable result of such use will be the freedom of the blacks. Slavery as a cause for the separation of the North and South has, therefore, disappeared. With diffidence Blair approaches the other issue—the question of Southern independence. With slavery gone, one object for which independence was coveted has disappeared. But in any case, independence, he insinuates, will be impossible. Either it will be bargained away in return for foreign aid and assistance, or taken away by the victorious march of Louis Napoleon [III]. There is but one method by which to prevent this disaster, and that is Union—a natural Union. [Spoke Blair:]

> "The people are one people, speak a common language, are educated in the same common law, are brought up in one common habitude, the growth of republican representative institutions, all fixed in freeholds rooted in the soil of a great luxuriant continent bound as one body by backbone mountains, pervaded in every member with gigantic streams running in every direction to give animation and strength like arteries and veins in the human system. Such an embodiment, in such a country, cannot be divided."

The analysis of the situation completed, Blair endeavored to give his solution for the problem. Slavery was to be abandoned; the Northern offer of amnesty was to be enlarged to include everyone engaged in the War of the Rebellion; and the union of North and South would be brought about through an armistice. Secret preliminaries to this armistice would enable to transport his army to the Mexican border. There he could secure the coöperation of [Mexican President Benito] Juarez, whose minister [to the United States, Mafias] Romero, "is intimate with my son, Montgomery, who is persuaded that he could induce Juarez to devolve all the power he can command on President Davis—a dictatorship, if necessary—to restore the rights of Mexico and her people." The North, moreover, although officially aloof, would send recruits for such an expedition. For this purpose "I think I could venture to pledge my son, [U.S.] General [Francis P.] Blair, [Jr.], now commanding a corps against the Confederacy."

To Jefferson Davis this plan ought to make an especial appeal. If he accepts it and thereby restores the Southern states without "proscription, conscription, or confiscation," as equals in the Union, he can write his name with those of [George] Washington and [Andrew] Jackson,

> "as a defender of the liberty of the country. If in delivering Mexico, he should mould its States in form and principle to adapt them to our Union and add a new Southern constellation to its benignant sky while rounding off our possession on the continent at the Isthmus, and opening the way to blending the waters of the Atlantic and Pacific, thus embracing our Republic in the arms of the ocean, he would complete the work of [Thomas] Jefferson, who first set one foot of our colossal government on the Pacific by a stride from the Gulf of Mexico. Such achievement would be more highly appreciated in the South, inasmuch as it would restore the equipoise between the Northern and Southern States if indeed such sectional distinctions could be recognized after the peculiar institution which created them had ceased to exist."

When the reading of this paper was finished, the two men discussed its provisions. Davis expressed his desire for reconciliation and reiterated his love for the old nation [that is, the U.S.A. as the Founders originally created it—a "confederate republic," as Washington referred to it, popularly nicknamed "The Confederate States of America"].[45] At the Battle of Bull Run, so near alike were the two flags, he said, that he had mistaken the Union one hanging limp at the staff, for his own. And of all the plans for reconciliation, the one Blair had proposed was the best.

There were two obstacles in the way—the feeling of vindictiveness which the war had aroused and the necessity of absolute honesty on the part of persons making such an agreement. Davis admitted that, in regard to the first consideration, the union of North and South in an aggressive war upon a foreign power, assailing the principles of government common to both sections, would be of great assistance. The feelings of resentment, moreover, both Blair and Davis agreed were stronger not in the army but in the politicians and profiteers and in the people at home who "brooded" over its disasters.

As to the second consideration, Davis and Blair again agreed in a fortunate distrust of [Lincoln's Secretary of State, William H.] Seward who was ambitious, selfish, perfidious, and designing although "he has good social feelings." But Blair gave Davis assurance that, if the plan were carried out, it would have to be carried out by Mr. Lincoln who was absolutely responsible and capable of "great personal sacrifices . . .", capable "of sacrificing a friend when he thinks it necessary for the good of the country."

Then the interview closed with Davis' assertion that, in order to bring about an understanding, he would appoint commissioners. As for his personal fame, a matter to which Blair had made allusion, he did not care for a great name; all he desired was to "restore the prosperity and happiness of his country. . . . For himself, death would end his cares, and that was very easy to be accomplished." On the following day he sent a note to Mr. Blair to be delivered to Mr. Lincoln.

The spectacle of those who had been most active in provoking war, now most ready to make peace, would probably amuse the sophisticated Seward. There are laughable incongruities in the sight of old F. P. Blair, who had talked so vehemently of "nullifiers" and "rebels," and who had urged a vigorous war as a means for restoring national harmony, now boasting of the Southern blood in his veins and urging Jefferson Davis to make peace. Even if four years of political struggle with conservatives [then the Democrats] and extremists [the socialists and communists in the then Liberal Republican Party,] had wrought this transformation, they had not diminished the astuteness and the subtlety of this master politician.

Blair's Mexican project is a marvelously adroit appeal to the Confederacy and to the personality of her President . With delicacy Blair points out the hopelessness of the situation for the Southern states by stressing their determination to use the slaves [by officially enlisting them in the Confederate military][46] and to secure foreign intervention. Then he eases their inevitable return into the Union by proposing a "joint crusade against foreign powers" and by arousing the hope that in the newly acquired territory the South may have an equipoise to the power of the North.

Then comes the appeal to Davis himself. He will protect the independence of the South no longer against the North but against Louis Napoleon [III], the real enemy; he may hold his head high in the accomplishment of this defense of free institutions; he may ally his name with those of Washington, Jefferson, and Jackson. Under the magic of Blair's words defeat takes on the aspect of victory.

On January 16, [1865,] Blair returned to Washington on the *Don*, the [U.S.] flagship of the Potomac flotilla. The reporters found him "silent but in good humor."

One reason for the elder Blair's taciturn good humor may have been the impression, which he had gained during his visits to Richmond, of affairs in the Confederate States of America. The Southern capital was, in truth, a city of sorrows and waning hopes. Every day the Federal armies were drawing nearer to the heart of the Confederacy and were taking in their march a fatal toll of men and of territory. Every day the resources of the Confederacy were being whittled away; and each dispatch from the various fronts seemed to tell the tale of a new and inescapable disaster. As if to increase the gloom which enshrouded the Southern cause, there was a spell of miserable weather. There were incessant rains; falling snow was turned into slush or ice by rapid alternation in the temperature. Even the clear days were robbed of their promise by the news which seeped in from defeated armies.

But the Confederacy was not in danger solely because of attacks from without. Such simply gave occasion and emphasis to the real causes of disintegration—the personal dislikes and the political differences within the Southern states. That internal dissensions should appear when a nation is threatened with disaster is a truism. But these dissensions were peculiarly dangerous for the Confederacy because that government was based upon a belief in the principles of separation and state individuality. Disunion, therefore, always had a theoretic justification and it would seem as if secessionists could not justly complain when various Southern states, in turn, talked of independent state action.

In this respect January 1865 witnessed one more step in the difficulties which the central government had had with North Carolina. In that state discontent with the Civil War had been brewing ever since 1862. There were plans for peace negotiations to be undertaken by North Carolina alone, and for a convention to carry North Carolina out of the Confederacy and back into the Union. People of this belief, denominating themselves "conservatives" and their opponents "destructives," were led by William W. Holden, the editor of the Raleigh *Standard*. In 1862, the conservative party had helped to elect as Governor of the state, Zebulon B. Vance, whose wholesale allegiance to the cause of his creators was sometimes a matter of doubt. But gubernatorial indecision could not stand in the way of the rising tide of peace sentiment. Holden, the shrewd and variable editor, who had once supported secession to the last ditch, had caught the drift of the current and converted himself into an earnest advocate of peace. His paper "took" like wildfire, and his subscription list increased enormously. Jonathan Worth, Public Treasurer of the state, was "for peace on *almost any terms*."

Zebulon B. Vance.

By January, 1864, there were open mass meetings for a peace convention—irrespective of what the central government might do—and petitions were circulated for the same end. But the possibilities of state action were checkmated by the rival political ambitions of Holden and Vance, both of whom ran for governor. Ultra-loyal Confederates saw little to choose between the two candidates, but rallied around Governor Vance as the less of two evils. His successful reëlection, however, did not make him appreciably less sensitive to the strength of the peace element. Indeed, he could not well ignore it, for its violence and intensity were uncontrollable. By the end of 1864 he was writing Jefferson Davis that it would be impossible to remove the "sources of discontent" in North Carolina, "except by making some effort at negotiation with the enemy.

    But the ablest advocate of independent state action was Georgia. To the supporters of the administration all the greatest malcontents of the South seemed to have gravitated to that particular region. There was Robert [A.] Toombs, "shifted from Secretary of State to subordinate General, and then to a militia officer under suspended Court Martial," there was Governor Joseph E. Brown and Judge Linton Stephens, and finally there was [Linton's brother] Alexander H. Stephens, Vice President of the Confederacy, who was disappointed because "he had been a cypher, when he expected to be the counsellor and brains of the Confederacy." Even the loyal support of Benjamin H. Hill, Senator from Georgia, could not compensate the administration for such disaffection. But Stephens did not explain his differences with the administration policy on the basis of personal pique or thwarted ambition. Rather, he placed it on the high ground of theory. The *a priori* grounds on which Stephens had based his feeble allegiance to the secession cause were violated by his fellow secessionists. Stephens' primary devotion had always been to the civil rights which the Federal constitution had embodied and consecrated; and, when he left the Union, he tried to the best of his ability to secure the perpetuation of those principles in his state and in the new nation. But he soon beheld in the Confederacy either the actuality or the possibility of conscription, impressments, suspension of *habeas corpus*, military arrests, and imprisonments, and the operation of martial law. The adoption of these arbitrary methods for the conduct of the war was clearly unnecessary in view of the exigencies of the conflict; their use could augur, therefore, only the intention of Jefferson Davis to create a centralized, consolidated, military despotism or to establish a personal dynasty. [Editor's note: As readers of my works know, this was as far from Davis' intention as could possibly be. Thus we must assign the origins of this ludicrous statement to the author's incomplete knowledge of both Davis and authentic Southern history. L.S.]

    Stephens was "wretched" at this perversion of Confederate war aims. It seemed to him that the ambition and zeal of the Southern President alone stood in the way of peace, and that, if he were willing to surrender the attainment of Southern independence and his own continuation in power, the guarantees of the civil and political rights which were so dear to the heart of Stephens, could once again be secured within the Federal Union.[47]

By the early summer of 1863 Stephens, whose role in the Confederacy had become one of habitual criticism, saw an opportunity to stay the march of the South toward the inevitable goal of a military despotism. Difficulties had arisen with the North over the exchange and treatment of prisoners and Stephens believed that he would be a fit emissary for the conduct of negotiations to bring about the amelioration of the situation. But this question of prisoners was only a minor point—an excuse for the discussion of the greater question of peace. [Wrote Stephens:]

> "I am not without hope that indirectly I could now turn attention to a general adjustment upon such basis as might ultimately be acceptable to both parties and stop the further effusion of blood in a contest so irrational, unchristian, and so inconsistent with all recognized American principles."

Although Stephens was unable to give any reasons for his optimistic faith in the possibility of peace, Davis was willing to adopt his suggestion. The dispatch of Stephens on a peace mission would at least serve to quiet the flood of his criticism and the victorious march of General Lee into Pennsylvania might fittingly be attended with the proffer of peace to a vanquished foe. But Davis' acceptance of Stephens' proposition hedged it about with so many restrictions that the Vice President would be powerless to effect any harm to the campaign of the Confederacy for independence. The Southern President thrusts the whole burden of seeking peace upon Stephens for in his own letter he says not a word about the larger aspects of the proposed mission, but simply details the problems connected with the question of prisoners. If Stephens talks of peace terms, it will evidently be upon his own responsibility.

As a credential for his errand, Davis gave Stephens a letter addressed to Lincoln. Every effort was made to cast this letter in a form which would be acceptable to the Northern President. Pains were taken to forestall a refusal to receive Stephens on the ground that such a reception would "involve a tacit recognition of the

Confederacy," and the letter was drawn up in duplicate, one copy of which was addressed to Abraham Lincoln as Commander-in-Chief of the land and naval forces of the North, and the other addressed to him as President, with the idea that the more acceptable form should be used. But here concession stopped. The letter to Lincoln as President of the United States was signed by Davis as President of the Confederate States. If the North should refuse this recognition, the whole idea of a conference must be abandoned. Such a "conference is admissible only on the footing of perfect equality," and Stephens was instructed to take care that "the equal rights of the Confederacy be always preserved."

Losing no time, Stephens proceeded by the steamer *Torpedo*, a vessel of the Confederate navy, to City Point. Once there, he applied to [U.S.] Admiral Samuel P. Lee for permission to proceed to Washington to deliver a letter from Jefferson Davis to Abraham Lincoln. Stephens neglected to state the object of his mission. The receipt of this request was the occasion for confusion at Washington. There were two cabinet meetings which served to air a quarrel between [U.S. Secretary of the Navy, Gideon] Welles and [U.S. Secretary of War, Edwin M.] Stanton as to which Department should be the medium of communication with the Southern emissary, to disclose the President's inclination to despatch someone to Fortress Monroe to discover Stephens' purposes, and finally to show the great diversity of opinion among members of the cabinet. Probably everyone was more interested in the news which came from Vicksburg and from Gettysburg. At last on July 6 [1863], a telegram was dispatched which stated that Stephens' request was inadmissible and that the regular "agents and channels are adequate for all needful military communication . . ." The Vice President returned disheartened and perplexed to the Confederacy.

The events of the summer and fall were not such as to strengthen his waning belief in the success of the Confederate cause. The last six months of that year unrolled before the South an unwelcome vista of military defeat. Gettysburg and Vicksburg were followed by Chattanooga and Missionary Ridge. Under Stephens' guidance, Georgia became a center of rising dissatisfaction.

In March, 1864, the Vice President of the Confederacy

delivered a remarkable address before the Georgia Legislature. It rehearsed his customary opposition to conscription and to the suspension of the right of *habeas corpus*; stated that he would not trust the "dictatorship" of the country to the President or anyone else; and implied in conclusion that Georgia might well assert its sovereignty rather than submit to a new "master." As a result of this extraordinary attack upon the President and his policies, the Georgia Legislature passed resolutions, sponsored by Linton Stephens, a brother of Alexander, on the suspension of *habeas corpus* and on the question of peace. The latter series, which were far more revolutionary in tone, asserted the general right of secession and attacked the Lincoln administration as despotic and tyrannous. This was a form of appeal to the peace party of the North [primarily members of the then Conservative Democratic Party]. The resolutions then went on to state that on a favorable opportunity the state organizations and the central government of the South should make an offer of peace to the North on the basis of the Declaration of Independence. Such an offer would have a desirable effect in the North, f or, even if it were refused, the peace party of the North would be encouraged and strengthened. In the South efforts for peace are thwarted only by men, "whose importance, or whose gains, would be diminished by peace, and men whose arbitrary designs would need cover under the ever-recurring plea of the necessities of the war."

If any new stimulus to Stephens' distrust of the administration was needed, it came from [U.S. Gen. William T.] Sherman's march into Georgia, the capture of Atlanta, and the threat which the Federal [U.S.] army presented to Georgia and to the Confederacy. Sherman, to be sure, did his best to capitalize the discontent of the state which he had invaded and sent a hearty invitation to Governor [Joseph E.] Brown and Stephens to confer with him as to the possibilities of peace. Both refused but with reservations. Brown expected that the last paragraph of his answer "as looking to a possible contingency, in which Mr. Davis would not be recognized as superior" would be attacked by administration supporters; and Stephens, perhaps influenced by Toombs, refused to participate in negotiations largely on the ground that he possessed no power to do so. Although they might refuse a conference with a Federal

[U.S.] general, they still dallied with the idea of separate state action, perhaps in conjunction with other states, as a means to circumvent the obstacles which Davis had placed in the sure way toward peace.

Jefferson Davis.

If the President and Vice President had hitherto veiled their hostility to each other from a sense of dignity as to what was becoming in the two leading executives of the Confederacy, that restraint was cast aside by the end of the year. In October Davis paid a visit to the Southern armies and on his return made an address at Augusta, Georgia, the heart of the enemy's country. He attacked the croakers [that is, Southern cynics and pessimists] who saw no hope in the Confederate cause, repudiated for himself any idea of negotiation except on the basis of a recognition of Southern independence, apologized for the harshness of Confederate legislation on the plea of necessity, and advised those who "can plan in their closets the campaigns of a general and write the State papers of an executive" to "go to the front and there give us the benefit of their services."

But Jefferson Davis could not stay in Georgia to excite the enthusiasm of the mob. He had to return to Richmond. Stephens remained on the job. The [re-]election of Lincoln swept away, once for all, his delusive hopes of peace through a victory of the Northern peace party. In a letter published in the *Augusta Constitutionalist*, he implied that Davis preferred the election of Lincoln to [U.S. Gen. George B.] McClellan—a statement which carried the further implication that Davis preferred war to peace. Linton Stephens introduced into the Georgia House of Representatives resolutions urging the calling of a convention of states to negotiate peace. This movement Davis met in a letter to certain members of the Georgia Senate. Any such step, as envisaged by the resolutions, seemed to Davis a logical absurdity. If a convention of all the states should assemble for the purpose of negotiating peace, it would meet under one of two conditions, for either the decisions of such a body would be binding upon all the states, or they would not be binding. In the former case, the South would be at the mercy of the North; in the latter case, the North would indirectly admit the right of the South for independence. Furthermore, a convention meeting simply for the purpose of negotiating peace, without any previous agreement as to whether or not its decisions would be binding, is a cumbersome method, infinitely inferior to individual negotiators. Jefferson Davis then strips the proposal of all its pretences and places his finger upon the real difficulty in the Stephens plan of negotiation—a difficulty parallel to that which bewildered northern Democrats—that is the unwillingness of the North to advance peace propositions acceptable to the South.

Stephens, meanwhile, had left Georgia for Richmond in order to assume his duties as presiding officer in the Senate. He was in a gloomy mood. The further suspension of the writ of *habeas corpus* seemed likely to be sanctioned by the House of Representatives and Stephens thought he might even resign the vice presidency and thus wash his hands clean from all complicity in the acts of the Davis dynasty. His temper, moreover, was not improved by the correspondence with the President over Stephens' accusation that the former preferred the election of Lincoln rather than McClellan. Each epistolary contestant found the activities of the other "strange" and Davis, on January 8 [1865], closed the controversy with the chiding statement that he would like to see Stephens "devoting your great and admitted ability exclusively to upholding the confidence and animating the spirit of the people to unconquerable resistance against their foes."

The dissatisfaction with the course of the war could not be confined to state capitals or to state politics. The craving for peace which had grown so rapidly in North Carolina and Georgia surged up to Richmond. January bore heavy witness to a gradual sapping of the Confederate morale by the personal bitterness and the petty bickerings of a discontented and apprehensive people. [Editor's note: This *Northern* view of the Southern people in early 1865 is not accurate. L.S.]. The croakers, hitherto somewhat restrained, increased in numbers and outspokenness. The discontent of this opposition found an expression, in the first place, in an attempt by the Confederate Congress to take the control of policy away from the President. There had always been a party of opposition to Davis; it had become more restive after the disasters of the summer of 1863; now it determined to save the country from the misfortunes of his rule.

It first attempted to interfere with the conduct of military affairs; a resolution was passed requesting the President to appoint Robert E. Lee, general-in-chief of all the Confederate armies, and to restore Joseph E. Johnston to the command of the army of the Tennessee. In civil affairs there was a similar interference. The Virginian delegation in the House of Representatives in an address to the President expressed a want of confidence in the cabinet and, as a result of their action, [James A.] Seddon, [C.S.] Secretary of War and a Virginian, felt compelled to resign. From another direction pressure was exerted to compel the President to make peace. The reassembling of Congress saw a flood of resolutions on the subject in the House of Representatives. In this movement Henry S. Foote, a Representative from Tennessee and a member of the Committee on Foreign Affairs, was a leader. Foote was an explosive person who had never been on completely friendly terms with Jefferson Davis. There had been personal differences in the old days when Davis and Foote were both Senators from Mississippi in the Federal Senate, and during the Civil War, especially in the later years, the latter "blew clouds of vituperative gas at President and Cabinet."

On December 1, 1864, Foote introduced a resolution calling for a convention of the Southern states in order either to devise measures for the more efficient prosecution of the war or so to alter the treaty-making powers of the government as "to secure as early a cessation of hostilities and restoration of peace as would be compatible with honor, safety, and the permanent happiness of the people of the said Confederate States." This motion was laid on the table. Two weeks later, Josiah Turner, Representative from North Carolina and likewise a member of the Committee on Foreign Affairs, introduced a resolution whose object was the appointment of thirteen commissioners, one from each of the Confederate states, who were to propose to the North a convention for the purpose of negotiating peace. After debate, the House referred this resolution, with others offered as amendments, to the Committee on Foreign Affairs.

These resolutions were only the surface indications of the forces which were working underground in the House of Representatives.

[John B.] Baldwin of Virginia was restive; [Arthur S. C.] Colyar, [John D. C.] Atkins, and [Thomas] Menees, all of Tennessee, were of the same opinion as their colleague Foote. They determined, if possible, to influence the deliberations of the Committee on Foreign Affairs in the direction of resolutions looking toward peace. Foote, however, could not harness his excitable nature to any more deliberate measures. The possibility of the passage of the act to suspend the writ of *habeas corpus* drew from him a threat to resign the seat which he occupied in the Confederate Congress. Fleeing from Richmond, he wrote a letter on December 24 [1864] from "the bank of the Potomac, in sight of the birthplace of [George] Washington, to the Speaker of the House, in which he resigned his seat and announced his intention of departing for the Northern capital to make peace. On this journey he was accompanied by his wife. For some reason she was allowed to pass through the Federal Lines; her husband, not so fortunate, was arrested by the Confederate military authorities and imprisoned at Fredericksburg. Jefferson Davis referred the question of privilege involved to the House of Representatives.

The insurgents, meanwhile, had won a partial victory in the House of Representatives. On January 12, 1865, John A. Orr of Mississippi, Chairman of the Committee on Foreign Affairs, introduced into secret session a series of resolutions which expressed a desire for peace, suggested as a method of negotiation a convention of all the states a convention which was merely to deliberate upon means for peace and make no final agreement, and finally called upon the President to allow the House, voting by states, to select three commissioners to proceed to Washington and there discover if such a convention could be assembled. If this method of peace making was unacceptable, the commissioners were to discuss other methods and particularly the possibility of a joint action to uphold the Monroe Doctrine in return for a "prompt recognition of the independence" of the Confederacy. By a narrow majority of four, the consideration of these resolutions was postponed until the disposal of a bill dealing with the military organization of the Confederacy. The debate on these resolutions, revived by an article in the *Sentinel* which denounced them as "treason!" again demonstrated the closeness of sentiment in the House and the fact that its members were still unwilling to force the President's hand in the matter of peace negotiations.

In the Senate, the chief ally of the discontents was naturally Alexander H. Stephens. He was privy to their desire to push through the lower House resolutions in favor of a peace convention. He may even have been the author of the resolutions which were presented on January 12 [1865]. In the Senate he lost no opportunity to express his dissatisfaction with the conduct of the administration. The debate over the suspension of the writ of *habeas corpus* was so manipulated as to prevent a statement of his views, an act which almost led him to resign. But the Senate assuaged his injured feelings by a resolution, passed unanimously, which requested him to present his opinions on the state of the country. In a long extempore address on January 6, he gave them his views "very freely."

Only a brief condensation of those frank remarks now remains. He advocated, however, that the policy of the administration "should be speedily and thoroughly changed" and, as suggestions for this revolution, proposed a Fabian military policy and a cultivation of the peace element in the North by means which are not at all explicit in his report of his own oration. Probably he advocated peace negotiations as a means for showing the North the real purpose of the Lincoln administration and the Northern President's desire to create a military despotism. Stephens saw in Presidents North and South nothing but dynasties and despotisms.

While the ferment of this discontent was brewing, Francis Preston Blair, Sr., paid his first visit to Richmond and read his editorial appeal to Jefferson Davis. Every aspect of the situation in the Confederate capital seemed to impel the President to consider favorably Blair's suggestions. The obstacle to previous negotiations—the question of Southern independence—was adroitly concealed by the Mexican project and, therefore, Davis could not be accused of inconsistency if he again entered upon negotiation. Thus, on the one hand, he was sheltered from the southern fire-eaters [diehard pro-South secessionists]. On the other hand, by making a sincere effort at peace, he could quiet the clamor of the peace crowd and ease the pressure which it was bringing to bear upon him. If, in the course of negotiations, it should again develop that the North would make no concession to Southern self-government, there would be renewed enthusiasm for the war. In any case the possibility of an armistice would be of military advantage. Accordingly, Davis assented to the "dreams of an old man."

F. P. Blair, Sr., on his return to Washington, carried with him a note written to him by Jefferson Davis. In it the Southern President asserted his willingness to dispense with forms and to send or receive commissioners. But the closing words ran,

> "That notwithstanding the rejection of our former offers, I would, if you could promise that a commissioner, minister, or other agent would be received, appoint one immediately, and renew the effort to enter into conference, with a view to secure peace to the two countries."

In his report to Lincoln, Blair had to give not only the results of his visit to Richmond, but also the first account of the proposals which he had laid before the Confederate President. With the Mexican project, as Blair had drawn it up, Lincoln would have nothing to do; but he was in other respects willing to continue negotiations. In turn he wrote a letter to Blair. This letter authorized him to tell Jefferson Davis that

> "I have constantly been, am now, and shall continue ready to receive any agent, whom he, or any other influential person now resisting the national authority, may informally send to me with the view of securing peace to the people of our one common country."

On the 20th of January Blair left Washington for Richmond on the *Don*.

Blair was soon back in Secessia, for on the 21st he presented Lincoln's reply to Jefferson Davis. There was still some ambiguity over the Mexican project, but Blair spoke of the President's reticence in that matter as due to his difficulties with the extremists [that is, the socialist-communist element in the then Liberal Republican Party] in [the U.S.] Congress; an armistice to carry out the objects which Blair and Davis had previously discussed would have, therefore, to be arranged by some military convention between Lee and Grant. Whatever may have been the actual situation, Davis was apparently left under the impression that the Mexican expedition was still a possibility.

On January 25 [1865], Blair returned from his second visit to the Confederacy. He had had quite a sojourn at Richmond and the nature of his errand was a subject of great curiosity and speculation there. It was known that he came on the question of peace and the extremist [Republican socialist-communist] press viewed with great alarm the cordiality with which, it was rumored, he was received by the President [Davis]. The *Richmond Examiner* thought that Blair was either a spy or a propagandist, a fit person in any case to be excluded from the country; and advised Jefferson Davis, if he must interview such persons, to depart permanently for the other side of the Potomac. The *Whig* lamented the increased power which Blair's mission gave to the Confederate peace crowd and dreaded a repetition of the "peace mania" which last summer "brought us to the verge of ruin." The *Sentinel*, the fiercest opponent of compromise, pictured peace on Northern terms as involving universal confiscation of property and judicial murders, and asserted that "All the dark and malignant passions of a vindictive people, drunk with blood and vomiting crime, will be unloosed upon us like bloodhounds upon their prey."

Blair enjoyed the greatest freedom in Richmond and he did not confine himself to conversation with Jefferson Davis. His acquaintance with Southerners was extensive and with this acquaintance, including as it did many officials of the Confederacy, he talked about the desirability of peace. The resources of the North, he pointed out, were overwhelming and there were vast reserves of manpower in Europe which could be utilized if the North promised European recruits a portion of Southern confiscated lands. The South might well submit before it was utterly exhausted. It is doubtful whether Blair had any closer connection with the Southern peace movement than that of general encouragement. Robert Ould, Commissioner of Exchange for prisoners, at whose home Blair spent his first visit in Richmond, testifies to the propriety of Blair's conversation and one of those who thought him a spy bears witness to Blair's silence rather than his loquacity.

Blair, meanwhile, had returned to Washington. On January 28 [1865] he gave the final report of his mission to Lincoln and he had again to utilize his gift for reconciling difficult situations. It was necessary to convince Lincoln that Davis would enter into negotiations with the purpose of uniting the two warring sections. Such had been the implication of the words at the end of Lincoln's letter of January 18—"securing peace to the people of our one common country." Davis had written earlier that negotiations should be entertained to "secure peace to the two countries." If the Civil War was to be brought to a conclusion, one of these two conceptions would have to surrender. Without the promise of such a surrender, negotiations would be fruitless. But this discrepancy between the two letters did not daunt Blair. He told Lincoln that Davis had read the letter of January 18 twice and "at the close of which he (Mr. Blair) remarked that the part about 'our one common country' related to the part of Mr. Davis' letter about 'the two countries,' to which Mr. Davis replied that he so understood it."

When Blair had departed from Richmond, Davis consulted Stephens concerning the advisability of entering into negotiations and concerning the personnel of the peace commission. Davis expressed himself as fully convinced that the administration would support Blair's proposals but he doubted the wisdom of making a military agreement which might result in reunion. Stephens was naturally in favor of a conference under any condition. The joint attack upon Mexico might not result in reunion; if it did, reunion would be on terms which would recognize the theoretical position of the Confederacy. Anyway, an armistice would be advantageous. Then Stephens turned to the question of emissaries. He first proposed Jefferson Davis himself, and then, when the President refused, suggested John A. Campbell, Assistant Secretary of War, General Henry L. Benning, ex-Justice of the Supreme Court of

Georgia, and Thomas S. Flournoy, a Virginian who was well known to President Lincoln. The qualifications of these men were their ability and the fact that their absence from the Confederacy would not attract attention. Just why Stephens had suddenly devised this latter criterion, after previously urging the departure of Jefferson Davis, is a problem. The interview terminated as members of the cabinet arrived to discuss, for the first time, the same situation.

The next day, January 28 [1865], the Vice President of the Confederacy was pained to learn that Davis and his cabinet had not seen fit to follow his advice as to the membership of the commission. To be sure, there was agreement as to Judge John A. Campbell, but the other members were Robert M. T. Hunter and Alexander H. Stephens. Stephens was in despair for Hunter and himself did not fulfill the qualification of being inconspicuous. Hunter was President *pro tempore* of the Senate, and he himself was Vice President and the presiding officer of the upper House. Their absence from Richmond would be sure to attract attention and arouse comment. He urged upon the President the advisability of changing so undesirable an arrangement, but Davis was obdurate. The selection of Stephens, displeasing as it was to him, should have been no surprise. The President's [Davis] acceptance of Blair's proposition was in part determined by the desire to answer the complaints of the malcontents and the critics of the [Davis] administration. If that purpose were to be fulfilled and if there were to be no charges of bad faith, it was important to entrust the conduct of negotiations to the proponents of peace. Of these Stephens was certainly the most outstanding.

Alexander H. Stephens.

Another of Stephens' colleagues, John Archibald Campbell, was also an advocate of peace. Campbell, appointed in 1853 to the Supreme Court of the United States, had resigned this position at the outbreak of the war and sadly [a Yankee term, L.S.] followed Alabama, his native state, in its withdrawal from the Union. Under the Confederacy he held no office until 1862 when he was appointed Assistant Secretary of War and placed largely in control of the relations of that Department with civilians. One of the motives which induced him to accept this position was the hope that he would be in a more influential position for promoting peace. By the end of 1864 he was pointing out the exhaustion of the Confederacy and urging members of Congress to take measures for negotiation. Finally in December, 1864, with the approval of Hunter, Seddon, and even Jefferson Davis, he sent a letter to an old colleague of his in the North, Judge Nelson. Campbell, asserting his belief that an "honorable peace" might be made, announced himself ready to confer informally for that purpose with Nelson or with Ewing of Ohio, Judge Curtis, or [U.S.] Secretary Stanton. Campbell would naturally be wholly unaccredited; his sole object was "simply to promote an interchange of views and opinions which might be productive of good and scarcely do harm." This letter Nelson showed to Stanton who gave a qualified approval of the project, but said that nothing could be done until the scheme of President Lincoln and of Francis P. Blair [Sr.] had been tried.

The third member of the commission, Robert Mercer Taliaferro Hunter, possessed a mellifluous name and the usual experience of a Virginian politician. He came from a family of the Virginian aristocracy—the F.F.V.'s—and his political career in that state had been shaped by this influence. Before the Civil War he had been first a Representative and then a Senator in the national Congress. There, as an exponent of [John C.] Calhoun's views on state's rights, he became more and more in sympathy with the ideas of such men as Jefferson Davis and Robert Toombs. It was logical, therefore, that in the Baltimore Convention of 1860 he should advocate the support of [John C.] Breckinridge and [Joseph] Lane, that he should think it advantageous for Virginia to secede if the cotton states left the Union, and that he should become Secretary of State in Davis' cabinet. In 1862 he left this office to his successor, Judah P. Benjamin, and entered the Confederate Senate as a member from Virginia. His life during the remainder of the war was not a happy one. Financial difficulties, always serious, were increased when Federal [U.S.] troops in1863 burned down the mill on his plantation and drove away his horses and cattle. Earlier he had been embittered by the loss of his eldest son. By 1865 he seemed to have become convinced that the further prosecution of the war was impossible. Mrs. Hunter was despondent, the remarks of F. P. Blair, Sr., transmitted to Hunter by another Confederate Senator, made a deep and gloomy impression, the conscription of boys as young as sixteen and the enrollment of negroes in the army were unpleasant prospects [false: nearly every Confederate officer was in favor of black enlistment. L.S.], the military situation of the Confederacy was increasingly unfavorable. In January Hunter was a frequent caller on Judge Campbell. A partisan observer explained the sudden activity of so fat a man as due to a desire to obtain news of approaching disasters in time to save somehow the remnants of his fortune. But Campbell and Hunter more likely were discussing means to obtain their common desire, the initiation of peace negotiations.

On the afternoon of January 28 [1865], the three commissioners met President Davis. He told them of the project which F. P. Blair, Sr., had presented to him but gave them no very exact account of how the joint arrangement as to Mexico was to be carried out. Then, on the night of the same day, Mr. Washington of the State Department delivered to Campbell the money for the expenses of the journey and the commissioners' letters of appointment. As he received them, Campbell remarked that their last sentence closed with the phrase, "the purpose of securing peace to the two countries," while the letter of Lincoln to F. P. Blair, Sr., which was to serve as their passport, spoke of "one common country." Campbell's observation disclosed the dilemma which confronted Davis. On the one hand, he desired the peace mission in order to silence the clamor of his foes and perhaps to salvage something by the delay of an armistice. It is inconceivable that he really believed that Lincoln would consent to disunion. On the other hand, Davis was determined to accept nothing short of independence for the Confederacy. Such had been the upshot of his conversation with Stephens, such were his verbal instructions to the commissioners by which they were allowed to make any sort of treaty other than one providing for the reconstitution of the Federal

Union, such had been the difficulty with [Judah P.] Benjamin over drawing up the letter of appointment. The Confederate Secretary of State had foreseen the unwisdom of being too explicit and had advocated vagueness and generalities. He had written,

> "In compliance with the letter of Mr. Lincoln, of which the foregoing is a copy, you are hereby requested to proceed to Washington city for conference with him upon the subject to which it relates."

To this form of appointment, Davis objected because it might apparently be misconstrued to be a confession that Davis was willing to sacrifice independence. The President rewrote the letters so as to read, "for informal conference with him upon the issues involved in the existing war, and for the purpose of securing peace to the two countries."

In truth there was no other course open with honor to the Confederate President. He had taken his oath of office to maintain and defend the government of the Confederacy. He could not violate that oath. As long as the army existed in the field and the people gave any support, he was determined to fight on. If the course of events had changed the determination of the people whom he represented he "should have bowed to their will, but would never have executed it."

It is interesting to speculate as to what the commissioners thought of the instructions which practically reduced their mission to an effort to secure an armistice and discover Northern peace terms. What did this delegation of confirmed peace men think of the proposal of no peace without independence? Stephens was convinced that they had no power to accomplish anything except the securing of an armistice, but whether he was pained at this limitation of their functions is problematical. His own thinking on the subject of peace seems somewhat akin to Horace Greeley's in its confusion. He had certainly envisaged, however, the possibility of reunion with eagerness and complacency. Campbell admits that a short while after the conference, he was in favor of reunion. Hunter's attitude seems a piece of his usual uncertainty. *In a later controversy with Jefferson Davis he announced that no one of the commissioners was in favor of reunion, and that a peace drawn up on that basis had no chance of acceptance* [my emphasis, L.S.]. Yet seven years earlier, he states that he was of the opinion that abolition and reunion should be accepted, and the best possible terms secured on the other points at issue. But whatever may have been their personal feelings, the commissioners accepted their appointment, and on January 29 [1865] reached the lines in the vicinity of Petersburg.

The scene now shifts to the Northern army. Under a flag of truce, Lieutenant Colonel [William H.] Hatch of the Confederate forces asked permission for three peace commissioners, on their way to Washington, to cross the lines "in accordance with an understanding claimed to exist with Lieutenant General Grant." Through the regular military hierarchy this request eventually reached headquarters only to find General Grant absent from the army and Major General Edward O. C. Ord, Commander of the Army of the James, the ranking officer on the spot. That afternoon the latter forwarded the despatch to Washington for instructions. Stanton, in reply, expressed no knowledge of any such arrangement and forbade the passage of the commissioners until the telegram had been acted upon by the President [Lincoln]. The President then formulated his course of action. As a result of an evening conference, he reached a decision to send a special messenger to the lines in order to examine the instructions of the Confederate commissioners and see if they were really authorized to make peace on the conditions which he had proposed. This decision showed that the President had not taken too seriously the assurances of the elder Blair, for only the previous day the latter had reported that Davis had understood Lincoln's position and accepted the phrase "our one common country."

Admirers of Stanton have wished to see in the President's caution in admitting the Confederate commissioners another evidence of the great War Secretary's influence. Undoubtedly Stanton, reflecting the extremist position, disliked all overtures for peace and distrusted all persons who thought peace was possible. He may have felt with other extremists [Republican socialists and communists] that the President was too apt to be swayed by the dictates of leniency and loving kindness; he certainly did not trust the Blairs. By 1865, however, Lincoln was unquestionably master of his own administration and his own grasp of peace possibilities, a grasp, strengthened by the previous peace negotiations, is sufficient to account for his unwillingness to embark upon further peace efforts without a definite clarification of the Southern independence issue.[48]

The bearer of the President's instructions was Major Thomas T. Eckert. Eckert had worked his way into the [U.S.] War Department through a knowledge of the telegraph. Stanton had made him a Major, given him a horse and carriage for his official duties, and placed him in complete charge of the telegraphs in the war offices. Over the telegraph Stanton loved to exercise a despotic control; and for this purpose Eckert, his grateful appointee, was an excellent instrument. Some of the latter's activities, indeed, seem those of an offensive busybody. On one occasion he took the liberty of withholding from transmittal communications from a certain New York politician to McClellan and of showing them to Stanton. At another time he delayed, on his own responsibility, the despatch of the order for the removal of General [George H.] Thomas until news of a victory by Thomas' army arrived.

On the morning of January 30 Eckert was given his instructions. He was to deliver to the commissioners a copy of Lincoln's letter to F. P. Blair, Sr., and to ask if they accepted its terms. If the answer was in the affirmative, the Confederates were to pass through the lines where they would be met for the purpose of an informal conference by a commissioner or commissioners from the North. If they did not accept these terms, Eckert was to refuse them safe conduct. But meanwhile affairs were taken out of the hands of Eckert and the Washington authorities by the return of Lieutenant General Grant to the headquarters of the army. Arriving on the morning of January 31 [1865], he was uninformed as to the previous correspondence between his subordinates and Washington, and confronted with a personal letter which the restless Confederate commissioners had dispatched to him the previous evening. This letter reiterated the desire of the commissioners to go to Washington to discuss terms of peace upon the basis of the letter of F. P. Blair, Sr., "of which we presume you have a copy"; and then added that, if this procedure is impossible, they wished to see Grant in person and confer with him on the subject of peace. Grant at once dispatched this note to the President

[Lincoln] and coupled it with the information that he had sent a staff officer to admit the Confederates.

In accordance with Grant's instructions, Lieutenant Colonel [Orville E.] Babcock of Grant's staff met the commissioners almost at sunset at the Petersburg lines. The commissioners walked across no man's land, covered with its mute testimony of the long battle which had been waged there, amid cheering by soldiers of both armies. As they boarded the train for City Point, there was again cheering.

It was late when they reached their destination. Babcock led them to the door of a log cabin, then knocked, and, when a voice replied, "Come in," opened the door and ushered in the commissioners. A plainly attired man was busy writing by the light of a kerosene lamp. The Confederates could hardly believe that they were in the presence of the commander of the Federal forces.

Grant's dispatch of the early morning, meanwhile, had arrived at Washington and had compelled an alteration in the plans for the treatment of the commissioners. Eckert, who had not yet departed, was, nevertheless, sent on his mission—a mission considerably attenuated by the fact that the commissioners had passed through the Union lines without his preliminary scrutiny; and Seward was despatched to Hampton Roads to confer with the peace emissaries once they were admitted. The President [Lincoln] evidently believed that the reception of the envoys by Grant was sufficient credential. The instructions to the Secretary of State were definite and a trifle peremptory. He was to lay down three indispensable conditions of peace:

> "1st. The restoration of the national authority throughout all the States.
> 2nd. No receding by the Executive of the United States, on the slavery question, from the position assumed thereon in the late annual message to Congress and in preceding documents.
> 3rd. No cessation of hostilities short of an end of the war and the dis-banding of all forces hostile to the government."

The Secretary was to hear what the commissioners had to say and then report to the President. He himself was authorized to take no action of any kind.

On February 1 [1865], the Confederate commissioners passed

the day pleasantly on one of General Grant's dispatch boats. They had conversations with many officers, among whom were [U.S.] General [George G.] Meade and General Grant, and they found that the desire for peace was prevalent.

In the afternoon, however, they were annoyed by the arrival of Major Eckert, who delivered his message from President Lincoln. The answer which the commissioners framed and which they handed to Eckert at six o'clock did not satisfy his matter of fact mind. The commissioners, indeed, had found it difficult to reconcile the discrepancy between Lincoln's letter and their instructions. Stephens observed that neither letter was correct as really thirty-six countries were involved. But theoretical distinctions aside, the difficulty had to be met. In their reply, therefore, the commissioners included a statement of their instructions and then said that

> "Our earnest desire is that a just and honorable peace may be agreed upon, and we are prepared to receive or to submit propositions which may possibly lead to the attainment of that end."

Eckert, however, was able to see only the difference between "one common country" and "two countries." He refused to let them go further.

General Ulysses Simpson Grant, however, [being a Southerner] had an independent nature. Already he had admitted the Confederate commissioners within his lines in a manner which was above quibbling about technicalities and instructions from Washington. In fact, he seemed positively eager to meet the commissioners, and they, on their side, were equally eager to arrange matters with him personally. A partial explanation of Grant's actions can be found in the fact that the Blairs had taken him into their confidence in the matter of their peace efforts. Old Blair [Francis, Sr.] had arranged with Grant the means by which the Mexican foray was to be carried out. In Richmond he had hinted to Jefferson Davis of the possibility of a military convention between Lee and the Federal commander. And then there was Mrs. Ulysses Simpson Grant, née Julia B. Dent, a descendant of an old Maryland family and a resident of St. Louis, whence the Blairs came. An officer told Hunter that Mrs. Grant thought that her husband ought to arrange an interview for the commissioners; that they were "good men" and their "intentions were praiseworthy"; that a conference with Mr. Lincoln might accomplish great good, especially if Seward were excluded. He would be likely to prevent a settlement by his *"wily tactics"* [my emphasis, L.S.]. This advice has a ring reminiscent of the Blairs. It is no wonder that the commissioners were as impressed by the friendliness of Mrs. Grant as they were by that of her husband. Both seemed eager for the conference to take place.

The commissioners, disappointed by Eckert, naturally turned their next efforts toward General Grant. At eight o'clock that evening he received a note from them which stated that

> "We desire to go to Washington City to confer informally with the President [Lincoln] personally, in reference to the matters mentioned in his letter to Mr. Blair of the 18th of January ultimo, without any personal compromise on any question in the letter. We have permission to do so from the authorities in Richmond."

Eckert was shown this note but he again gave his refusal and then dashed to the telegraph office to transmit his reports to Stanton and Lincoln. He closed the latter message with the statement that since he had complied with his instructions, he would return to Washington on the next day. As far as he was concerned the incident was closed. A half hour later, Grant, in a circumspect telegram to Stanton, said that, as a result of his conversations with Hunter and Stephens (Campbell was ill), he was convinced that the "intentions" of the commissioners were "good" and "their desire sincere to restore peace and union." Although he recognized the difficulties in the way of receiving them, he did not think it wise to have them go back to Richmond without meeting some one of authority. In fact, he was "sorry that Mr. Lincoln cannot have an interview" with them. As for their instructions, their letter to Grant was all the President had asked for, even if they had used different language to Eckert.

On the morning of February 2 the various participants in this negotiation transferred their activities to Fortress Monroe. First of all went Eckert in consequence of a command sent by Seward on the previous evening; and then followed the commissioners. Grant, without waiting to hear from Washington, had determined to send them since "they have accepted the proposed terms"; but, before their departure, a telegram arrived from Washington saying that Lincoln would be a party to the conference. Grant, showing his gratification at the good news, announced the President's determination to the commissioners, and soon afterwards the *Mary Martin*, a dispatch boat, headed away from City Point for Hampton Roads. There the commissioners arrived in the course of the afternoon.

Lincoln, meanwhile, had about made up his mind to recall both Seward and Eckert in view of the latter's report, when he received Grant's telegram of the night before. The news it contained not only led him to alter his decision in regard to the recall of Seward, but also induced him to join the latter at Hampton Roads. With an attaché of the White House, the President left by train for Annapolis where he boarded the *Thomas Colyar*. Late that evening he arrived at Fortress Monroe and went at once aboard the *River Queen*, the vessel by which Seward had come down earlier and upon which he was now awaiting the arrival of his chief.

Abraham Lincoln and his family.

On the morning of February 3 [1865], occurred the Hampton Roads Conference. The Confederate commissioners went on board the *River Queen*, which was decked with flags and anchored about fifty rods from the shore, and were ushered into the cabin where the actual meeting was to take place. Seward and the President entered soon after. These five men, with the addition of a colored servant who came in occasionally with refreshments and with things to smoke, were the only ones present at the famous Hampton Roads Conference.

The conversation opened with an exchange of pleasantries

between Stephens and Lincoln. They recalled the old days when they were members of a club to secure the election of [Zachary] Taylor; Lincoln asked after various acquaintances in the Confederacy; both talked of their services in Congress. These reminiscences served as a graceful reminder of the former days of harmony and good feeling, and eased the conversation into a discussion of how they might be restored.

Lincoln, at the outset, demanded the unequivocal restoration of the Union and at once Stephens tried to divert the consideration of this point by alluding to Blair's Mexican project. The President replied that, while Blair meant well, he had no official authority whatever. The project could not be carried out by granting an armistice unless a previous pledge was given that the Union would be restored . This pledge the commissioners were not able to give. Then, in accordance with a previous understanding among themselves to ferret out the possible bases for peace even if they could not secure an armistice, Campbell asked what the terms for reconstruction of the Union would be. The immediate pursuit of this subject was prevented by Seward who asked Stephens to elaborate his Mexican project as it had a "philosophical basis." Stephens then developed his favorite theory as to how such a joint operation would serve to unite the two countries. There would first be a secret military agreement between the North and South providing for the location of troops, the division of tariff receipts, and for other necessary arrangements. Then the two nations would turn their common forces upon the enemy. Such a proceeding would have the practical value of uniting the two sections in one common purpose; it would also have the theoretical value of stressing the principle of the Monroe Doctrine the right of self-government—a principle which would gradually be recognized as the correct one for the settlement of the differences between the North and the South. "This great law of the System would effect the same results in its organization, as the law of gravitation in the material world"; it would pull the states together.

The other commissioners, less abstruse, thought that the joint assertion of the Monroe Doctrine would approximately result in the end foreseen by Stephens. Campbell said that such a project would bring about reunion; and Hunter, although he thought

Southern independence might still be retained, believed a close military and commercial alliance would eventuate.

Seward and Lincoln spoke for the Union. Although they both disliked the presence of the French in Mexico, their objections to the Mexican project were fundamental and numerous. The former attacked Stephens' reasoning on practical grounds. The right of self-government violated the law of self preservation. For instance, could the whole United States allow Louisiana, which controlled the mouth of the Mississippi, to govern itself independently to the extent of forming an alliance with foreign countries?

Then there were the details of the military arrangements. Lincoln saw that the formulation of an agreement would lead to bickering and jealousy and besides he had no power to make such an agreement. The right to declare war lay with Congress; the Senate had a share in the making of treaties. In any case he had no intention of making such a convention without first securing an unconditional recognition of the Union. To do otherwise would be to recognize the Confederacy and the justice of their status in rebellion against the national authority.

Hunter, who had been much pained by Stephens' earlier remarks, now broke into the conversation. The South was not a unit in support of the proposed Mexican procedure. As for himself, he did not lay claim to the whole country or entirely approve of a war waged for policy rather than for honor as the Mexican project envisaged. Hunter, in fact, was under the impression that the commissioners were not empowered to enter into any agreement involving the coöperation of Northern and Southern arms, for the subjugation of Mexico.

The discussion now returned to the bases of a possible reconstruction. Seward opened the question by quoting from the President's message of the previous December the parts which reiterated his purpose to end the war only on the acceptance of the Congressional and Executive acts in regard to emancipation. Campbell replied with a query about confiscation. Seward answered that this was a question for the courts, but that Congress would be liberal in restoration and indemnity. Hunter raised the question of the status of West Virginia. Would it continue to be independent or would it be reunited with Virginia? Lincoln leaned to the former opinion. *Then arose the question of the Southern slave and the real effect of the emancipation proclamation upon him. As to the application of the proclamation, Lincoln felt that it was a war measure and as such it would be inoperative in time of peace. As far as he could tell, it applied only to the number of slaves which had already been freed by it—a number which Seward estimated at 200,000* [my emphasis, L.S.]. Although the proclamation would not be withdrawn, its applicability was to be determined by the courts and the courts might do anything.

Then Seward produced the Thirteenth Amendment. The commissioners deduced from his conversation that he did not take it very seriously. Stephens believed that Seward thought that, if the Southern states made peace and reëntered the Union they could defeat the amendment by their votes. *Campbell said Seward thought the amendment was a war measure and the demand for it would cease with peace although the extremist [Republican socialists and communists] sentiment in the North was growing. Lincoln had a different proposal. He began by admitting that the emancipation proclamation had been forced upon him; that he had adopted it solely as a war measure. His own belief was that the government in time of peace had no power over slavery except in the territories. He, nevertheless, did believe in the rightfulness of eventual emancipation everywhere. Even then it would cause suffering, but that suffering was inevitable* [my emphasis, L.S.].

To Hunter, Lincoln's attitude and the story of the Illinois farmer and the hogs, which he told to illustrate it, seemed harsh and ruthless. [In essence, Lincoln told this story to illustrate his true sentiment toward freed slaves: "Let 'em root or perish."][49] Then Lincoln advised Stephens to return to his native state, and induce it to withdraw active support from the war and ratify the Thirteenth Amendment "prospectively, so as to take effect—say in five years." But *whatever method of freeing the slaves was followed, all the commissioners, Northern and Southern, recognized the evils of immediate emancipation* [my emphasis, L.S.].

The discussion of the main points at issue was now concluded and attention was directed informally to various aspects of the peace situation. The commissioners thought that Lincoln should make some preliminary agreement with the Southern states in case they should wish to return to the Union. Hunter said there had been precedents for such an action. [King] Charles I had made a treaty with rebels. Lincoln referred the question of history to Seward and replied that "all he knew of Charles I was that he lost his head." Hunter remarked with intensity that to give up all arms and all guarantees of fair treatment was "unconditional submission." Seward replied that they did not use that word; the South would have all the safeguards of the constitution and the courts. Lincoln said that in the exercise of powers delegated to him by the various confiscation and penal acts, he would be very lenient. As for the readmission of the states into the Union, he could not tell what Congress would do; he disapproved of their policy in regard to the already reconstructed states. For himself, moreover, he would be willing to be taxed in order to compensate owners for their freed slaves; *the North was as much responsible for slavery as the South* [my emphasis, L.S.]. Some had even proposed $400,000,000 as a proper amount. But the President could not answer for others as to such compensation. As for Seward's attitude on the same subject, the commissioners derived different impressions. Stephens thought that Seward was in favor of compensation; but the other two Southerners inferred that Seward regarded the military expenditures of the North as enough of a debt to incur in behalf of abolition.

The conference had now lasted for four hours and there was a pause in the conversation. The commissioners arose and talked over matters of smaller import, such as the exchange of prisoners. Stephens asked the President to reconsider the possibility of an armistice and received a noncommittal answer. Lincoln and Seward left the cabin; Babcock escorted the Confederates to their boat.

In the afternoon the President left for Annapolis and Washington; the commissioners departed for City Point and Richmond. The Hampton Roads Conference was over.

The Southern commissioners returned very much sobered. Stephens realized the grave military situation of the South, intensified by the loss of Fort Fisher, which protected the Confederacy's last outlet to the world, and saw that the cause of the country was lost without peace. There should be another mission to the North for which the possibilities of success would be greater if it were less public.

Campbell saw the impossibility of another campaign and thought that the Conference had offered some terms less bitter than total subjugation. But the opinions of Hunter differed slightly from those held by his confrères. The Hampton Roads Conference had angered him, for Lincoln's terms, involving as they did complete submission, seemed unnecessarily harsh. Still even his uncertain nature realized the difficulties in the way of military success. For the moment, it was a question which road—peace or war—led to the less gloomy prospect.

He seemed willing to be influenced in either direction. But these differences and timidities of opinion found no replica in the mind of Jefferson Davis. Conscious of his own severe sincerity of purpose and of act, he could not ascribe a similar quality to Lincoln. Lincoln, he thought, had acted in bad faith; the statements of the Southerners, especially as regards the Monroe Doctrine, would be used by the Northern commissioners to create international hostility against the South. Such considerations, however, were purely secondary ones. The vital fact was that the North offered to the South at Hampton Roads unconditional submission. Jefferson Davis could not in honor accept such a termination to the war. The only choice was a continuation of the struggle.

To further such a purpose the Hampton Roads Conference could be utilized. The first difficulty was the report to be made by the commissioners. Two of them were certainly unwilling to participate in a design to lead the South into a new war fury. Besides, the conference had been confidential. The result of this conflict was a simple statement signed by all three commissioners. It said that Lincoln's bases for peace were unaltered from those laid down in his December message to Congress; no treaty or armistice could be granted to the Confederate states; Lincoln would use the powers entrusted to him liberally; and "during the conference the proposed amendment to the Constitution of the United States, adopted by Congress on the 31st ult., was brought to our notice." Although this report omitted several qualifications of importance, it did not prejudice the case for peace or for war. The Presidential message which transmitted the report to the Senate and the House of Representatives of the Confederate States, however, infused color and vigor into its matter of fact assertions. The North refused to give any terms or guarantees other "than those which the conqueror may grant, or to permit us to have peace on any other basis than our unconditional submission to their rule. . . ."

On the evening of the same day, February 6, occurred a gigantic mass meeting at the African Church. Over two hours before the speaking was scheduled to begin, every seat was taken and fears were entertained as to the safety of the galleries . [C.S.] General [William] Smith of Virginia opened the meeting and then came Davis. For three quarters of an hour he held his audience mastered. Newspaper accounts of the speech are inadequate, for they give no hint of his eloquence, of his emotion and of his magnetic power. He hurled defiance at the North, and said that as far as he was concerned, he would rather give up a thousand lives than independence. Carried away by the enthusiasm of the President, the audience adopted resolutions spurning "with indignation due to so gross an insult" the terms which Lincoln proffered, declaring the circumstances under which the terms were offered

> "add to the outrage and stamp it as a designed and premeditated indignity to our people," and asserting "that in the presence, and in the face of the world, reverently invoking thereto the aid of Almighty God, we renew our resolve to maintain our liberties and independence; and to this we mutually pledge our lives, our fortunes, and our sacred honor."

The press, which during the week of negotiations had held its judgment in suspense, now unleashed all its fury. The *Enquirer* said "the prospects of war are much brighter—cannot be darker than those of peace." The *Examiner* saw the Confederacy with three unconquered armies, an uncaptured capital, and an almost uninvaded country. The *Whig* concluded that "to talk now of any other arbitrament than that of the sword is to betray cowardice or treachery."

But the deep tragedy of those days when the President [Davis] and his followers were determined upon immolating their cause and their country was made still deeper by the fact that the South was not a united nation. Stephens refused to address the meeting at the African Church, had a last interview with Davis, and then returned sadly to Georgia.

Campbell's voice was silent.

As for Hunter, his easily influenced nature allowed him to be the presiding officer at a second meeting in the African Church. A day or two later, he had again become convinced that peace was necessary and he turned savagely upon the administration.

The Hampton Roads Conference had delivered the Southern cause into the hands of those who were bent upon the perpetuation of the war for Southern independence. In the North the negotiations had dangerously strengthened the extremist element [the socialist-communist wing of the then Liberal Republican Party].

When the elder Blair moved to and fro on his missions of intrigue and reconciliation, when commissioners from the Confederacy crossed the Federal lines, when Lincoln himself finally departed for Hampton Roads, the radicals [socialists and communists] in the Republican party became thoroughly alarmed. The Committee on the Conduct of the War saw that the Union cause was betrayed and that their own influence was diminished. Stanton was rumored to be disturbed by these new peace efforts. In Baltimore, [Rev. Henry Ward] Beecher addressed a great audience. He painted a picture of a procession of justice

> "with malefactors of the blackest dye, criminals against a nation's life and against humanity, marching to the gibbet, and broken into by people who would stay the execution and let the criminals loose."

A voice in the audience shouted "Blair, Blair," and the crowd became riotous with indignation. The radicals [Republican socialists and communists] were organizing opposition to the leniency of the President [Lincoln].

On February 3, Lincoln had left Hampton Roads for Annapolis. There were crowds at the railroad station in the latter place, eager to learn the results of the negotiation.

On the 4th of February [1865], Lincoln was back in Washington. The next day there was a cabinet meeting. Lincoln proposed an offer of $400,000,000 for the slaves of the Confederates if armed resistance would cease before April. This sum was to be divided into two portions, the first to be paid on April 1, and the second on

July 1, if the slavery amendment was adopted. All political offenses were to be pardoned and all property subject to confiscation was to be freed from that liability. But this offer was disapproved by the cabinet. Congress could not pass such an act before adjournment, and an offer of compensation should not be made until the war was ended by force of arms.

Until the war was ended by force of arms was the result in the North, as it was in the South, of the Hampton Roads Conference.

On February 4, Stanton had telegraphed Grant, at the direction of the President, that nothing should prevent the continuance of his "military plans or operations."

William H. Seward.

In Congress the radicals [Republican socialists and communists] were jubilant. The Hampton Roads Conference had put an end to the talk of peace by negotiations and determined that peace should come only by military victory. In response to the demands of Congress, Lincoln submitted a report on the preliminaries to the negotiations and on the conference itself. On the former point the report was well documented and explicit; on the latter, it was brief. Lincoln and Seward had acted only on the points laid down in the President's memorandum to his Secretary of State.

The Southerners were evasive on the question of reunion and desired a postponement, "which course, we thought, would amount to an indefinite postponement. The conference ended without result." But no event passes without some result.

The Hampton Roads Conference was the last considerable effort to make peace by agreement and to end the war by negotiation. But the President [Davis] of the crumbling Confederacy could not bring himself to make the sacrifice of the ideals and of the cause of the South which such a peace involved.

He elected to take a last desperate chance for success or failure. Humiliating as the Northern terms must have seemed, it would have been the part of wisdom, if not of honor, to have yielded [a Yankee view]. His decision increased the strength of the extreme group in the North [Republican socialists and communists] by furnishing renewed evidence of the unrighteousness of the Confederacy; and, by assenting to a continuation of the war, he made a military peace inevitable. Thus Lincoln's task of reconciliation, of "malice toward none; with charity for all" was made extremely difficult.

It is interesting to speculate as to the course of events if Lincoln had returned from Hampton Roads with the definite acceptance by the Confederate commissioners of his terms of peace. But such speculation is idle. For Appomattox Court House, the tragedy at Ford's Theater, and the days of reconstruction were to determine the peace terms of the American Civil War.[50] — EDWARD CHASE KIRKLAND, AMERICAN HISTORIAN & VERMONT COPPERHEAD

Old Dominion Line steamer at Hampton Roads, Virginia, circa 1905.

Battle of Hampton Roads, showing the fight between the ironclad frigate C.S.S. *Virginia* (formerly the U.S.S. *Merrimack*) and the ironclad warship U.S.S. *Monitor*, Hampton Roads, Virginia, March 9, 1862.

SECTION TWO

Reports of C.S. & U.S. Officials & Participants

2. ACCOUNT OF THE CONFERENCE BY JEFFERSON DAVIS

☛ ... [After numerous communications between Francis P. Blair, Sr. and President Lincoln,] it only remained for me to act upon the letter of Mr. Lincoln [to Mr. Blair, which read:]

> "Washington, January 18, 1865. F. P. Blair, Esq. Sir, you having shown me Mr. Davis's letter to you of the 12th instant, you may say to him that I have constantly been, am now, and shall continue ready to receive any agent whom he or any other influential person now resisting the national authority may informally send to me with the view of securing peace to the people of our one common country. Yours, etc., A. Lincoln."

I determined to send, as commissioners or agents for the informal conference, Messrs. Alexander H. Stephens, R. M. T. Hunter, and John A. Campbell.

A letter of commission or certificate of appointment for each was prepared by the Secretary of State in the following form:

> "In compliance with the letter of Mr. Lincoln, of which the foregoing is a copy, you are hereby requested to proceed to Washington City for conference with him upon the subject to which it relates," etc.

This draft of a commission was, upon perusal, modified by me so as to read as follows:

> "Richmond, January 28, 1865. In conformity with the letter of Mr. Lincoln, of which the foregoing is a copy, you are requested to proceed to Washington City for an informal conference with him upon the issues involved in the existing war, and for the purpose of securing peace to the two countries."

Some objections were made to this commission by the United States officials, because it authorized the commissioners to confer for the purpose "of securing peace to the two countries"; whereas the letter of Mr. Lincoln, which was their passport, spoke of "securing peace to the people of our one common country." But these objections were finally waived.

Jefferson Davis.

The letter of Mr. Lincoln expressing a willingness to receive any agent I might send to Washington City, a commission was appointed to go there; but it was not allowed to proceed farther than Hampton Roads, where Mr. Lincoln, accompanied by Mr. Seward, met the commissioners. *Seward craftily proposed that the conference should be confidential, and the commissioners regarded this so binding on them as to prevent them from including in their report the discussion which occurred. This enabled Mr. Seward to give his own version of it in a dispatch to the United States Minister to the French Government, which was calculated to create distrust of, if not hostility to, the Confederacy on the part of the power in Europe most effectively favoring our recognition* [my emphasis, L.S.]. Why Mr. Lincoln changed his purpose, and, instead of receiving the commissioners at Washington, met them at Hampton Roads, I can not, of course, explain. Several causes may be conjecturally assigned. The commissioners were well known in Washington, had there held high positions, and, so far as there was any peace party there, might have been expected to have influence with its members; but a more important inquiry is: If Mr. Lincoln previously had determined to hear no proposition for negotiation, and to accept nothing less than an unconditional surrender, why did he propose to receive informally our agent? If there was nothing to discuss, the agent would have been without functions.

I think the views of Mr. Lincoln had changed after he wrote the letter to Mr. Blair of June 18th, and that the change was mainly produced by the report which he made of what he saw and heard at Richmond on the night he staid there. Mr. Blair had many acquaintances among the members of the Confederate Congress; and all those of the class who, of old, fled to the cave of Adullam, "gathered themselves unto him."

Mr. Hunter, in a published article on the peace commission, referring to Mr. Blair's visit to Richmond, says:

> "He saw many old friends and party associates. Here his representations were not without effect upon his old confederates, who for so long had been in the habit of taking counsel with him on public affairs."

He then goes on to describe Mr. Blair as revealing dangers of such overwhelming disaster as turned the thoughts of many Confederates toward peace more seriously than ever before. That Mr. Blair saw and noted this serious inclining of many to thoughts of peace, scarcely admits of a doubt; and, if he believed the Congress to be infected by *a cabal undermining the Executive* [my emphasis, L.S.][51] in his efforts successfully to prosecute the war, Mr. Lincoln may be naturally supposed thence to have reached the conclusion that he should accept nothing but an unconditional surrender, and that he should not allow a commission from the Confederacy to visit the United States capital.

[After the conference, the] report of the [three] commissioners, dated February 5, 1865, was as follows:

> "To the President of the Confederate States: Sir: Under your letter of appointment of the 28th ult. we proceeded to seek 'an informal conference' with Abraham Lincoln, President of the United States, upon the subject mentioned in the letter. The conference was granted and took place on the 30th ult., on board of a steamer anchored in Hampton Roads, where we met President Lincoln and the Hon. Mr. Seward, Secretary of State of the United States. It continued for several hours, and was both full and explicit. We learned from them

that the message of President Lincoln to the Congress of the United States, in December last, explains clearly and distinctly his sentiments as to the terms, conditions, and method of proceeding by which peace can be secured to the people, and we were not informed that they would be modified or altered to obtain that end. We understood from him that no terms or proposals of any treaty, or agreement looking to an ultimate settlement, would be entertained or made by him with the authorities of the Confederate States, because that would be a recognition of their existence as a separate power, which under no circumstances would be done; and, for a like reason, that no such terms would be entertained by him for the States separately; that no extended truce or armistice (as at present advised) would be granted or allowed without a satisfactory assurance in advance of the complete restoration of the authority of the Constitution and laws of the United States over all places within the States of the Confederacy; that whatever consequences may follow from the reëstablishment of that authority must be accepted; but that individuals subject to pains and penalties under the laws of the United States might rely upon a very liberal use of the power confided to him to remit those pains and penalties if peace be restored.

"During the conference, the proposed amendment to the Constitution of the United States adopted by Congress on the 31st ultimo was brought to our notice.

"This amendment provides that neither slavery nor involuntary servitude, except for crime, should exist within the United States, or any place within their jurisdiction, and that Congress should have power to enforce this amendment by appropriate legislation. Very respectfully, etc., Alexander H. Stephens, R. M. T. Hunter, John A. Campbell."

Thus closed the conference, and all negotiations with the Government of the United States for the establishment of peace. Says Judge Campbell, in his memoranda:

"In conclusion, Mr. Hunter summed up what seemed to be the result of the interview: that there could be no arrangements by treaty between the Confederate States and the United States, or any agreements between them; that there was nothing left for them but unconditional submission."

By reference to the message of President Lincoln of December 6, 1864, which is mentioned in the report, it appears that the terms of peace therein stated were as follows:

"In presenting the abandonment of armed resistance to the national authority on the part of the insurgents, as the only indispensable condition to ending the war on the part of the Government, I retract nothing heretofore said as to slavery. I repeat the declaration made a year ago, that 'while I remain in my present position I shall not attempt to retract or modify the emancipation proclamation, nor shall I return to slavery any person who is free by the terms of that proclamation, or by any act of Congress.'

"If the people should, by whatever mode or means, make it an executive duty to reënslave such persons, another, and not I, must be their instrument to perform it."

On the 4th of March, 1861, President Lincoln appeared on the western portico of the Capitol at Washington, and in the presence of a great multitude of witnesses took the following oath:

"I do solemnly swear that I will faithfully execute the office of President of the United States, and will, to the best of my ability, preserve, protect, and defend the Constitution of the United States."

The first section of the fourth article of the Constitution of the United States is in these words:

"No person held to service or labor in one State, under the laws thereof, escaping into another, shall, in consequence of any law or regulation therein, be discharged from such service or labor, but shall be delivered up on claim of the party to whom such service or bor may be due."

The intelligent reader will observe that the words of this section, "in consequence of any law or regulation therein," embrace a President's emancipation proclamation, as well as any other regulation therein. Thus the Constitution itself nullified Mr. Lincoln's proclamation, and made it of no force whatever. Yet he assumed and maintained, with all the military force he could command, that it set every slave free. Which is the higher authority, Mr. Lincoln and his emancipation proclamation or the Constitution? If the former, then what are constitutions worth for the protection of rights?

Again he says:

"Nor shall I return to slavery any person who is free by the terms of that proclamation or by an act of Congress."

But the Constitution says he shall return them—

"but shall be delivered up on claim of the party to whom such service is due."

Who shall decide? Which is sovereign, Mr. Lincoln and his proclamation or the Constitution? The Constitution says:

"This Constitution, and the laws of the United States which shall be made in pursuance thereof, shall be the supreme law of the land."

Was it thus obeyed by Mr. Lincoln as the supreme law of the land? It was not obeyed, but set aside, subverted, overturned by him. But he said in his oath:

"I do solemnly swear that I will, to the best of my ability, preserve, protect, and defend the Constitution of the United States."

Did he do it? Is such treatment of the Constitution the manner to preserve, protect, and defend it? Of what value, then, are paper constitutions and oaths binding officers to their preservation, if there is not intelligence enough in the people to discern the violations, and virtue enough to resist the violators?

Again the report says:

"We understood from him that no terms or proposals of any treaty or agreement looking to an ultimate settlement would be entertained or made by him with the authorities of the Confederate States, because that would be a recognition of their existence as a separate power, which under no circumstances would be done; and, for a like reason, that no such terms would be entertained by him for the States separately."

Now the Constitution of the United States says, in Article X:

"The powers not delegated to the United States by the Constitution, nor prohibited by it to the States, are reserved to the States respectively, or to the people."

Within the purview of this article of the Constitution the States are independent, distinct, and sovereign bodies—that is, in their reserved powers they are as sovereign, separate, and supreme as the Government of the United States in its delegated powers. One of these reserved powers is the right of the people to alter or abolish any form of government, and to institute a new one such as to them shall seem most likely to effect their safety and happiness; that power is neither "delegated to the United States by the Constitution nor prohibited by it to the States." On the contrary, it is guaranteed to the States by the Constitution itself in these words:

> "The powers not delegated to the United States by the Constitution, nor prohibited by it to the States, are reserved to the States respectively, or to the people."

Mark the words, "are reserved to the States respectively, or to the people." No one will venture to say that a sovereign State, by the mere act of accession to the Constitution, delegated the power of secession. The assertion would be of no validity if it were made for the question is one of fact as to the powers delegated or not delegated to the United States by the Constitution. It is absurd to ask if the power of secession in a State is delegated to the United States by the Constitution, or prohibited by it to the States. No trace of the delegation or prohibition of this power is to be found in the Constitution. It is, therefore, as the Constitution says, "reserved to the States respectively, or to the people."

The Convention of the State of New York, which ratified the Constitution of the United States on July 26, 1788, in its resolution of ratification said:

> "We do declare and make known . . . that the powers of Government may be reassumed by the people, whensoever it shall become necessary to their happiness; that every power, jurisdiction, and right, which is not by the said Constitution clearly delegated to the Congress of the United States, or to the departments of the Government thereof, remains to the people of the several States, or to their respective State governments, to whom they may have granted the same. . . . Under these impressions, and declaring that the rights aforesaid can not be abridged or violated," etc., etc., "we, the said

delegates, in the name and in behalf of the people of the State of New York, do, by these presents, assent to and ratify the said Constitution."

With this and other conditions stated in the resolution of ratification, it was accepted and approved by the other States, and New York became a member of the Union. The resolution of Rhode Island asserts the same reservation in regard to the reassumption of powers.

It is unnecessary to examine here whether this reserved power exists in the States respectively or in the people; for, when the Confederate States seceded, it was done by the people, acting through, or in conjunction with, the State, and by that power which is expressly reserved to them in the Constitution of the United States. When Mr. Lincoln, therefore, issued his proclamation calling for seventy-five thousand men to subjugate certain "combinations too powerful to be suppressed by the ordinary course of judicial proceedings," he not only thereby denied the validity of the Constitution, but sought to resist, by military force, the exercise of a power clearly reserved in the Constitution, and reaffirmed in its tenth amendment, to the States respectively or to the people for their exercise. But, *in order to justify his flagrant disregard of the Constitution, he contrived the fiction of "combinations," and upon this basis commenced the bloody war of subjugation with all its consequences. Thus, any recognition of the Confederate States, or of either of them, in his negotiations, would have exposed the groundlessness of his fiction. But the Constitution required him to recognize each of them, for they had simply exercised a power which it expressly reserved for their exercise. Thus it is seen who violated the Constitution, and upon whom rests the responsibility of the war* [my emphasis, L.S.].

It has been stated above that the conditions offered to our soldiers whenever they proposed to capitulate, were only those of subjugation. When [Confederate] General [Simon B.] Buckner, on

February 16, 1862, asked of [U.S.] General [Ulysses S.] Grant to appoint commissioners to agree upon terms of capitulation, he replied:

> "No terms, except unconditional and immediate surrender, can be accepted."

When [Confederate] General [Robert E.] Lee asked the same question, on April 9, 1865, General Grant replied:

> "The terms upon which peace can be had are well understood. By the South laying down their arms, they will hasten that most desirable event, save thousands of human lives and hundreds of millions of property not yet destroyed."

When [U.S.] General [William T.] Sherman made an agreement with [Confederate] General [Joseph E.] Johnston for formal disbandment of the army of the latter, it was at once disapproved by the Government of the United States, and Sherman therefore wrote to Johnston:

> "I demand the surrender of your army on the same terms as were given to General Lee at Appomattox, on April 9th, purely and simply."

It remains to be stated that the Government which spurned all these proposals for peace, and gave no terms but unconditional and immediate surrender, was instituted and organized for the purposes and objects expressed in the following extract, and for no others:

> "We, the people of the United States, in order to form a more perfect union, establish justice, insure domestic tranquillity, provide for the common defense, promote the general welfare, and secure the blessings of liberty to ourselves and our posterity, do ordain and establish this Constitution for the United States of America."[52] —
PRESIDENT JEFFERSON DAVIS, CONFEDERATE STATES OF AMERICA

3. ACCOUNT OF THE CONFERENCE BY JOHN H. REAGAN
☛ Vice-President [Alexander H.] Stephens, as shown in his *History of the War Between the States*, and in utterances after the fall of

Vicksburg and the drawn battle at Gettysburg, and even before that, seemed to think something could be done to arrest the carnage of war by negotiations; and offered his service for that purpose in June, 1863. He evidently believed there was some possibility of favorable results from an effort at that time. After this matter had been discussed between them, the [Confederate] President [Jefferson Davis] gave him authority to go to Washington and see whether anything could be done. The authority he had from the President was to endeavor to secure a renewal of the cartel for the exchange of prisoners; but the discussion, as shown in Mr. Stephens's book, indicated that he hoped to offer suggestions looking to a cessation of hostilities. While it is not stated by him or by the President in their printed accounts about the matter, I understood at the time that the Vice-President hoped for some good effect on account of the fact that he and [U.S.] President [Abraham] Lincoln had been associated as Whig members of Congress, and as friends before the war, and that he might, because of that, be in a better position to invite the attention of Mr. Lincoln to pacific measures. He went to the Federal lines, but was refused permission to proceed to Washington.

In his history (Vol. II, p. 561) he uses this language, referring to what he hoped to accomplish:

> But if Mr. Lincoln could be prevailed on to agree to such a conference, then the object proposed, besides effecting, if possible, the general amelioration of prisoners, and the mitigation of the horrors of war as conducted by the Federals [U.S. government and military officials], was to use the occasion for effecting also, if possible, other material results which might open the way for future negotiations that might eventually lead on to an amicable adjustment. . . . In this view Mr. Davis did not concur. He did not believe that the road to peace lay in that way. He did not think that anything towards its ultimate obtainment could be effected on this line of external policy indicated by me.

But his book shows that after the siege of Vicksburg and the battle of Gettysburg, he himself had lost confidence in the scheme. However, it was finally agreed between them that he should undertake the trip to Washington; but this programme was superseded by the Hampton Roads Conference, growing out of the

Hon. Francis P. Blair's intercession.

On the 12th of January, 1865, the venerable Francis P. Blair [Sr.], by permission of the Federal and Confederate authorities, visited President Davis at Richmond, Virginia, in the interest of peace between the United States and the Confederate States. He disavowed any authority from the Government of the United States to act for it. His idea seems to have been to secure a conference between the military authorities of the two governments; and to arrange a plan, without any formal negotiations, by which the armies of the two countries could be united and sent to Mexico to enforce the Monroe Doctrine against the Government of the Emperor Maximilian. After this conference, Mr. Davis gave Mr. Blair a letter stating that he had no desire to throw obstacles in the way of negotiations for the restoration of peace between the two countries, and that he was ready to send commissioners for that purpose whenever he had reason to suppose they would be received. Mr. Blair having returned to Washington, on the 13th of January President Lincoln addressed a note to him in which he referred to the letter of President Davis, and expressed his willingness to receive any agent whom Mr. Davis might send him, with a view of securing peace to our common country.

John H. Reagan.

Upon learning of this disposition, Mr. Davis determined to send as Commissioners, for an informal conference, Vice President Stephens, the Hon. R. M. T. Hunter, president of the Confederate Senate and former United States Senator; and the Hon. John A.

Campbell, formerly a justice of the Supreme Court of the United States. The following is the commission under which they were to act:

> Richmond, January 23, 1865. In conformity with the letter of Mr. Lincoln, you are requested to proceed to Washington City for an informal conference upon the issues involved in the existing war, and for the purpose of securing peace to the two countries.

Mr. Lincoln changed his purpose, and, instead of receiving them at Washington, met them at Hampton Roads. The Confederate Commissioners were met there also by Secretary of State W. H. Seward on the part of the United States.

During recent years there has been an extensive discussion through the public prints of the questions which rose at the Hampton Roads Conference. It has been asserted over and over that President Lincoln offered to pay $400,000,000 for the slaves of the South to secure an end of the war; and that he held up a piece of paper to Mr. Stephens, saying: "Let me write the word Union on it, and you may add any other conditions you please, if it will give us peace." I am probably not using the exact words which were employed, but I am expressing the idea given to the public, in the discussion. It has frequently been alleged that Mr. Stephens said these offers were made. *This has been repeated by citizens of acknowledged ability and high character, and it has been said that these offers could not be acceded to because the instructions given to the Commission by President Davis prevented it. The purpose of urging these untrue statements seems to have been to induce the public to believe that Mr. Davis could have obtained peace on almost any terms desired and $400,000,000 for the Southern slaves if he would have consented to a restoration of the Southern States to the Union; and that, because of this, he was responsible for the losses of life and property caused by the continuance of the war* [my emphasis, L.S.].

I shall submit evidence which will prove that no such propositions were ever made. This course is rendered necessary and just, both for the truth of history, and to vindicate the action of President Davis and his Cabinet. For, *undoubtedly, one of the purposes of insisting that such offers were made is to mislead the public as to the truth* [my emphasis, L.S.].

The following is the report of the Confederate Commissioners to President Davis as to what occurred at the Conference held on the 5th of February [1865]:

"Richmond, Va., February 5, 1865. To the President of the Confederate States—Sir: Under your letter of appointment of the 28th ult. we proceeded to seek an 'informal conference' with Abraham Lincoln, President of the United States, upon the subject mentioned in the letter. The conference was granted and took place on the 3rd inst. on board of a steamer in Hampton Roads, where we met President Lincoln and the Hon. Mr. Seward, Secretary of State of the United States. It continued for several hours and was both full and explicit.

"We learned from them that the message of President Lincoln to the Congress of the United States in December last explains clearly and distinctly his sentiments as to the terms, conditions, and methods of proceeding by which peace can be secured to the people, and we were not informed that they would be modified or altered to obtain that end. We understand from him that no terms or proposals of any treaty or agreement looking to an ultimate settlement would be entertained or made by him with the Confederate States, because that would be a recognition of their existence as a separate power, which under no circumstances would be done, and for this reason that no such terms would be entertained by him from the States separately, that no extended truce or armistice, as at present advised, would be granted without a satisfactory assurance in advance of a complete restoration of the authority of the United States over all places within the States of the Confederacy.

"That whatever consequences may follow from the reestablishment of that authority must be accepted, but that individuals, subject to pains and penalties under the laws of the United States, might rely upon a very liberal use of the power confided to him to remit those pains and penalties if peace be restored.

"During the conference the proposed amendment to the Constitution of the United States, adopted by Congress on the 31st ult., was brought to our notice. This amendment declares that neither slavery nor involuntary servitude, except for crimes, should exist within the United States or any place within their jurisdiction and that Congress should have power to enforce this amendment by appropriate legislation. Of all the correspondence that preceded the conference herein mentioned and leading to the same you have been informed. Very respectfully your obedient servants, Alexander H. Stephens, Robert M. T. Hunter, John A. Campbell."

Complaint has been made that Mr. Davis, by the wording of his instructions to the Commission, prevented them from making peace on any other terms than upon the condition of the independence of the Confederate Government; and that but for this condition, peace might have been secured at the Hampton Roads Conference. The official papers of that conference show that no terms could have been obtained or considered other than the unconditional surrender of the Confederate authorities. Mr. Davis knew the Vice-President's strong inclination to make peace on such terms as could be had. This is evidenced by Mr. Stephens's *History of the War Between the States*, and by his many statements to others; and it is fair to presume that the limitation put upon the power of these Commissioners was for the purpose of making it certain that they should agree to nothing less than either the recognition of the independence of the Confederacy, or at least the securing of protection against the unlawful domination of its enemies. There was a wide divergence of views between the President and Vice-President on this subject. Mr. Stephens never seemed to realize that there was no time, while we had fighting armies in the field, that the people and the Army would have permitted an unconditional surrender if the President had been so inclined; nor would Mr. Davis at any time have consented to surrender while we had armies in the field able and willing to prolong the contest, rather than submit to *Federal wrongs* [my emphasis, L.S.].

It is seen that the Confederate Commissioners say that no terms or proposals of any treaty or agreement would be entertained by President Lincoln with the authorities of the Confederate States, or with any of the States separately, and that no truce or armistice would be allowed without satisfactory evidence, in advance, of the complete restoration of the authority of the Constitution and laws of the United States over all places within the States of the Confederacy. This report was signed by Mr. Stephens, Mr. Hunter, and Judge Campbell. It shows conclusively that unconditional surrender, in advance of any negotiations, was the only condition whereby the war could be ended. And Judge Campbell, in his memoranda relating to this Conference, says that:

> In conclusion, Mr. Hunter summed up what seemed to be the result of the interview: that there could be no arrangements by treaty

between the Confederate States and the United States, or any agreement between them; there was nothing left for them but unconditional submission.

On the 6th of February, 1865, President Davis sent the report of the Commissioners to the Confederate Congress, with a message in which he used this language:

> I herewith transmit for the information of Congress the report of the eminent citizens above named, showing that the enemy refused to enter into negotiations with the Confederate States, or any of them separately, or to give our people any other terms or guaranties than those which the conquerors may grant, or to permit us to have peace on any other basis than our unconditional submission to their rule, coupled with the acceptance of their recent legislation on the subject of the relations between the black and white population of each State.

In his *History of the War Between the States* (Vol. II, pp. 599-626) Vice-President Stephens gives a carefully compiled account of what was done at the conference; and in this he shows plainly and fully the distinct refusal of President Lincoln to recognize, or in any form to make or agree to any terms for peace with the Government of the Confederate States, or with any of the States separately, except upon the condition that they should, before any other measure should be considered, recognize and accept the Constitution and laws of the United States, and trust to Congress as to what disposition was to be made of the Confederacy, their people, and property. There is no word in his long account of any proposition as to the payment of $400,000,000 for the slaves, or of President Lincoln's writing the word Union on a sheet of paper and allowing Mr. Stephens or any one else to determine the terms and conditions upon which the war should be ended.

The joint resolutions, expressing the sense of the Confederate Congress on the subject of the Peace Commission, are as follows:

> Whereas, the Congress of the Confederate States have ever been desirous of an honorable and a permanent settlement, by negotiation, of all matters of difference between the people of the Confederate States of America and the Government of the United States; and to this end provided, immediately on its assembling at Montgomery in February, eighteen hundred and sixty-one, for the sending of three

commissioners to Washington, to negotiate friendly relations on all questions of disagreement between the two Governments, on principles of right, justice, equity and good faith; and, whereas, these having been refused a reception, Congress again, on the fourteenth of June, eighteen hundred and sixty-four, adopted and published a Manifesto to the civilized world, declaring its continued desire to settle, without further shedding of blood, upon honorable terms, all questions at issue between the people of the Confederate States and those of the United States, to which the only response received from the Congress of the United States has been, the voting down, by large majorities, all resolutions proposing an amicable settlement of existing difficulties; and, whereas, the President has communicated to this Congress that, in the same spirit of conciliation and peace, he recently sent Vice-President Stephens, Senator Hunter, and Judge Campbell to hold conference with such persons as the Government of the United States might designate to meet them; and, whereas, those eminent citizens, after a full conference with President Lincoln and Secretary Seward, have reported that they were informed explicitly that the authorities of the United States would hold no negotiations with the Confederate States, or any of them separately; that no terms, except such as the conqueror grants to the subjugated, would be extended to the people of these States; and that the subversion of our institutions, and a complete submission to their rule, was the only condition of peace: Therefore,

Section First. Resolved by the Congress of the Confederate States of America, that while Congress regrets that no alternative is left to the people of the Confederate States but a continuance of the war or submission to terms of peace alike ruinous and dishonorable, it accepts in their behalf the issue tendered them by the authorities of the United States Government, and solemnly declares that it is their unalterable determination to prosecute the war with the United States until that power shall desist from its efforts to subjugate them, and the independence of the Confederate States shall have been established.

Section Second. Resolved, that the Congress has received with pride the numerous noble and patriotic resolutions passed by the Army, and in the gallant and unconquered spirit which they breathe, coming from those who have for years endured dangers and privations, it sees unmistakable evidence that the enthusiasm with which they first dedicated their lives to the defense of their country is not yet extinct, but has been confirmed by hardships and suffering into *a principle of resistance to Northern rule* [my emphasis, L.S.], that will hold in contempt all disgraceful terms of submission; and for these expressions in camp, as well as for their noble acts in the field, our soldiers deserve, and will receive the thanks of the Country.

Section Third. Resolved, that the Congress invite the people of these States to assemble in public meetings, and *renew their vows of devotion to the cause of independence; to declare their determination to maintain their liberties* [my emphasis, L.S.]; to pledge themselves to do all in their power to fill the ranks of the Army; and to provide for the support of the families of our soldiers, and to cheer and comfort, by every means, the gallant men, who, for years, through trials and dangers, have vindicated our rights on the battlefield.

Section Fourth. Resolved, that, invoking the blessing of God, and confiding in the justice of our cause, in the valor and endurance of our soldiers, and in *the deep and ardent devotion of our people to the great principles of civil and political liberty for which we are contending* [my emphasis, L.S.]. Congress pledges itself to the passage of the most energetic measures to secure our ultimate success. T. S. Bocock, Speaker of the House of Representatives. R. M. T. Hunter, President pro tempore of the Senate. Approved 14th March, 1865. Jefferson Davis.

So it is seen that we have the report of the Confederate Commissioners to the President, the message of the President to Congress, the joint resolutions of the two Houses of the Confederate Congress, and the evidence of Mr. Stephens's history of what occurred at that Conference to prove that no such offers were made by Mr. Lincoln.

While it may seem unnecessary, I will go further and add to these testimonials those of President Lincoln and Secretary Seward.

Mr. Lincoln at first determined to send Secretary of State Seward to meet the Confederate Commissioners, and on the 31st of January, 1865, furnished him with instructions for his Government, which contained these provisions:

> You will make known to them that three things are indispensable, to wit: 1, the restoration of the national authority throughout all the States; 2, no receding by the Executive of the United States, on the slavery question, from the position assumed thereon in the late message to Congress, and in preceding documents; 3, no cessation of hostilities short of an end of the war and the disbanding of all forces hostile to the Government.

In Mr. Lincoln's annual message to Congress dated December 5th, 1864, he says:

> At the last session of Congress a proposed amendment of the

Constitution abolishing slavery throughout the United States passed the Senate, but failed of the requisite two-thirds vote of the House of Representatives. Although the present is the same Congress, and nearly the same members, and without questioning the wisdom and patriotism of those who stood in opposition, I venture to recommend the reconsideration and passage of the measure at the present session.

And the same message contained the following:

In presenting the abandonment of armed resistance to the national authority, on the part of the insurgents, as the only indispensable condition to ending the war on the part of the Government, I retract nothing heretofore said as to slavery. I repeat the declaration made a year ago, that while I remain in my present position I shall not attempt to retract or modify the Emancipation Proclamation, nor shall I return to slavery any person who is free by the terms of that proclamation, or by any of the acts of Congress. If the people should, by whatever mode or means, make it an executive duty to re-enslave such persons, another, and not I, must be their instrument to perform it.

The [final] proclamation here referred to by President Lincoln was that of January 1, 1863, for which [the preliminary proclamation] that of September 22, 1862, had prepared the way. In that of the later date he declared:

That on the 1st day of January, 1863, all persons held as slaves within any State or designated part of a State, the people whereof shall be in rebellion against the United States, shall be then, thenceforward, and forever free.

Charles F. Adams, Sr.

In the face of his annual message of December 5, 1864, and of these two proclamations, how could President Lincoln have proposed to pay $400,000,000 for the slaves he had already set free, and did not intend to return to a condition of slavery? And how could he have said that if he were allowed to write the word Union on a piece of blank paper the Confederate Commissioners might name any terms they pleased to end the war?

On the 7th of February, 1865, Mr. Seward addressed a communication to the Hon. Charles Francis Adams [Sr.], the Minister Plenipotentiary of the United States to Great Britain, giving, for his information, an account of what occurred at the Hampton Roads Conference. This letter, it will be observed, was written four days after that Conference. In it, among other things, he said that President Lincoln announced to the Confederate Commissioners:

> That we can agree to no cessation or suspension of hostilities, except on the basis of the disbandment of the insurgent forces, and the restoration of the national authority throughout all the States in the Union. Collaterally, and in subordination to the proposition which he thus announced, the anti-slavery policy of the United States was reviewed in all its bearings, and the President announced that he must not be expected to depart from the positions he had assumed in his Proclamation of Emancipation, and other documents, as these positions were reiterated in his last annual message. It was further declared by the President that the complete restoration of national authority everywhere was an indispensable condition to any assent on our part to whatever form of peace might be proposed. The President assured the other party that while he must adhere to these positions, he would be prepared, as far as power was lodged with the Executive, to exercise it liberally. His power, however, is limited by the Constitution; and when peace should be made, Congress must necessarily act in regard to appropriations of money and the admission of representatives from the insurrectionary States. The Richmond party [the three Confederate commissioners] was then informed that Congress had, on the 31st ultimo, adopted by a Constitutional majority a joint resolution submitting to the several States the proposition to abolish slavery throughout the Union, and that there is every reason to expect that it will be accepted by three-fourths of the States, so as to become a part of the organic law.

I have not access to the *Life of Lincoln* by [John G.] Nicolay and [John] Hay, but I am informed that it fully sustains the views I am presenting on this question.

While it is true that some respectable men have asserted that Mr. Stephens told them of Mr. Lincoln's alleged offer,—and I have all their statements in writing or print, there must have been some misunderstanding as to his language, for he was an honorable and truthful man, and a man of too much good sense to have made such allegations in the face of such record as is here presented. Among those who assert that Mr. Stephens made one or the other of those statements are the Hon. Henry Watterson, editor of the Courier-Journal; the Rev. E. A. Green, of Virginia; Dr. R. J. Massey, of Georgia; and Mr. [Clark] Howell. Any impartial person who may read the statements of Mr. Green will see his gross ignorance of the matters of which he writes, and any one who will read what he says and what Dr. Massey says will see that *the main purpose with them was to throw discredit on President Davis for not making peace on terms which, as the evidence shows, were not offered, and which we were fully informed could not be allowed the Confederates. And it is also clear that a prime object with Dr. Massey was to lionize Mr. Stephens while discrediting Mr. Davis* [my emphasis, L.S.].

Among those who say Mr. Stephens denied making these statements are the Rev. F. C. Boykin of Georgia; Mr. R. F. Littig of Mississippi; Hon. James [L.] Orr of South Carolina, who was at that time associated with Vice-President Stephens as a member of the Confederate Senate; Hon. Frank B. Sexton, then a member of the Confederate Congress; Col. Stephen W. Blount of Texas, who had been a schoolmate, and was a friend to Mr. Stephens, who, in answer to Blount's inquiry, wrote that he never made any such remark; Mr. Charles G. Newman, of Arkansas; and Governor A. H. Garland, of Arkansas, who was at the time of the Conference a member of the Confederate Senate, and the roommate of Mr. Stephens, and who has been United States Senator, and Attorney-General of the United States. Governor Garland says that on the return of the Confederate Commissioners Mr. Stephens told him no terms of peace could be had except upon unconditional submission of the Confederates.

It is not pleasant to have to consider such a conflict of statements. It has arisen between men of ability and character in the discussion of one of the important historical questions which grew out of the great contest. And *the published statements show that there was an extensive effort being made to pervert and falsify the history of that important conference so as to cast public censure on President Davis for not terminating the war upon conditions which were not offered* [my emphasis, L.S.].

I also have a letter from Senator [George G.] Vest of Missouri, who was then a Confederate Senator, in which he says:

> "R. M. T. Hunter, who was President *pro tempore* of the Confederate Senate, told me in detail what occurred at the Fort Monroe Conference, and it agrees with your statements. No more truthful and conservative man than Hunter ever lived."

The message of Mr. Lincoln of March 6, 1862, and his conference with border State representatives, at that time, and the statements he made to Mr. Stephens at the Hampton Roads Conference, and perhaps other expressions of his, showed, I think, his personal willingness that compensation should have been made for the slaves of the South, but the message referred to, and the conference which followed, were in March of the second year of the war; his suggestion then was that the border States of the Confederacy should adopt a general plan of emancipation upon the basis of compensation, and that if this was done it would defeat the purpose of the Southern States. *It was a bid to the border States to desert their Southern sister States* [my emphasis, L.S.]. Those representing the border States declined to act on this suggestion, for it was only a suggestion; for them to have acted in advance of any move by the Northern States, and with no assurance that if they should adopt such a policy it would ever be accepted by the North would have been a species of madness. This, however, had no direct relation to what occurred at Hampton Roads.

I have no doubt that Mr. Stephens recited the statement made by President Lincoln at that conference to the effect that he, personally, would have no objection to an arrangement for compensation for the slaves if that would end the war, and that he knew persons who would be willing to pay $400,000,000 for that purpose. This is probably the basis and the only basis for the stories so often repeated about his offering at that conference to pay $400,000,000 if it would end the war. And when Mr. Stephens spoke of these two things, his hearers, I must suppose, misunderstood him, or misconstrued his words. It is better to view it thus and to assume that the stories referred to had their origin in that way than to believe that wilful misstatements were made.

I served with Mr. Stephens in the Congress of the United States four years before the war. We served together in the Provisional Congress of the Confederacy; were thrown together more or less during the war; and we served together in [the U.S.] Congress for several years after the war. I always regarded him as an upright, honorable man. I was his friend, and admired his genius and ability, though I thought during the war, and have not changed my opinion, that he had very impracticable views as to the methods of conducting the war. And I fear from his writings and from the statements attributed to him by others that during the latter part of the war, and after it closed, *he allowed his great name and influence to give too much encouragement to malcontents, who caused embarrassment to the Confederate Government, and who endeavored to cast unjust reflections on the policy, actions and services of President Davis, his Cabinet and the Confederate Congress* [my emphasis, L.S.].⁵³ — FORMER C.S. POSTMASTER GENERAL JOHN HENNIGER REAGAN

4. ACCOUNT OF THE CONFERENCE BY ALEXANDER H. STEPHENS

☞ . . . After Mr. Lincoln's telegram to him that he would meet us at Fortress Monroe, which General Grant brought to us himself, with evident indications of high gratification, he immediately started us on one of his despatch boats. We reached the Roads in the evening of the same day. We remained on board the steamer which anchored near the Fort [Monroe]. Mr. Lincoln arrived in another steamer during the night, which anchored not far off. Mr. Seward, as is known, had been sent on a day or two in advance. So much then for the first point as to the objects, and how I became connected with this Conference.

We come now to the Conference itself, and what occurred at it.

The interview took place in the Saloon of the steamer [*River Queen*], on board of which were Mr. Lincoln and Mr. Seward, and which lay at anchor near Fortress Monroe. The Commissioners were conducted into the Saloon first. Soon after, Mr. Lincoln and Mr. Seward entered. After usual salutations on the part of those who were previously acquainted, and introductions of the others who had never met before, conversation was immediately opened by the revival of reminiscences and associations of former days.

Alexander H. Stephens.

This was commenced by myself addressing Mr. Lincoln, and alluding to some of the incidents of our Congressional acquaintance—especially, to the part we had acted together in effecting the election of General [Zachary] Taylor in 1848. To my remarks he responded in a cheerful and cordial manner, as if the remembrance of those times, and our connection with the incidents referred to, had awakened in him a train of agreeable reflections, extending to others. Mutual inquiries were made after the fate and well-being of several who had been our intimate friends and active associates in a "Congressional Taylor Club," well-known at the time. I inquired especially after Mr. Truman Smith, of Connecticut, and he after Mr. [Robert A.] Toombs, William Ballard Preston, Thomas S. Flournoy, and others. With this introduction I said in substance: Well, Mr. President, is there no way of putting an end to the present trouble, and bringing about a restoration of the general good feeling and harmony then existing between the different States and Sections of the country?

Mr. Seward said: It is understood, gentlemen, that this is to be an informal Conference. There is to be no clerk or secretary—no writing or record of anything that is said. All is to be verbal.

I, speaking for the Commissioners, said that was our understanding of it. To this all assented, whereupon I repeated the question.

Mr. Lincoln in reply said, in substance, that there was but one way that he knew of, and that was for those who were resisting the laws of the Union to cease that resistance. All the trouble came from an armed resistance against the National Authority.

But, said I, is there no other question that might divert the attention of both Parties, for a time, from the questions involved in their present strife, until the passions on both sides might cool, when they would be in better temper to come to an amicable and proper adjustment of those points of difference out of which the present lamentable collision of arms has arisen? Is there no Continental question, said I, which might thus temporarily engage their attention? We have been induced to believe that there is.

Mr. Lincoln seemed to understand my allusion instantly, and said in substance: I suppose you refer to something that Mr. [Francis P.] Blair [Sr.] has said. Now it is proper to state at the beginning, that whatever he said was of his own accord, and without the least authority from me. When he applied for a passport to go to Richmond, with certain ideas which he wished to make known to me, I told him flatly that I did not want to hear them. If he desired to go to Richmond of his own accord, I would give him a passport; but he had no authority to speak for me in any way whatever. When he returned and brought me Mr. [Jefferson] Davis's letter, I gave him the one to which you alluded in your application for leave to cross the lines. I was always willing to hear propositions for peace on the conditions of this letter and on no other. The restoration of the Union is a *sine qua non* with me, and hence my instructions that no conference was to be held except upon that basis.

From this I inferred that he simply meant to be understood, in the first place, as disavowing whatever Mr. Blair had said as coming authoritatively from him; and, in the second place, that no arrangement could be made on the line suggested by Mr. Blair, without a previous pledge or assurance being given, that the Union was to be ultimately restored.

After a short silence, I continued: But suppose, Mr. President, a line of policy should be suggested, which, if adopted, would most probably lead to a restoration of the Union without further bloodshed, would it not be highly advisable to act on it, even without the absolute pledge of ultimate restoration being required to be first given? May not such a policy be found to exist in the line indicated by the interrogatory propounded? Is there not now such a Continental question in which all the parties engaged in our present war feel a deep and similar interest? I allude, of course, to Mexico, and what is called the "Monroe Doctrine," the principles of which are directly involved in the contest now waging there. From the tone of leading Northern papers and from public speeches of prominent men, as well as from other sources, we are under the impression that the Administration at Washington is decidedly opposed to the establishment of an Empire in Mexico by France, and is desirous to prevent it. In other words, they wish to sustain the principles of the Monroe Doctrine, and that, as I understand it, is, that the United States will maintain the right of Self-government to all Peoples on this Continent, against the dominion or control of any European power.

Mr. Lincoln and Mr. Seward both concurred in the expression of opinion that such was the feeling of a majority of the people of the North.

Could not both Parties then, said I, in our contest, come to an understanding and agreement to postpone their present strife, by a suspension of hostilities between themselves, until this principle is maintained in behalf of Mexico; and might it not, when successfully sustained there, naturally, and would it not almost inevitably, lead to a peaceful and harmonious solution of their own difficulties? Could any pledge now given, make a permanent restoration or re-organization of the Union more probable, or even so probable, as such a result would?

Mr. Lincoln replied with considerable earnestness, that he could entertain no proposition for ceasing active military operations, which was not based upon a pledge first given, for the ultimate restoration of the Union. He had considered the question of an Armistice fully, and he could not give his consent to any proposition of that sort, on the basis suggested. The settlement of our existing difficulties was a question now of supreme importance, and the only basis on which he would entertain a proposition for a settlement was the recognition and re-establishment of the National Authority throughout the land.

These pointed and emphatic responses seemed to put an end to the Conference on the subject contemplated in our Mission, as we had no authority to give any such pledge, even if we had been inclined to do so, nor was it expected that any such would really be required to be given.

Judge [John A.] Campbell then inquired in what way the settlement for a restoration of the Union was to be made? Supposing the Confederate States should consent to the general terms as stated by Mr. Lincoln, how would the re-establishment of the National Authority take place? He wished to know something as to the details.

These inquiries were made by him upon the line agreed upon by the Commissioners before, that if we failed in securing an Armistice, we would then endeavor to ascertain on what terms the Administration at Washington would be willing to end the war.

Mr. Seward said, he desired that any answer to Judge Campbell's inquiries might be postponed, until the general ideas advanced by me might be more fully developed, as they had, as he expressed it, "a philosophical basis." All seemed to acquiesce in this suggestion.

I then went quite at large into the development of my views, which briefly stated in substance amounted to this: That the Monroe Doctrine, as it was called, so far as it commended itself to my favor, assumed the position, that no European Power should impose Governments upon any Peoples on this Continent against their will. This principle of the Sovereign right of local Self-government, was peculiarly and specially sacred to the people of the United States, as well as to the people of the Confederate States. It was the one on which all our Institutions, State, and National, were based. At that time, the Emperor of France [Napoleon III] was attempting to violate this great principle, which was so sacred alike to the Belligerents on both sides of our contest. Now, if we could in any way agree to suspend our present strife, for the maintenance and vindication of this principle as to Mexico, might, and would not, the result most probably be, not only the allowance of time for the blood of our people on both sides to cool towards each other, but the leading of the public mind, on both sides, to a clearer understanding of those principles which ought to constitute the basis of the settlement of our own difficulties, and on which the Union should be ultimately restored?

A settlement of the Mexican question in this way, it seemed to me, would necessarily lead to a peaceful settlement of our own. I went on to give it as my opinion that, whenever it should be determined and firmly established that this right of local Self-government is the Principle on which all American Institutions rest and shall be maintained, all the States might reasonably be expected, very soon, to return, of their own accord, to their former relations to the Union, just as they came together at first by their own consent, and for their mutual interests. Others, too, would continue to join it in the future, as they had in the past. This great law of the System would effect the same certain results in its organization, as the law of gravitation in the material world.

In a word, I presented briefly, but substantially in outline, . . . our system of Government, . . . and showed how we might become, in deed and in truth, an Ocean-bound Federal Republic, under the operation of this *Continental Regulator*—the ultimate absolute Sovereignty of each State. This inherent and natural right of all States and Peoples, to govern themselves as they please, in my judgment, was not only the foundation upon which our Institutions were based in the beginning, but constituted the only sure ground of permanent peace and harmony in all parts of the country, consistent with the preservation of the liberties of each, even under a re-organized Union of the States. This Mexican question, therefore, might, it seemed to me, afford a very opportune occasion for reaching a proper solution of our own troubles without any further effusion of fraternal blood.

Mr. Seward [like Lincoln, a Liberal or Left-winger] said, in substance, that the ideas as presented had something specious about them in theory; but, practically, no system of Government founded upon them could be successfully worked. The Union could never be restored or maintained on that basis. Suppose, said he, a State under such a system, having within her limits and jurisdiction an important point, or port on the sea coast, should be induced by some foreign Power to abandon the Union so sovereignly entered into, and after setting herself up as an Independent Nation, should enter into a treaty with such foreign Power at enmity, or even at war with the other members of the Union—thus, giving their enemies an assumed rightful foothold in their vicinity, and by which great and irreparable injuries might be inflicted upon them. Could this be tolerated by them, for a moment? Suppose, for instance, Louisiana, holding the mouth of the Mississippi, and controlling the commerce of its immense Valley, and for which the United States paid so much, should, as she might, under this theory and doctrine, withdraw at pleasure, and form an alliance with a foreign enemy in time of war. Could the United States tolerate, for a moment, the recognition of any such right on her part? Self-defence, if nothing else, would compel them to interfere, and prevent such withdrawal, and the formation of such an alliance. Self-preservation is the first law of Nature, which applies to Nations as well as to individuals. No Government could have any stability or usefulness founded upon any such principle.

To this I replied, that it was not my purpose to do more than present briefly the outlines of the basis on which a settlement should be made, and how the Mexican question could be made subservient in bringing the public mind to that result. It was not my intention to argue the general principles as matters of fact or feasible theory. I granted that what he said was the legitimate effect of the System with some limitations. But, said I, in the supposed case of the State at the mouth of the Mississippi; if her Confederates would so act towards her as to make it her interest to remain in the Confederation, as it was when she joined it, she would never think of leaving it, or forming any alliance with a foreign inimical Power. She would abhor and spurn such an idea if presented. The object of all such Unions is the best interests of all the States composing them. This was the object of our Union. It was this that caused its formation. So long as this end is attained, there need be no apprehension of Separation, or foreign alliance by any of them; but if the other States so act toward any one of their Confederates as to render it more to her interest to be out of the Union than in it, then she ought to quit it. The same doctrine stated by him, in reference to all the States jointly, applied with equal force to each State separately. Self-preservation is as much the first law of Nature to any one of the States of the Union as another or all the others combined. The principle of self-preservation applied to every State, singly, in all such associations. It is only with a view to the better securing of the self-preservation of each State separately, that all such associations are formed. It was true, I admitted, if a State should wantonly, and without just cause, quit any association of this sort, and form an alliance with a foreign inimical Nation, and with hostile intent, then that would, of course, be a just cause of war on the part of her former Confederates. All that I granted; but urged that, if perfect justice should be done to the State in the supposed case, the great law of self-preservation and interest would restrain her from any such course. This might be regarded as one of the most immutable of those laws which regulate human societies in their voluntary relations towards each other.

Dropping further remarks on that point, Mr. Seward proceeded to inquire of me, something of the details of the plan I had in view for effecting the proposed purpose. What would be the general situation of affairs in the meantime, especially in States where there were two sets of Authorities—one recognized by the Confederate States and one adhering to the National Government? How would the laws be administered in the meantime in those States? and how was the object suggested to be practically accomplished?

What he meant by presenting this question, after Mr. Lincoln had virtually closed all further conference on that subject, I did not perceive, but proceeded to answer him in a general way, by stating that I had no fixed plan, but there were several which might be suggested, and stated one, amongst other ways, by which it might be effected. The suggestions I made on this point, as of my own accord, were the same which had been communicated to me as coming from Mr. Blair. The whole, I said, could be easily arranged by a Military Convention. This could be made to embrace, not only a suspension of actual hostilities on all the frontier lines, but also other matters involving the execution of the laws in the States referred to. Whatever disposition of troops on both sides might be necessary for the purpose, could be easily arranged in the same way. This Convention being known, however, only to the Authorities at Richmond and Washington. All these matters of detail, I said, could be easily adjusted, if we should first determine upon an Armistice for that purpose. If there was a will to do it, a proper way could easily be made clear.

Mr. Hunter said, that there was not unanimity in the South upon the subject of undertaking the maintenance of the Monroe

Doctrine, and it was not probable that any arrangement could be made by which the Confederates would agree to join in sending any portion of their Army into Mexico. In this view he expressed the joint opinion of the Commissioners; indeed, we had determined not to enter into any agreement that would require the Confederate arms to join in any invasion of Mexico.

Mr. Lincoln and Mr. Seward stated that the feeling in the North was very strong for maintaining the Monroe Doctrine.

The conversation was again diverted from that view of the subject by Mr. Lincoln. He repeated that he could not entertain a proposition for an Armistice on any terms, while the great and vital question of re-union was undisposed of. That was the first question to be settled. He could enter into no treaty, convention or stipulation, or agreement with the Confederate States, jointly or separately, upon that or any other subject, but upon the basis first settled, that the Union was to be restored. Any such agreement, or stipulation, would be a *quasi* recognition of the States then in arms against the National Government as a separate Power. That he never could do.

I stated that as President, being Commander-in-Chief of the Armies of the United States, he might, without doubt, enter into a *Military* Convention. The arrangement suggested contemplated nothing but a Military Convention between the two Parties at war. All that was suggested could be easily effected in that way, if there was a willingness on both sides.

Mr. Lincoln admitted that a Military Convention could be properly entered into by him as President for some of the purposes proposed, but repeated his determination to do nothing which would suspend military operations, unless it was first agreed that the National Authority was to be re-established throughout the country.

Judge Campbell now renewed his inquiry how restoration was to take place, supposing that the Confederate States were consenting to it?

Mr. Lincoln replied: By disbanding their armies and permitting the National Authorities to resume their functions.

Mr. Seward interposed and said, that Mr. Lincoln could not express himself more clearly or forcibly in reference to this question, than he had done in his message to Congress in December before, and referred specially to that portion in these words:

> "In presenting the abandonment of armed resistance to the National Authority, on the part of the insurgents, as the only indispensable condition to ending the war on the part of the Government, I retract nothing heretofore said as to Slavery. I repeat the declaration made a year ago, that, 'while I remain in my present position, I shall not attempt to retract or modify the Emancipation Proclamation, nor shall I return to slavery any person who is free by the terms of that Proclamation, or by any of the Acts of Congress.' If the people should, by whatever mode or means, make it an Executive duty to reenslave such persons, another, and not I, must be their instrument to perform it."
>
> "In stating a single condition of peace, I mean simply to say that the war will cease on the part of the Government whenever it shall have ceased on the part of those who began it."

After referring to this and stating its substance from memory, Mr. Seward went on to illustrate the meaning, by saying that the war would cease whenever the civil officers of the Federal Government should be permitted to discharge their duties under the laws of the United States—in other words, whenever the due execution of the laws of the United States should be submitted to in the Confederate States.

Judge Campbell said that the war had necessarily given rise to questions which must, it seemed to him, require stipulation or agreement of some sort, or assurances of some sort, which ought to be adjusted understandingly, before a harmonious restoration of former relations could properly be made. He alluded to the disbandment of the army, which would require time, and the disposition of its supplies. He alluded to the Confiscation Acts on both sides, and stated that property had been sold under them, and the title would be affected by the facts existing when the war ended, unless provided for by stipulations.

Mr. Seward replied, that as to all questions involving rights of property, the courts would determine; and that, Congress would, no doubt, be liberal in making restitution of confiscated property, or providing indemnity, after the excitement of the times had passed off.

I asked Mr. Lincoln what would be the status of that portion of the Slave population in the Confederate States, which had not then become free under his Proclamation; or in other words, what effect that Proclamation would have upon the entire Black population? Would it be held to emancipate the whole, or only those who had, at the time the war ended, become actually free under it?

Mr. Lincoln said, that was a judicial question. How the Courts would decide it, he did not know, and could give no answer. *His own opinion was, that as the Proclamation was a war measure, and would have effect only from its being an exercise of the war power, as soon as the war ceased, it would be inoperative for the future. It would be held to apply only to such slaves as had come under its operation while it was in active exercise* [my emphasis, L.S.].[54] This was his individual opinion, but the Courts might decide the other way, and hold that it effectually emancipated all the slaves in the States to which it applied at the time. So far as he was concerned, he should leave it to the Courts to decide. He never would change or modify the terms of the Proclamation in the slightest particular.

Mr. Seward said there were only about two hundred thousand slaves, who, up to that time, had come under the actual operation of the Proclamation, and who were then in the enjoyment of their freedom under it; so, if the war should then cease, the status of much the larger portion of the slaves would be subject to judicial construction. Mr. Lincoln sustained Mr. Seward as to the number of slaves who were then in the actual enjoyment of their freedom under the Proclamation. Mr. Seward also said, it might be proper to state to us, that Congress, a day or two before, had proposed a Constitutional Amendment [the Thirteenth Amendment] for the immediate abolition of slavery throughout the United States, which he produced and read to us from a newspaper. *He said this was done as a war measure. If the war were then to cease, it would probably not be adopted by a number of States, sufficient to make it a part of the Constitution* [my emphasis, L.S.]; but presented the case in such light as clearly showed his object to be, to impress upon the minds of the Commissioners that, if the war should not cease, this, as a war measure, would be adopted by a sufficient number of States to become a part of the Constitution, and without saying it in direct words, left the inference very clearly to be perceived by the

Commissioners that *his opinion was, if the Confederate States would then abandon the war, they could of themselves defeat this amendment, by voting it down as members of the Union. The whole number of States, it was said, being thirty-six, any ten of them could defeat this proposed amendment* [my emphasis, L.S.].

I inquired how this matter could be adjusted, without some understanding as to what position the Confederate States would occupy towards the others, if they were then to abandon the war. Would they be admitted to representation in Congress?

Mr. Lincoln very promptly replied, that his own individual opinion was, they ought to be. He also thought they would be; but he could not enter into any stipulation upon the subject. His own opinion was, that when the resistance ceased and the National Authority was recognized, the States would be immediately restored to their practical relations to the Union. This was a form of expression repeatedly used by him during the conversation, in speaking of the restoration of the Union. He spoke of it as a "restoration of the States to their practical relations to the Union."

Upon my urging the importance of some understanding on this point, even in case the Confederate States should entertain the proposition of a return to the Union, he persisted in asserting that he could not enter into any agreement upon this subject, or upon any other matters of that sort, with parties in arms against the Government.

Mr. Hunter interposed, and in illustration of the propriety of the Executive entering into agreements with persons in arms against the acknowledged rightful public authority, referred to repeated instances of this character between Charles I, of England, and the people in arms against him.

Mr. Lincoln in reply to this said: I do not profess to be posted in history. On all such matters I will turn you over to Seward. All I distinctly recollect about the case of Charles I, is, that he lost his head in the end.

This was the familiar manner in which Mr. Lincoln,,throughout the conversation, spoke of and to Mr. Seward. In the same familiar manner he addressed me throughout, as was his custom with all his intimate acquaintances when in Congress.

I insisted that if he could, as a war measure, issue his

Proclamation for Emancipation, which he did not venture to justify under the Constitution on any other grounds, he could certainly, as a like war measure, or as a measure for putting an end to the war rather, enter into some stipulation on this subject.

He [Lincoln] then went into a prolonged course of remarks about the Proclamation. He said it was not his intention in the beginning to interfere with Slavery in the States; that he never would have done it, if he had not been compelled by necessity to do it, to maintain the Union; that the subject presented many difficult and perplexing questions to him; that he had hesitated for some time, and had resorted to this measure, only when driven to it by public necessity; that he had been in favor of the General Government prohibiting the extension of Slavery into the Territories, but did not think that that Government possessed power over the subject in the States, except as a war measure; and that he had always himself been in favor of emancipation, but not immediate emancipation, even by the States. Many evils attending this appeared to him [my emphasis, L.S.].

After pausing for some time, his head rather bent down, as if in deep reflection, while all were silent, he rose up and used these words, almost, if not, quite identical:

Stephens, if I were in Georgia, and entertained the sentiments I do—though, I suppose, I should not be permitted to stay there long with them; but if I resided in Georgia, with my present sentiments, I'll tell you what I would do, if I were in your place: I would go home and get the Governor of the State to call the Legislature together, and get them to recall all the State troops from the war; elect Senators and Members to Congress, and ratify this Constitutional Amendment [Thirteenth Amendment] prospectively, so as to take effect—say in five years. Such a ratification would be valid in my opinion. I have looked into the subject, and think such a prospective ratification would be valid. Whatever may have been the views of your people before the war, they must be convinced now, that Slavery is doomed. It cannot last long in any event, and the best course, it seems to me, for your public men to pursue, would be to adopt such a policy as will avoid, as far as possible, the evils of immediate emancipation. This would be my course, if I were in your place.

Mr. Seward also indulged in remarks at considerable length on the progress of the Anti-Slavery sentiment of the country, and stated that what he had thought would require forty or fifty years of agitation to accomplish, would certainly be attained in a much shorter time.

Judge Campbell inquired of Mr. Seward if he thought that agitation upon the subject of the political relations between the two races would cease upon the emancipation of the Blacks—the point to which heretofore it had been entirely confined.

Mr. Seward replied, perhaps not, or possibly not.

Other matters were then talked over relating to the evils of immediate emancipation, if that policy should be pressed, especially the sufferings which would necessarily attend the old and the infirm, as well as the women and children, who were unable to support themselves. These were fully admitted by Mr. Lincoln, but in reference to them, in that event, he illustrated all he could say by telling the anecdote, which has been published in the papers, about the Illinois farmer and his hogs. The conversation then took another turn.[55]

Mr. Hunter inquired of Mr. Lincoln, what would be the result of a restoration of the Union, according to his idea, as to Western Virginia. Would the "Old Dominion" be restored to her ancient boundaries, or would Western Virginia be recognized as a State in the restored Union?

Mr. Lincoln said he could only give an individual opinion, which was, that Western Virginia would be continued to be recognized as a separate State in the Union.

Mr. Hunter after this went into a sort of recapitulation of the subjects talked over in the interview, and the conclusions which seemed to be logically deducible from them; which amounted to nothing as a basis of peace, in his judgment, but an unconditional surrender on the part of the Confederate States and their people. There could be no agreement, no treaty, nor even any stipulations as to terms—nothing but unconditional submission. A good deal of force was given to the points in this summation by the tone in which the whole was expressed.

Mr. Seward promptly replied by insisting that no words like unconditional submission had been used, or any importing, or justly implying degradation, or humiliation even, to the people of the Confederate States. He wished this to be borne in mind.

Mr. Hunter repeated his view of the subject. What else could be made of it? No treaty, no stipulation, no agreement, either with the Confederate States jointly, or with them separately, as to their future position or security! What was this but unconditional submission to the mercy of conquerors?

Mr. Seward said they were not conquerors further than they required obedience to the laws. The force used was simply to maintain National Authority in the execution of laws. Nor did he think that in yielding to the execution of the laws under the Constitution of the United States, with all its guarantees and securities for personal and political rights, as they might be declared to be by the Courts, could be properly considered as unconditional submission to conquerors, or as having anything humiliating in it. The Southern people and the Southern States would be under the Constitution of the United States, with all their rights secured thereby, in the same way, and through the same instrumentalities, as the similar rights of the people of the other States were.

Mr. Hunter said: But you make no agreement that these rights will be so held and secured!

Mr. Lincoln said that so far as the Confiscation Acts, and other penal acts, were concerned, their enforcement was left entirely with him, and on that point he was perfectly willing to be full and explicit, and on his assurance perfect reliance might be placed. He should exercise the power of the Executive with the utmost liberality. *He went on to say that he would be willing to be taxed to remunerate the Southern people for their slaves. He believed the people of the North were as responsible for slavery as the people of the South, and if the war should then cease, with the voluntary abolition of slavery by the States, he should be in favor, individually, of the Government paying a fair indemnity for the loss to the owners. He said he believed this feeling had an extensive existence at the North* [my emphasis, L.S.]. He knew some who were in favor of an appropriation as high as Four Hundred

Millions of Dollars for this purpose. I could mention persons, said he, whose names would astonish you, who are willing to do this, if the war shall now cease without further expense, and with the abolition of slavery as stated. But on this subject he said he could give no assurance—enter into no stipulation. He barely expressed his own feelings and views, and what he believed to be the views of others upon the subject.

Mr. Seward said, that the Northern people were weary of the war. They desired peace and a restoration of harmony, and he believed would be willing to pay as an indemnity for the slaves, what would be required to continue the war, but stated no amount.

After thus going through with all these matters, in a conversation of about four hours, of which I have given you only the prominent leading points, and these in substance only, there was a pause, as if all felt that the interview should close. I arose and stated that it seemed our mission would be entirely fruitless, unless we could do something in the matter of the Exchange of Prisoners. This brought up that subject.

Mr. Lincoln expressed himself in favor of doing something on it, and concluded by saying that he would put the whole matter in the hands of General Grant, then at City Point, with whom we could interchange views on our return. Some propositions were then made for immediate special exchanges, which were readily agreed to.

I then said: I wish, Mr. President, you would re-consider the subject of an Armistice on the basis which has been suggested. Great questions, as well as vast interests, are involved in it. If, upon so doing, you shall change your mind, you can make it known through the Military.

Well, said he, as he was taking my hand for a farewell leave, and with a peculiar manner very characteristic of him: Well, Stephens, I will re-consider it, but I do not think my mind will change, but I will re-consider.

The two parties then took formal and friendly leave of each other, Mr. Lincoln and Mr. Seward withdrawing first from the saloon together. Col. [Orville E.] Babcock, our escort, soon came in to conduct us back to the steamer on which we came.

During the interview, no person entered the saloon, besides the parties named, except a colored servant or steward, who came in occasionally to see if anything was wanted, and to bring in water, cigars, and other refreshments.

This is as full and accurate an account as I can now give of the origin, the objects, and conduct of this Conference, from its beginning to its end. In giving it, as stated before, I have not undertaken to do more than to present substantially, what verbally passed between all the parties therein mentioned.

At City Point we again had an interview with Gen. Grant. He evidently regretted very much that nothing had been accomplished by the Conference. The subject of the Exchange of Prisoners was then mentioned to him, and what Mr. Lincoln said about it, when he expressed a like willingness for an immediate and general Exchange. That subject was then left with him and our Commissioner of Exchange, Col. [Robert] Ould. Thus ended this Mission.

It now remains according to the order prescribed, to say something of its results. A consideration of these will necessarily bring us to the close of the war, for the end was now rapidly approaching.

On the return of the Commissioners to Richmond, everybody was very much disappointed, and no one seemed to be more so than Mr. Davis. *He thought Mr. Lincoln had acted in bad faith in the matter* [my emphasis, L.S.], and attributed this change in his policy to the fall of Fort Fisher, in North Carolina, which occurred on the 15th of January, after Mr. Blair's first visit to Richmond. The fall of this Fort was one of the greatest disasters which had befallen our Cause [self-government according to the Constitution][56] from the beginning of the war—not excepting the loss of Vicksburg or Atlanta. Forts Fisher and Caswell guarded the entrance to the Cape Fear River, and prevented the complete blockade of the port of Wilmington, through which a limited Foreign Commerce had been carried on during the whole time. It was by means of what cotton could thus be carried out, that we had been enabled to get along financially, as well as we had; and at this point also, a considerable number of arms and various munitions of war, as well as large supplies of subsistence, had been introduced. All other ports, except Wilmington, had long since been closed by Naval siege.

Forts Jackson and St. Philip, which guarded the mouth of the Mississippi [River] and the entrance to New Orleans, had been captured in March, 1862. Fort Pulaski, at the mouth of the Savannah [River], had fallen on the 12th of April, in the same year; and Fort Macon in North Carolina, a month or two earlier. Forts Gaines, Powell, and Morgan, at Mobile, had also fallen in August, 1863. Fort Sumter, at Charleston, it is true, had still held out, and had never been taken, but the harbor there had been virtually closed by a strict blockade; so that the closing of the port of Wilmington was the complete shutting out of the Confederate States from all intercourse by sea with Foreign Countries. The respiratory functions of External Trade, so essential to the vitality of all Communities, had been performed for the whole Confederacy, mainly, for nearly three years, through the small aperture of this little Port, choked to wheezing as it was, by a cordon of armed ships, drawn around its neck. The passing in and out of necessary Commerce at this place, all the time, was very much like breathing through a quill in extreme cases of quinsy or croup; still, as such breathing often saves life, so this channel of External Trade was of the utmost importance to us at that time. The closing of this Port, therefore, and the great advantage against us secured by it, was what Mr. Davis supposed to be the cause of a change of policy on the part of the [Lincoln] Administration at Washington.

We reported to him, verbally, all that had occurred at the Conference, and much more minutely in detail than I have given it [here]. . . . In this report to him, I gave it as my opinion, that if he were not himself mistaken as to Mr. Blair's knowledge of the policy of the Administration at Washington, and of his being in its confidence; in other words, if there was *really* at that time, entertained by Mr. Lincoln, any such views as those suggested by Mr. Blair, I was not at all disappointed myself at the result of the interview at Fortress Monroe. I thought the publicity of the Mission was enough to account for its failure, without attributing it to any bad faith, either on the part of Mr. Blair or Mr. Lincoln; that I had expressed the opinion to Judge Campbell and Mr. Hunter, when we saw our departure announced in the papers as it was, (the whole North being in a stir upon the subject by the time we reached City

Point), that this would most probably defeat our accomplishing anything, even if Mr. Lincoln really intended to do anything on that line; and that it was in this view of the subject *solely*, I had made the request of him, at the close of the interview, to *reconsider* the matter of the Armistice.

I called Mr. Davis's attention specially to the fact, that in reply to that request Mr. Lincoln declared he *would reconsider* it; and notwithstanding the qualification with which he made the declaration, yet I thought if there ever had been *really* anything in the *projèt*, Mr. Davis would still hear from it in a quiet way through the Military, after all the then "hubbub" about Peace Negotiations had subsided. In this view of the subject, I gave it to him as my opinion, that there should be no written report by the Commissioners touching the Conference, especially as a full disclosure of its real objects could not, with propriety, then be made; and that any report without this, however consistent with the facts, as far as they should be set forth, would fail to give full information upon the exact posture of the affairs to which it related, by which the public mind in reference to it would be more or less misled.

He insisted that a written report should be made, and the other Commissioners concurring with him, I again yielded my views on that point, and joined them in the Report which you have seen, believing, as I did, that if I declined, more harm would certainly result from a misconstruction of my course and reasons in the matter, than would by conforming to his views and those of my Colleagues.

The question then was, what was next to be done?

Mr. Davis's position was, that inasmuch as it was now settled beyond question, by the decided and pointed declarations of Mr. Lincoln, that there could be no Peace short of Unconditional Submission on the part of the People of the Confederate States, with an entire change of their Social Fabric throughout the South, the People ought to be, and could be, more thoroughly aroused by Appeals through the Press and by Public Addresses, to the full consciousness of the necessity of renewed and more desperate efforts, for the preservation of themselves and their Institutions. By these means they might yet be saved from the most humiliating threatened degradation. In these lay the only hope left of escaping such a Calamity. He himself seemed more determined than ever to fight it out on this line, and to risk all upon the issue.[57] — VICE-PRESIDENT ALEXANDER HAMILTON STEPHENS, CONFEDERATE STATES OF AMERICA

5. ACCOUNT OF THE CONFERENCE BY JOHN A. CAMPBELL

☛ The conference was opened by some conversation between Mr. Stephens and President Lincoln relative to their connection as members of a committee or association to promote the election of General [Zachary] Taylor as President, in 1848. The composition of the association, the fate of different members (Freeman Smith and Mr. [Robert A.] Toombs, and others), the time that the parties had served in Congress together, when Mr. Hunter and Mr. Seward became members of the Senate, and other personal incidents, were alluded to. After this the parties approached the subject of the conference. At a very early stage in the conversation Mr. Lincoln announced with some emphasis that until the national authority be recognised within the Confederate States, that no consideration of any terms or conditions could take place.

Mr. Stephens then suggested if there could not be some plan devised by which that question could be adjourned, and to let its settlement await the calm that would occur in the passions and irritations that the war had created; that it was important to divert the public mind from the present quarrel to some matter in which the parties had a common feeling and interest, and mentioned the condition of Mexico as affording such an opportunity.

Mr. Lincoln answered that the settlement of the existing difficulties was of supreme importance, and that he was not disposed to entertain any proposition for any armistice or cessation of hostilities until they were determined by the reëstablishment of the National authority over the United States; that he had considered the measure of an armistice fully. He would not consent to a proposition of the kind.

Mr. Campbell asked in what manner was reconstruction to be effected, supposing that the Confederate authorities were consenting to it.

John A. Campbell.

Mr. Seward requested that the answer to this question might be deferred until Mr. Stephens could develop his ideas more fully, as they had a philosophical basis. He had proposed to divert the public mind from the existing troubles.

Mr. Stephens then proceeded at some length to express his opinions upon the so-called Monroe doctrine, and his assent to it; that the establishment of an empire in Mexico was in hostility to that doctrine, and was an offence against the Confederate States as much as against the United States; that he was favorable to an appropriation of the whole of the North American continent by the States of *the two confederacies* [my emphasis, L.S.], and to exclude foreigners from a control over it; that there might be a union of power for that object, and in the course of that union fraternal feelings would arise, and a settlement might be acceptably made; that the conquest of Mexico would introduce a new element, and would require modifications of the existing system, etc.

Mr. Seward interposed, and made inquiries as to what would be the status quo during the period employed in the consummation of the enterprise. He referred to the arrangements concerning the tariff; the government of the territory of the Confederate States in the occupation of the respective authorities; the case when two governments existed in the same State, one recognised by the United States, and the other in the Confederacy.

This was answered by statements that a military convention might be entered into which could provide for all these subjects; that the troops on either side might be withdrawn into ascertained stations or posts; and that the duties collected might be arranged in the agreement; and that the government of the State recognised by the Confederacy should be supreme in the States.

This branch of the discussion was closed by Mr. Lincoln, who answered that it could not be entertained; that there could be no war without the consent of Congress [yet Lincoln sent U.S. troops into the South *without* the consent of Congress], and no treaty without the consent of the Senate of the United States; that he could make no treaty with the Confederate States, because that would be a recognition of those States, and that this could not be done under any circumstances; that unless a settlement were made there would be danger that the quarrel would break out in the midst of the joint operations; that one party might unite with the common enemy to destroy the other; that he was determined to do nothing to suspend the operations for bringing the existing struggle to a close to attain any collateral end. Mr. Lincoln in this part of the conversation admitted that he had power to make a military convention, and that his arrangements under that might extend to settle several of the points mentioned, but others it could not.

The question was renewed as to how the matter was to be accomplished, supposing that the Confederate States were consenting.

He answered: By disbanding the troops and permitting the national authorities to resume their functions.

Mr. Seward said that Mr. Lincoln could not express himself more aptly than he had done in his message to Congress in December last, and recited a portion of that message, and specified the mode by saying that where there was a custom-house that officer would be appointed to collect duties, and appointments to the post-offices, courts, land offices, etc., should be made and the laws submitted to.

It was replied that the separation and the war had given rise to questions and interests which it would be necessary to provide for by stipulations and to adjust before a restoration of former relations could be efficiently made; that the disbandment of the army was a delicate and difficult operation, and that time was needed for this; that Confiscation Acts had been passed and property sold under them, and the title would be affected by the facts existing, when the war ended, unless provided for by stipulation.

The reply to this was that as to all questions involving rights of property, the courts could determine them, and that Congress would no doubt be liberal in making restitution of confiscated property, or by indemnity, after the passions that had been excited by the war had been composed. Special reference was made as to the effect of the President's proclamation. He said that there were different opinions as to its operation; that some believed that it was not operative at all, others that it operated only within the circle which had been occupied by the army, and others believed that it was operative everywhere in the States to which it applied; that this would be decided by the courts when cases arose; that he would not modify any portion of it.

Mr. Seward produced the proposed amendments to the Constitution that had been adopted the 31st of January, and which had not been seen by the Commissioners. *He said that these were passed as a war measure and under the predominance of revolutionary passion, and if the war were ended it was probable that the measures of the war would be abandoned* [my emphasis, L.S.]. He alluded to the power of such passions in precipitating emancipation measures in Maryland and Missouri; that the most extreme views in a revolution were sure to acquire predominance, and that the more moderate parties were always overborne, as they had been in those States.

Mr. Hunter spoke of the cruelty of such measures, to the slave population especially, in localities in which the men had been removed; that the women and children were a tax on their masters, and if emancipated, would be helpless and suffering [my emphasis, L.S.].

To this Mr. Lincoln replied with a story of a man who had planted potatoes for his hogs and left them in the ground to be rooted for. The ground froze, but the master said the hogs must root *nevertheless*. ["Let 'em root or perish," were Lincoln's words.]

Mr. Seward was asked if he supposed the slavery agitation would end with emancipation; if there would not be agitation as to the status of the slave. He assented that it was quite possible.

Mr. Hunter inquired of Mr. Lincoln, if the State of Virginia were to return to the Union, would it be with her ancient limits. The answer to this was, that the question would have to be settled by other departments of the Government, but that in his opinion

Western Virginia would remain as she is.

In the course of the conversation Mr. Hunter remarked that there had been numerous instances in which the parties to contests similar to this had conferred through commissioners, and had made agreements in reference to matters in dispute, and instanced the case of Charles I, and the Parliament in Great Britain.

Mr. Lincoln replied, "All that he knew of Charles I was, that he lost his head."

To another historical instance, cited by Mr. Stephens in another connection, he expressed unfeignedly his ignorance of history, and referred him to Mr. Seward for that kind of discussion.

In conclusion Mr. Hunter summed up what seemed to be the result of the interview: That there could be no arrangements by treaty between the Confederate States and the United States, or any agreements between them.

That there was nothing left for them but unconditional submission.

Mr. Seward remarked that they had not used the word submission, or any word that implied humiliation to the States, and begged that it should be noted. Mr. Lincoln in the course of his remarks had said that the laws relative to confiscation and to pains and penalties had left the matter in his hands, and that he could express himself freely as to them. That he would say that the power granted to him would be very liberally exerted. That he could not answer what Congress would do as to the admission of members of Congress; that it was their business to decide upon that, and that they had rejected members who, in his opinion, ought to have been admitted.

Reference was made to Mr. Blair. It was said by Mr. Lincoln that doubtless the old man meant well, but that he had given him no authority to make any proposition or statement to any one; that he had stopped him from proceeding when he commenced to tell him of his business in Richmond.

Mr. Hunter stated that in candor he should say, that upon the subject of Mexico there was diversity of sentiment in the Confederate States, and that it was not probable that any arrangement could be made for her invasion without much opposition.

Mr. Seward had evidently encouraged Mr. Stephens in his remarks upon the general subject, and sympathised apparently in his general views, and represented that there was a very strong feeling in the Northern States on the subject. He, or Mr. Lincoln, had remarked that there never was a question upon which the Northern mind seemed to be more harmonious.

Upon the observation of Mr. Hunter before stated, they qualified what had been previously said on that subject, and stated that there was a strong feeling in the North that the affairs in Mexico were not right, and that something ought to be done.

Mr. Seward remarked that their foreign relations were complicated and that the feeling of the United States was as strong against England as against France; that they were in the situation that they were in prior to the war of 1812, with a cause of war against both nations, and uncertain against which to proceed; that it might be they would be decided by the ancient grudge against Great Britain.

I have stated the import of the conference generally, without introducing what was said by the different members of the Commission, except when their remarks were direct and pointed to some particular subject.

My own purpose was to ascertain if practicable the precise views of Messrs. Lincoln and Seward as to the manner in which reconstruction would be effected, and the rights that would be secured to the Southern States in the event that one should take place.

I expressed the opinion that an agreement to go upon an enterprise against Mexico, leaving the strongholds of the Confederacy in the hands of the enemy, would lead inevitably to reconstruction.

Mr. Hunter expressed the opinion that it might lead to independence with a close alliance, sufficient to arrange satisfactorily all questions of trade and intercourse, and for defence against foreign aggression.

Both *[parties]* agreed that in the present temper of both nations that a reunion would *not* be profitable to either, and should *not* be desired by either [my emphasis, L.S.].

Mr. Seward at one time said that the Northern States were

weary of war, and would be willing to pay what they would probably be required to pay on account of its continuance, but did not explain himself further on this subject.

Mr. Lincoln stated that he regarded the North to be as much responsible for slavery as the South, and that he would be rejoiced to be taxed on his little property for indemnities to the masters of slaves [my emphasis, L.S.].

Mr. Seward remarked that the North had already paid on that account. These observations were incidentally made, and did not seem to have any reference to the general subject. They were not intended apparently as the ground of any proposition.

Mr. Stephens requested President Lincoln to reconsider his conclusion upon the subject of a suspension of hostilities.

Mr. Lincoln replied that he would reconsider it as asked, but as at present advised he could not promise any consent to such a proposal; that he had maturely considered of the plan, and had determined that it could not be done.

At the commencement of the conference it was understood that it was to be free and open, that none of the parties were to be held to anything they had said, and that the whole was to be in confidence. February 1865.[58] — C.S. ASSISTANT SECRETARY OF WAR JUDGE JOHN ARCHIBALD CAMPBELL

6. ACCOUNT OF THE CONFERENCE BY ROBERT M. T. HUNTER

☞ We met Mr. Lincoln and Mr. Seward aboard the steamer, and soon the conference was commenced by Mr. Stephens, who seemed impressed with the idea that secession was the true *conservative* [my emphasis, L.S.] remedy for sectional difference, and appeared to be animated by the hope that he could convince the President [Lincoln] and Secretary of the truth of this view. Never was hope more mistaken. Although polite, neither countenanced the idea for a moment.

He next proposed another subject upon which he seemed to rely with even more confidence. He revived the old Monroe doctrine, and suggested that a reunion might be formed on the basis of uniting to drive the French out of America, and uniting to organize this continent for Americans. This was received with even less favor than I expected. Both [Lincoln and Seward] expressed their aversion to any occupancy of Mexico by the French, but if they felt any doubt, expressed none as to the capacity of the United States Government to drive the French away. Mr. Blair, while in Richmond, talked of this as a probable basis of reunion. Mr. Lincoln was evidently afraid that he had uttered sentiments for which he could not be responsible, and earnestly disclaimed having authorized his mission—whether this was true I had my doubts then and now.

Robert M. T. Hunter.

It is impossible but that Mr. Lincoln must have felt anxiety on the subject of peace. If he knew of our destitution he gave no sign of it, but he did not press the peace as I had supposed he would. He distinctly affirmed that he would not treat except on the basis of reunion and the abolition of slavery. *Neither Lincoln nor Seward showed any wise or considerate regard for the whole country, or any desire to make the war as little disastrous to the whole country as possible. If they entertained any such desires they made no exhibition. Their whole object seemed to be to force a reunion and an abolition of slavery. If this could be done, they seemed to feel little care for the distress and suffering of the beaten party* [my emphasis, L.S.]

Mr. Lincoln, it is true, said that a politician on his side had declared that $400,000,000 ought to be given by way of compensation to the slaveholders, and in this opinion he expressed his concurrence.

Upon this Mr. Seward exhibited some impatience and got up to walk across the floor, exclaiming, as he moved, that in his opinion the United States had done enough in expending so much money on the war for the abolition of slavery, and had suffered enough in enduring the losses necessary to carry on the war.

> "Ah, Mr. Seward," said Mr. Lincoln, "you may talk so about slavery, if you will; but *if it was wrong in the South to hold slaves, it was wrong in the North to carry on the slave trade and sell them to the South (as it is notorious that they did, he might have added), and to have held on to the money thus procured without compensation, if the slaves were to be taken by them again* [my emphasis, L.S.]."

Mr. Lincoln said, however, that he was not authorized to make such a proposition, nor did he make it. It was evident that both the President and Secretary were afraid of the extreme men of their party [that is, the socialist and communist members of the then Left-wing Republican Party].

Certain objects were to be secured, and when once obtained it was no consideration with their party whether the sufferings of the conquered party were to be mitigated or any relief was to be afforded. And yet to statesmen and benevolent men, it was obvious that both parties were to be benefitted by affording the conquered party some relief for their prostration.

The reaction of the sufferings of the South upon the North has been obvious enough for many years. The English Government in its scheme of West India emancipation saw the necessity of some relief to all parts of the country. It ought to have been obvious enough to wise and considerate statesmen that some relief was the policy here, too. But the [Liberal] North, when placed in power, seemed to be insensible to these views, and *desired to punish those who had been defeated in the contest. To do this they seemed willing to make their losses irretrievable* [my emphasis, L.S.].

The armistice was promptly opposed by the President and Secretary of State. If the only objects were to re-establish the Union and abolish slavery, they were right. If, however, they had any desire for the general good, and to procure relief for parties suffering, as ought to have been felt by men fit to govern such a country and to understand its wants, their views would have been different.

We had tried to intimate to [U.S.] General Grant before we reached Old Point, that a settlement generally satisfactory to both sides could be more easily effected through him and [C.S.] General Lee by an armistice than in any other way. The attempt was in vain. Lee had too much principle probably to have yielded to such a suggestion, and if Grant would have suffered no principle to restrain him if he had seen his way clear, he had not the ability to weigh truly his responsibility or to understand his opportunities. Generals who are so often accused and blamed for usurping power often see the best way out of difficulties. Had Caesar or Napoleon been in command of the Union forces there is little doubt but that some settlement would have been made to have relieved us of much of our difficulty. When a general knows what to do he is often more reliable than the politicians in civil war. England, probably, was better managed by [Oliver] Cromwell than would have been done by the general voice of her civilians. Politicians often make more fatal inroads on the bulwarks of national liberty than military commanders. It is doubtful whether a Government formed by the Roman Senate would have been better than Scylla's [an mythical ancient Greek monster], and Napoleon's constitutions were probably preferable to what the civilians would have given them. Civil wars often produce emergencies which create new and unexpected wants, and in these I have no doubt but that Napoleon was a more reliable counsellor than Lieges [his subjects].

Complications are sometimes produced by the sword that can only be cut by the sword. In this very case some compensation for the negroes taken away would have been both just and politic. Through a truce or armistice it might have been effected, but otherwise it seems not.

With regard to the Monroe doctrine, out of which I feared some complications might arise, as Blair had seemed to favor it very much, I took occasion to say to Mr. Lincoln that I differed much from Mr. Stephens, and so in my opinion did many of our people, who would be found unwilling to kindle a new war with the French on any such pretence. That for one I laid no such claims to the right of exclusive possession of the American continent for the American people, as had been done by others. That many of us would be found unwilling to have a war upon a mere question of policy rather than of honor or right. That although we would hear and communicate whatever was said to us on this question, we were not instructed to treat upon it. Nor for one was I prepared to do so.

I asked him, however, to communicate the terms, if any, upon which he would negotiate with us. He said he could not treat with us with arms in our hands; in rebellion, as it were, against the Government.

I did not advert to the fact that we were with arms in our hands upon this occasion when we came to treat with him, but I replied this had been often done, especially by Charles I, when at civil war with the British Parliament. He laughed, and said that "Seward could talk with me about Charles I, he only knew that Charles I had lost his head." I said not for that, but because he made no satisfactory settlement at all. But it was of no use to talk with him upon this subject. *It was evident that both he and Seward were terribly afraid of their constituents* [my emphasis, L.S.]. They would hint at nothing but unconditional submission, although professing to disclaim any such demand. Reunion and submission seemed their sole conditions.

Upon the subject of a forfeiture of lands, Mr. Lincoln said it was well known that he was humane and not disposed to exact severe terms. It was then that I expressed myself more freely on the subject of the negotiation and the condition of affairs. It seemed, I said, that nothing was left us but absolute submission both as to rights and property, a wish to impose no unnecessary sacrifice on us as to landed property on the part of one branch of our Government, but no absolute assurance as to this. I might have said it was the expression of an absolute determination not to treat at all, but to demand a submission as absolute as if we were passing through the Candine forks.

Such a rebuke to negotiation after a civil war of half this magnitude in any European nation, probably would have called down the intervention of its neighbors; nor is it probable that the parties to a civil war in any civilized European nation could have met for purposes of adjustment without some plan of relief or amelioration on the part of the stronger in favor of the weaker.

Mr. Seward, it is true, disclaimed all demand for unconditional submission. But what else was the demand for reunion and abolition of slavery, without any compensation for negroes or even

absolute safety for property proclaimed to have been forfeited?[59] —
C.S. SENATOR ROBERT MERCER TALIAFERRO HUNTER

7. ACCOUNT OF THE CONFERENCE BY ABRAHAM LINCOLN

☞ On the morning of the 3rd [of February 1865], the three gentlemen, Messrs. Stephens, Hunter, and Campbell, came aboard of our steamer, and had an interview with the Secretary of State [Seward] and myself, of several hours' duration. No question of preliminaries to the meeting was then and there made or mentioned. No other person was present; no papers were exchanged or produced; and it was, in advance, agreed that the conversation was to be informal and verbal merely.

Abraham Lincoln.

On our part, the whole substance of the instructions to the Secretary of State, herein before recited, was stated and insisted upon, and nothing was said inconsistent therewith; while, by the other party, it was not said that in any event or on any condition, they ever would consent to re-union; and yet they equally omitted to declare that they never would so consent. They seemed to desire a postponement of that question, and the adoption of some other course first which, as some of them seemed to argue, might or might not lead to re-union; but which course, we thought, would amount to an indefinite postponement. The conference ended without result.

The foregoing, containing as is believed all the information sought, is respectfully submitted.[60] — PRESIDENT ABRAHAM LINCOLN, UNITED STATES OF AMERICA, FEBRUARY 10, 1865.

8. ACCOUNT OF THE CONFERENCE BY WILLIAM H. SEWARD

☞ To Mr. [Charles Francis] Adams [Sr.], Department of State, Washington, February 7, 1865. Sir: It is a truism that in times of peace there are always instigators of war. So soon as a war begins there are citizens who impatiently demand negotiations for peace. The advocates of war, after an agitation, longer or shorter, generally gain their fearful end, though the war declared is not unfrequently unnecessary and unwise. So peace agitators in time of war ultimately bring about an abandonment of the conflict, sometimes without securing the advantages which were originally expected from the conflict.

The agitators for war in time of peace, and for peace in time of war, are not necessarily, or perhaps ordinarily, unpatriotic in their purposes or motives. Results alone determine whether they are wise or unwise. The treaty of peace concluded at Guadalupe Hidalgo [1848] was secured by an irregular negotiator, under the ban of the government. Some of the efforts which have been made to bring about negotiations with a view to end our civil war are known to the whole world, because they have employed foreign as well as domestic agents. Others, with whom you have had to deal confidentially, are known to yourself, although they have not publicly transpired. Other efforts have occurred here which are known only to the persons actually moving in them and to this government. I am now to give, for your information, an account of an affair, of the same general character, which recently received much attention here, and which, doubtless, will excite inquiry abroad.

A few days ago Francis P. Blair, [Sr.] Esq., of Maryland, obtained from the President [Lincoln] a simple leave to pass through our military lines, without definite views known to the government. Mr. Blair visited Richmond, and on his return he showed to the President a letter which Jefferson Davis had written to Mr. Blair, in which Davis wrote that Mr. Blair was at liberty to say to President Lincoln that Davis was now, as he always had been, willing to send commissioners, if assured they would be received, or to receive any that should be sent; that he was not disposed to find obstacles in forms. He would send commissioners to confer with the President, with a view to a restoration of peace between the two countries, if he could be assured they would be received. The President thereupon, on the 18th of January, addressed a note to Mr. Blair, in which the President, after acknowledging that he had read the note of Mr. Davis, said that he was, is, and always should be willing to receive any agents that Mr. Davis or any other influential person now actually resisting the authority of the government might send to confer informally with the President, with a view to the restoration of peace to the people of our one common country. Mr. Blair visited Richmond with this letter, and then again came back to Washington.

On the 29th instant we were advised from the camp of Lieutenant General [Ulysses S.] Grant that Alexander H. Stephens, R. M. T. Hunter, and John A. Campbell were applying for leave to pass through the lines to Washington, as peace commissioners, to confer with the President. They were permitted by the Lieutenant General to come to his headquarters, to await there the decision of the President. [U.S.] Major [Thomas T.] Eckert was sent down to meet the party from Richmond at General Grant's headquarters. The major was directed to deliver to them a copy of the President's letter to Mr. Blair, with a note to be addressed to them, and signed by the major, in which they were directly informed that if they should be allowed to pass our lines they would be understood as coming for an informal conference, upon the basis of the aforenamed letter of the 18th of January to Mr. Blair. If they should express their assent to this condition in writing, then Major Eckert was directed to give them safe conduct to Fortress Monroe, where a person coming from the President would meet them. It being thought probable, from a report of their conversation with Lieutenant General Grant, that the Richmond party would, in the manner prescribed, accept the condition mentioned, the Secretary of State was charged by the President with the duty of representing this government in the expected

William H. Seward.

informal conference.

The Secretary [that is, Seward himself] arrived at Fortress Monroe in the night of the first day of February. Major Eckert met him in the morning of the second of February with the information that the persons who had come from Richmond had not accepted, in writing, the condition upon which he was allowed to give them conduct to Fortress Monroe. The major had given the same information by telegraph to the President [Lincoln], at Washington. On receiving this information, the President prepared a telegram directing the Secretary to return to Washington. The Secretary was preparing, at the same moment, to so return, without waiting for instructions from the President; but at this juncture Lieutenant General Grant telegraphed to the Secretary of War [Edwin M. Stanton], as well as to the Secretary of State, that the party from Richmond had reconsidered and accepted the conditions tendered them through Major Eckert, and General Grant urgently advised the President to confer in person with the Richmond party. Under these circumstances, the Secretary, by the President's direction, remained at Fortress Monroe, and the President joined him there on the night of the 2nd of February. The Richmond party was brought down the James river in a United States steam transport during the day, and the transport was anchored in Hampton Roads.

On the morning of the 3rd the President, attended by the Secretary [Seward], received Messrs. Stephens, Hunter, and Campbell on board the United States steam transport *River Queen*, in Hampton Roads. The conference was altogether informal. There was no attendance of secretaries, clerks, or other witnesses. Nothing was written or read. The conversation, although earnest and free, was calm, and courteous, and kind on both sides.

The Richmond party [Confederate commissioners] approached the discussion rather indirectly, and at no time did they either make categorical demands, or tender formal stipulations, or absolute refusals. Nevertheless, during the conference, which lasted four hours, the several points at issue between the government and the insurgents were distinctly raised, and discussed fully, intelligently, and in an amicable spirit. What the insurgent party seemed chiefly to favor was a postponement of the question of separation, upon which the war is waged, and a mutual direction of efforts of the government, as well as those of the insurgents, to some extrinsic policy or scheme for a season, during which passions might be expected to subside, and the armies be reduced, and trade and intercourse between the people of both sections resumed. It was suggested by them that through such postponement we might now have immediate peace with some, not very certain, prospect of an ultimate satisfactory adjustment of political relations between this government and the States, section, or people now engaged in conflict with it.

This suggestion, though deliberately considered, was nevertheless regarded by the President as one of armistice or truce, and he announced that we can agree to no cessation or suspension of hostilities, except on the basis of the disbandment of the insurgent forces, and the restoration of the national authority throughout all the States in the Union. Collaterally, and in subordination to the proposition which was thus announced.

The anti-slavery policy of the United States was reviewed in all its bearings, and the President announced that he must not be expected to depart from the positions he had heretofore assumed in his proclamation of emancipation and other documents, as these positions were reiterated in his last annual message. It was further declared by the President that the complete restoration of the national authority everywhere was an indispensable condition of any assent on our part to whatever form of peace might be proposed. The President assured the other party that, while he must adhere to these positions, he would be prepared, so far as power is lodged with the Executive, to exercise liberality. His power, however, is limited by the Constitution, and when peace should be made, Congress must necessarily act in regard to appropriations of money and to the admission of representatives from the insurrectionary States.

The Richmond party were then informed that Congress had, on the 31st ultimo, adopted by a constitutional majority a joint resolution submitting to the several States the proposition to abolish slavery throughout the Union [Thirteenth Amendment], and that there is every reason to expect that it will be soon accepted by three-fourths of the States, so as to become a part of the national organic law.

The conference came to an end by mutual acquiescence, without producing an agreement of views upon the several matters discussed, or any of them. Nevertheless, it is perhaps of some importance that we have been able to submit our opinions and views directly to prominent insurgents [Confederates], and to hear them in answer in a courteous and not unfriendly manner. I am, sir, your obedient servant.[61] — U.S. SECRETARY OF STATE WILLIAM HENRY SEWARD

Victorian advertisement for the April-May 1893 "International Naval Rendezvous," with an aerial view of the world renowned waterways of Hampton Roads, Virginia. The event featured boat and ship displays, parades, and yacht races.

The U.S.S. *Malvern* docked at Hampton Roads, December 1864, two months prior to the Hampton Roads Conference.

Hampton Roads, Virginia, in 1890, 35 years after the Hampton Roads Conference.

SECTION THREE

Myths, Lies, & Defamation: The Controversy

SECTION THREE

9. BEGINNINGS OF THE LEGEND

☛ It is common to hear that President Lincoln at the Hampton Roads Conference during the War between the States said to Vice President Stephens something like this: "Let me write 'Union' at the top of a sheet of paper, and you may write after it whatever you please."

The effect of the story as it is generally told is to make a good impression about President Lincoln and a bad impression about President Davis; the one big-souled and yielding and the other blind and self-destructive.

The beginnings of the story seem to have been very early. The conference was held on February 3, 1865, and on February 6 the Louisville *Democrat* contained this item:

> "According to the *Herald's* (New York) correspondent, the President (Lincoln) is reported to have proposed to Messrs. Stephens, Hunter, and Campbell (Confederate commissioners) that if they were prepared to promise the return of their States to the Union he was ready to wave all minor questions but that of Chief Magistrate of the republic, sworn to maintain the Union and laws."

Then in the Augusta (Ga.) *Chronicle and Sentinel* there appeared in the issue of June 7, 1865, what purported to be an interview with Vice President Stephens about the Hampton Roads Conference. (It will be shown later that Mr. Stephens repeatedly and even bitterly complained about the incorrectness and injustice of this article.)

Then Judge John H. Reagan in his "Memoirs" (page 177) mentions the names of four persons who averred that Mr. Stephens

Julian Shakespeare Carr, former Commander-in-Chief of the United Confederate Veterans.

himself was the original author of the story—to wit: The Hon. Henry Watterson, of Kentucky; the Rev. E. A. Green, of Kentucky; Dr. R. J. Massey, of Georgia; and Mr. [Clark] Howell, of Georgia. These persons are quoted as saying that they heard Mr. Stephens himself expressly assert it.

In addition to these, Mr. Henry Watterson, in the Louisville *Courier-Journal* of June 20, 1916, avers that Mr. Stephenson the night of his arrival in Richmond from Hampton Roads told this story to "Mr. Felix G. de Fontaine, with whom he lodged and who, when the facts were disputed, made oath to the truth of them." In the same editorial Mr. Watterson says Mr. Stephens said it to him personally.

So the authorship of this story about Union and the sheet of paper is charged to Mr. Alexander H. Stephens, Vice President of the Confederacy and a member of the Hampton Roads Conference.

The purpose of this paper is to examine the available sources of information and follow the data to such a conclusion as the records may warrant. In its preparation the following have been examined and are the basis of its conclusions:

- Augusta *Chronicle and Sentinel*, June 7, 1865.
- Louisville *Democrat*, February 6, 1865.
- Louisville *Courier-Journal*, May 2, 1916.
- Louisville *Courier-Journal*, June 20, 1916.
- Lincoln's "Message to House," February 10, 1865 ("War of the Rebellion," Series I, Volume XLVI, page 505).
- Lincoln's "Instructions to Seward," January 31, 1865 ("War of the Rebellion," Ibid).
- "Lincoln's Life," by Nicolay and Hay, Volume X.
- Seward's "Letter to Adams" ("War of the Rebellion," Series III, Volume IV, pages 1163-1164).
- "Report of Confederate Commissioners," February 5, 1865 ("War of the Rebellion," Series I, Volume XLVI, page 446).
- Davis's "Message to Congress." February 6, 1865 ("War of the Rebellion," Series I, Volume XLVI, page 446).
- Davis's *The Rise and Fall of the Confederate Government*, Volume II, pages 611-620.
- Stephens's "War between the States," Volume II, Chapter XIII. Published 1870.
- Stephens's "Pictorial History of the United States."
- Stephens's "Recollections," diary kept while a prisoner at Fort Warren; sixteen references to Hampton Roads Conference.

- "Stephens's Letters and Speeches," by Henry Cleveland, pages 198-200. Published 1866.
- "Stephens's Life," by Pendleton, pages 330-342. Published 1908.
- Stephens's five articles in controversy with B. H. Hill in Atlanta *Herald*, April 17, May 8, 25, 31, June 5, 1874.
- Campbell's "Recollections." (*Southern Magazine*, December 1874, page 191.)
- Hunter's "Account." ("Southern Historical Society Papers," Volume III, page 175, April 1877.)
- Goode's "Account." "The Forum." (Volume XXIX, pages 92-103, March 1900.)
- Hill's "Life, Letters, and Speeches," page 399.
- Hill's "Unwritten History of Hampton Roads Conference," Atlanta *Herald*, May 3, 1874.
- Reagan's "Memoirs," Chapter XIII. Published 1906.
- Gordon's "Reminiscences."
- Watterson's "Might-Have-Beens of History," *Courier-Journal* May 2 and June 20, 1916.

This conference was held February 3, 1865. Its object was to find, if possible, some terms of ending the war between the Northern and Southern States. It was brought about by Francis P. Blair, Sr., an influential journalist of Washington. He was a native of Abingdon, Va., had lived in Kentucky, but was at this time a citizen of Maryland. He was a Democrat [at that time a Conservative] and had been a personal friend of President Davis, but had supported Lincoln for President and fellowshipped with the North during the war.

Blair thought peace might be brought about by getting the two governments to suspend hostilities against each other and join their forces in a common campaign against Maximilian [I] and the French in Mexico in an application of the Monroe Doctrine. He surmised that by the time this task should be finished and because it would have been jointly done the animosities between the two sections would be so assuaged that the North and South could settle their differences without further bloodshed. He presented his idea first of all to President Lincoln, who gave him a passport to Richmond. There he laid his project before President Davis in a private interview. Mr. Davis first satisfied himself that he was an informal, though unofficial, representative of President Lincoln, made a written memorandum of the interview, submitted the same to Blair for his approval of its correctness, and on January 12, 1865, gave him a note, in which he said:

> "I am willing now, as heretofore, to enter into negotiations for the restoration of peace."

Blair received this note, took it to Washington, and showed it to President Lincoln. He then brought back to Richmond a note dated January 18, 1865, in which Mr. Lincoln said:

> "I have constantly been, am now, and shall continue ready to receive any agent whom he or any other influential person now resisting national authority may informally send me with a view of securing peace to the people of our common country."

The way was thus cleared for both Presidents to appoint conferees and arrange for the meeting.

President Davis appointed three commissioners: Vice President Alexander H. Stephens, Senator Robert M. T. Hunter, and Assistant Secretary of War John A. Campbell. He thus intrusted the mission to the gentleman most likely to succeed. All three of them were known to the public as critics of Mr. Davis's administration of Confederate affairs. They persistently believed that the war could be settled by negotiation if only a fair trial were made. They were at least in as good favor at Washington as any men who could be selected, particularly Mr. Stephens. He and Mr. Lincoln had been fellow Whigs and personal friends, and Mr. Lincoln had expressed a desire that he might have him as a member of his Cabinet. He [Stephens] had been opposed to secession from the beginning and had all along been an aggressive advocate of peace by negotiation. The Northern papers of the day were diligently circulating the report that he was on the eve of severing his connection with the Richmond government and the cause of the South. Mr. Hunter was a leading malcontent in the Confederate Senate, and Mr. Lincoln was known to entertain a very high regard for Judge Campbell. Mr. Davis, furthermore, knew that he himself was bitterly disliked at Washington, and this animosity toward him personally would likely handicap any negotiations for peace. He also well understood that if the conference should fail all the blame and censure would be heaped upon him. So he selected conferees who could most likely get favorable terms for the South. He gave his commissioners the following instructions:

> "Richmond January 28, 1865. In conformity with the letter of Mr. Lincoln, of which the foregoing is a copy, you are to proceed to Washington City for an informal conference with him upon the issues involved in the existing war and for the purpose of securing peace to the two countries. With great respect, your obedient servant, Jefferson Davis."

He thus left his commissioners untrammeled. The conference they were to go to was to be "informal." The matters they were to confer about were "the issues involved in the existing war." The object which they were to seek was "peace to *the two countries* [my emphasis, L.S.]." There were no supplementary oral instructions which "tied their hands." Their powers were unqualified except by the terms of the President's written note. There were "two countries" at the moment this note was given, but he did not bind the commissioners to make such a settlement as would leave "two countries" in existence after the conference. The clause about the "two countries" was merely descriptive of the status quo at the beginning of the conference.

President Lincoln appointed as his representative his Secretary of State, W. H. Seward, known by every one to be unusually astute, if not foxy, and bitterly hostile to the South. He gave him the following instructions, specifically defining what he was to require as "indispensable":

> "Executive Mansion, January 31, 1865. Hon. William H. Seward, Secretary of State: You will proceed to Fortress Monroe, Va., there to meet and informally confer with Messrs. Stephens, Hunter, and Campbell on the basis of my letter to F. P. Blair, Esq., of January 18, 1865, a copy of which you have. You will make known to them that three things are indispensable—to wit: (1) the restoration of the national authority throughout all the States; (2) no receding by the executive of the United States on the slavery question from the position assumed thereon in the late annual message to Congress and in the preceding documents; (3) no cessation of hostilities short of an end of the war and the disbanding of all the forces hostile to the government. You will inform them that all propositions of theirs not

inconsistent with the above will be considered and passed upon in a spirit of sincere liberality. You will hear all that they may choose to say and report to me. You will not assume to definitely consummate anything. Yours, etc., Abraham Lincoln."

Mr. Seward was thus instructed by his President to require three things as "indispensable" preliminaries to any subsequent terms: (1) Submission, (2) emancipation, (3) disbandment of the Southern armies. Nothing was to be entertained "inconsistent" with these demands.

After many difficulties and much dispatching, the conference was held, not at Washington, but at Hampton Roads [Virginia] on February 3, 1865. When the Confederate commissioners reached the place of meeting, they found that President Lincoln himself had joined Mr. Seward.

The conference was held in the saloon of the *River Queen*, a small steamer, anchored out in the stream for the sake of greater privacy. The meeting lasted for four hours. It was held behind closed doors. Messrs. Lincoln, Seward, Stephens, Hunter, and Campbell were all present throughout the entire time. Besides these five, no other person entered the room, except that once a negro servant came in and was promptly sent out. *At the outset the wily Seward proposed that there be no secretary and nothing like minutes [notes]. So no written memorandum of anything said or done was made at the time* [my emphasis, LS].

What, then, did transpire at this conference? What terms of peace were offered to the Confederate commissioners? It would seem to be easy to answer this question, because every member of the conference, the only ones who could possibly know, has written and printed and given to the public each his own account of what did occur. And every one of these accounts agree. There is no variation as to the substantive terms that were there proposed. And yet there has been much discussion down to the present day as to what was precisely proposed to the South at that conference. Some contend that the only terms offered were "unconditional submission." Others contend that President Lincoln said to Mr. Stephens, the chairman of the Confederate representatives, words to this effect: "Stephens, let me write 'union,' and you can write after it what you please." And so the great-hearted and generous-minded Lincoln offered them reconciliation and peace on their own terms!

Now let us carefully examine all the available sources of information on this subject and accept the conclusion to which they lead.

PRESIDENT LINCOLN'S ACCOUNT

The contemporary newspapers of the day filled all the public mind with conjectural reports of what had taken place at Hampton Roads. For example, the Louisville *Democrat* in its issue of February 6, 1865, contained this item:

> "According to the *Herald's* correspondent, the President is reported to have proposed to Messrs. Stephens, Hunter, and Campbell that if they were prepared to promise the return of their States to the Union he was ready to waive all minor questions but that of Chief Magistrate of the republic, sworn to maintain the Union and laws."

Then the *Herald* under the same date gives another current report to the effect that "no concession or promise was made by him [Lincoln] in the least degree yielding."

These conflicting newspaper stories led the Federal House of Representatives on February 8 to pass a resolution, requesting President Lincoln himself to give a true account of what did happen at Hampton Roads. He complied with this request, and on February 10 sent an official message to the House, purporting to give a correct account of the matter. In this message he first quotes all the letters and telegrams and communications leading up to the conference and then concludes with these words:

> "On the morning of the 3rd the gentlemen, Messrs. Stephens, Hunter, and Campbell, came aboard our steamer and had an interview with the Secretary of State and myself of several hours' duration. No question of preliminaries to the meeting was then and there made or mentioned. No other person was present. No papers were exchanged or produced, and it was in advance agreed that the conversation was to be informal and verbal merely. On my part the whole substance of the instructions to the Secretary of State, hereinbefore recited, was stated and insisted upon, and nothing was said inconsistent therewith. . . . The conference ended without result. The foregoing, containing, as is believed, all the information sought, is respectfully submitted."[62]

Mr. Lincoln being the reporter, what did he offer at Hampton Roads? He says, "On my part . . . nothing was said inconsistent" with his instructions to Secretary Seward, and he had instructed Seward to demand three things: (1) Submission to national authority, (2) emancipation of the negroes, (3) disbandment of Confederate armies. But if he said, as is alleged, "Let me write 'union,' and you can write what you please," he said something seriously "inconsistent"with his instructions to Secretary Seward, and his message was not honest and truthful. It is unbelievable that Mr. Lincoln did thus misrepresent the facts to the House. What he himself substantively says he demanded at Hampton Roads was equal to "unconditional submission."

SECRETARY SEWARD'S ACCOUNT
This is found in a letter to Charles Francis Adams [Sr.], United States Minister to London. This letter was dated February 7, 1865, four days after the conference, and is printed in the "War of the Rebellion," Series III, Volume IV, pages 1163-1164. In it Mr. Seward says:

> "The President 'announced that we can agree to no cessation or suspension of hostilities except on the basis of the disbandment of the insurgent forces and the restoration of national authority throughout all the States in the Union. Collaterally . . . the President announced that he must not be expected to depart from the positions he had heretofore assumed in his proclamation of emancipation. . . . It was further declared by the President that the complete restoration of the national authority everywhere was an indispensable condition of any assent on our part to whatever form of peace might be proposed.'"

This is not the entire letter, but there is nothing in it which can possibly be construed as inconsistent with what is quoted. Mr. Seward here asserts that the President announced as "indispensable" preconditions: (1) "The disbandment of the insurgent forces," (2) the maintenance of "his proclamation of emancipation," and (3) "the complete restoration of the national authority." All of this means "unconditional submission"and is absolutely inconsistent with anything even approximating, "You can have union on your own terms."

REPORT OF THE CONFEDERATE COMMISSIONERS

On their return from the Hampton Roads Conference the three Confederate commissioners made a unanimous report [for President Davis] of what took place at the meeting. As you read it, as copied below, notice whether there is anything in it that even sounds like Lincoln saying, "Stephens, let me write 'union,' and you can write what you please":

"Richmond, Va., February 5, 1865. To the President of the Confederate States—Sir: Under your letter of appointment of the 28th ult. we proceeded to seek an 'informal conference' with Abraham Lincoln, President of the United States, upon the subject mentioned in the letter. The conference was granted and took place on the 3rd inst. on board of a steamer in Hampton Roads, where we met President Lincoln and the Hon. Mr. Seward, Secretary of State of the United States. It continued for several hours and was both full and explicit.

"We learned from them that the message of President Lincoln to the Congress of the United States in December last explains clearly and distinctly his sentiments as to the terms, conditions, and methods of proceeding by which peace can be secured to the people, and we were not informed that they would be modified or altered to obtain that end. We understand from him that no terms or proposals of any treaty or agreement looking to an ultimate settlement would be entertained or made by him with the Confederate States, because that would be a recognition of their existence as a separate power, which under no circumstances would be done, and for this reason that no such terms would be entertained by him from the States separately, that no extended truce or armistice, as at present advised, would be granted without a satisfactory assurance in advance of a complete restoration of the authority of the United States over all places within the States of the Confederacy.

"That whatever consequences may follow from the reestablishment of that authority must be accepted, but that individuals, subject to pains and penalties under the laws of the United States, might rely upon a very liberal use of the power confided to him to remit those pains and penalties if peace be restored.

"During the conference the proposed amendment to the Constitution of the United States, adopted by Congress on the 31st ult., was brought to our notice. This amendment declares that neither slavery nor involuntary servitude, except for crimes, should exist within the United States or any place within their jurisdiction and that Congress should have power to enforce this amendment by appropriate legislation. Of all the correspondence that preceded the conference herein mentioned and leading to the same you have been informed. Very respectfully your obedient servants, Alexander H. Stephens, Robert M. T. Hunter, John A. Campbell."[63]

These three signers were competent to tell what transpired at the Hampton Roads Conference, because they were there from its beginning to its end and participated in all its deliberations. Their summing up of the matter was deliberate and was submitted as their official account of what took place. They had every reason to believe that whatever they said would affect the conduct of the President of the Confederacy, of his Congress, of his military department, and react upon the public sentiment of the Southern people. We must believe that their report was serious and that they intended to put Mr. Davis in possession of the exact state of Mr. Lincoln's mind as to the ending of the hostilities between the two sections. We cannot imagine that they were trifling or suppressive or duplicitous. We must hold such gentlemen under such circumstances to have been sincere and honest and fully conscious in this account. Any other view is a grave aspersion upon them.

They formally and officially informed Mr. Davis that Mr. Lincoln would entertain no "terms," or "conditions," or "methods of proceeding," or "proposals," or "agreement," or "truce,"or "armistice" "without a satisfactory assurance in advance of a complete restoration of the authority of the United States over all places within the States of the Confederacy." This can mean nothing else under the circumstances but that the Confederate government must first surrender before Mr. Lincoln would consider Blair's project of applying the Monroe Doctrine to Maximilian [I] and Mexico or anything else. Their report assured Mr. Davis that Mr. Lincoln was implacable and determined to drive the war, without any interruption whatsoever, to utter subjugation. This would not have been true had Mr. Lincoln at any time or in any manner said in words or in substance: "Give me union on your own terms."

Moreover, the three Southern members of this conference were critics and opponents of Mr. Davis's administration. Mr. Stephens was the ringleader of the malcontents and obstructionists at Richmond and soon after this conference left the Confederate Capitol and went to his home in Georgia to nurse his dissatisfaction and disgust with Mr. Davis's conduct of affairs. He and Hunter and

Campbell and their like-minded associates were in favor of trying to settle the controversy by some diplomatic compromise, while Mr. Davis felt consistently and persistently persuaded that it would have to be fought to a finish. If, therefore, Mr. Lincoln had said at Hampton Roads, "Let me write 'Union,' and you can write anything else you want," it is inconceivable that these gentlemen, struggling as they had been for some compromise, would not have promptly and avariciously seized upon it, committed the country to it there and then, rushed back to Richmond, proclaimed it, capitalized it, and set to work to put it through. But they did not pursue this course. They came back with the lugubrious report that they found Mr. Lincoln implacable and that he would consider nothing but the complete surrender of the Southern States.

REPORT OF PRESIDENT DAVIS

The Confederate Commissioners not only made their written report of the conference to President Davis, but Mr. Stephens says:

> "We reported to him verbally all that had occurred at the conference and much more minutely in detail than I have given you."

We may assume that Mr. Davis had full and free interviews with his commissioners after their return to Richmond and that they put him in possession of the minutest inside details of all that was said and done at the meeting. Mr. Stephens says that they withheld nothing, and it is unthinkable that such honorable gentlemen would have kept back one iota of important information. Did they tell Mr. Davis that Mr. Lincoln had said that the Confederate government could have union on its own terms?

If they did, Mr. Davis deliberately falsified to the House of Representatives, for on February 6 he sent to that body a formal message in which he said:

> "The enemy refused . . . to permit us to have peace on any other basis than our unconditional submission to their rule."[64]

To sustain this interpretation, he laid before the body the written report of the three Confederate commissioners, in which Messrs. Stephens and Hunter and Campbell said:

"We understand from him (Lincoln) that no terms or proposals of any treaty or agreement looking to an ultimate settlement would be entertained or made by him with the Confederate States."

Messrs. Davis and Stephens and Hunter and Campbell are equally guilty of the grossest misrepresentation and shameful dishonesty if they knew that Mr. Lincoln had said that they could have union on their own terms.

Jefferson Davis.

Having sent this account to the House of Representatives, Mr. Davis straightway called for a mass meeting of citizens in the African church, the largest building in Richmond, and made what Mr. Stephens called the most Demosthenian speech since the days of Demosthenes, in which he told his hearers that the Hampton Roads Conference had demonstrated the diplomatic hopelessness of their cause and called upon the country to make a last desperate military effort. Mr. Stephens himself gave up in despair and went to his home in Crawfordsville, Ga. This is all incredible upon the supposition that Mr. Lincoln had said to all the commissioners or to any one of them at Hampton Roads: "You can have union on your own terms."

Did Messrs. Stephens, Hunter, and Campbell consciously misrepresent Mr. Lincoln and impose upon Mr. Davis? They were honorable gentlemen. Did Mr. Davis misrepresent Messrs. Stephens and Hunter and Campbell and impose first upon the Confederate House of Representatives and then upon the public? The thing is unbelievable.

When Mr. Davis sent to the Confederate Congress the report of the Hampton Roads commissioners, the Senate and the House passed joint resolutions. The preamble recited the previous efforts which the government had made to get peace by negotiations and then said concerning the Hampton Roads effort:

> "They (the commissioners), 'after a full conference with President Lincoln and Secretary Seward, have reported that they were informed explicitly that the authorities of the United States would hold no negotiations with the Confederate States or any of them separately that no terms, except such as the conqueror grants to the subjugated, would be extended to the people of these States and that the subversion of our institutions and a complete submission to their rule was the only condition of peace.'"

Then the Congress passed the resolutions, accepting the issue, calling upon the army and the people to redouble their efforts, and invoking the help of Almighty God. Mr. Stephens was President of the Senate, and Mr. Hunter was a member of it; and we are seriously asked to believe that they sat there and heard this false interpretation of Mr. Lincoln and the conference and saw this desperate action of their Congress without opening their mouths to inform those bodies that they could have union on their own terms. One cannot believe that Mr. Stephens was so guilty.

In reviewing this whole Hampton Roads affair in 1881, when he was writing his great history, Mr. Davis says:

> "I think the views of Mr. Lincoln had changed after he wrote the letter to Mr. Blair of June 18, and the change was mainly produced by the report of what he saw and heard at Richmond on the night he (Blair) stayed there."[65]

It is perfectly certain that Mr. Lincoln had some terms in his mind when he first sent Blair to Mr. Davis. They were probably concessory in their nature. The report somehow got out that he might be in a yielding frame of mind when he should meet the commissioners from the South. Hence the newspapers of the North were circulating it, and when the conference was over the House of Representatives called upon him to report exactly what had been done. Mr. Davis thinks that what he learned from Mr. Blair about the desperate condition of the Confederacy caused him to change his mind. It is also likely that in the interim while the conference was being arranged for he also felt the spirit and temper of those about him who wore implacable toward the South. At any rate, Mr. Davis says that the President of the United States declared at the conference that he would accept nothing but "unconditional surrender." We may fairly suppose that after the lapse of so many years, when writing about it with the war all over, he would have said something about Mr. Lincoln's generous attitude at Hampton Roads if he had ever been told by any of the commissioners that the President of the United States had said to any one of them that the Confederacy could have union on its own terms.

THE STORY OF ALEXANDER H. STEPHENS

At the time and later a great many divergent reports were spread abroad as to what did actually occur at the Hampton Roads Conference. Mr. Stephens, one of the principal actors in it (and because of these variant reports), devotes the whole of his twenty-third chapter in the second volume of his history of the "War between the States" (published in 1870) to the Hampton Roads Conference. He undertook to give the substance of what each member of the conference said with considerable detail and in the order of each speaker. His chief object was to make public the internal facts of the meeting and clear all misunderstandings and misrepresentations. At the close of his narrative he wrote:

> "This is as full account as I can now give of the origin, the objects, and the conduct of this conference from its beginning to its end."[66]

The following is a fair summary of his long account:

> Stephens: "Well, Mr. President, is there no way of putting an end to the present trouble?"
> Lincoln: "There is but one way: those who are resisting the laws of the Union must cease their resistance."
> Campbell: "How can a restoration to the Union take place, assuming that the Confederate States desire it?"
> Lincoln: "By disbanding their armies and permitting the national authorities to resume their functions."
> Hunter: "Then there can be no agreement, no treaty, no stipulation—nothing but unconditional surrender?"
> Seward: "No words like 'unconditional surrender' have been used."
> Hunter: "But you decline to make any agreement with us, and

that is tantamount to 'unconditional surrender.'"
Lincoln: "The executive would exercise the powers of his office with great liberality."
Stephens: "Mr. President, I hope you will reconsider."
Lincoln: "Well, Stephens, I will reconsider, but I do not think I will change my mind."

Boil down this long narrative of Mr. Stephens to a single terse phrase and put that phrase in the mouth of Mr. Lincoln at the conference, and it is not "Union on your terms," but it is "Union on terms of the complete surrender of the South."[67]

A publication appeared in the Augusta (Ga.) *Chronicle and Sentinel* on June 7, 1865, purporting to give Mr. Stephens's version of the Hampton Roads Conference. It was republished in many other papers. Mr. Stephens in his "Recollections," a diary which he kept while a prisoner in Fort Warren, makes sixteen entries concerning the Hampton Roads Conference, several of them bewailing this newspaper article. He describes it as "a discordant jumble of facts which presents almost anything but the truth."[68]

His early biographer, Henry Cleveland, who wrote in 1866, while Mr. Stephens was still alive and accessible, says:

"He (Mr. Stephens) has often been heard to say that his views in consenting to take part in that conference can never be fully understood without a knowledge of the true objects contemplated by the authors of the mission. These he has never disclosed and does not yet feel himself at liberty to disclose. . . . The report (of the commissioners) contains the exact truth touching the points embraced in it but the real object of that mission was not embraced in it. This was verbally and confidentially communicated."[69]

This biographer says that "he (Mr. Stephens) has on several occasions told a few particular friends some things that transpired." Then he adds:

"Particularly the agreeableness of the interview, the courteous bearing of Mr. Lincoln and Mr. Seward but he has always objected to giving the public any account whatever beyond that contained in the official report of the commissioners."

Finally, in 1870 Mr. Stephens told his whole story of the

conference in his history and failed to put in it anything like the story of the sheet of paper and union on any terms.

JUDGE CAMPBELL'S ACCOUNT
This is to be found in the *Southern Magazine* for December 1874, page 191. This careful, judicious, and judicial gentleman says:

> "In conclusion, Mr. Hunter summed up what seemed to be the result of the interview: that there could be no agreements by treaty between the Confederate States and the United States or any agreements between them; that there was nothing left for them but unconditional submission."

According to this member of the commission, they got nothing at Hampton Roads, when all the four hours' conversation was boiled down to its essence, but a proposition of "unconditional submission." This, however, would not be true if Mr. Lincoln said anything approximating, "Let me write 'Union,' and you can write after it what you please."

SENATOR HUNTER'S ACCOUNT
Both Mr. Stephens in his history and Judge Campbell in his "Recollections" represent Senator Hunter as summing up and reducing to a nutshell the sum and substance of all that had been proposed in the four-hour conference. Consequently great weight ought to be attached to his account of the meeting. It is to be found in the "Southern Historical Society papers," Volume III, pages 168-176. It was written in April 1877.

Mr. Hunter opens his narrative with some account of the occasion and origin of the conference. Then he says that Mr. Stephens seemed "possessed with the idea that secession was the true remedy for sectional difference," but neither Mr. Lincoln nor Mr. Seward "countenanced the idea for a moment." Then Mr. Stephens "revived the old Monroe Doctrine and suggested that a reunion might be formed on the basis of uniting to drive the French out of America," but Mr. Hunter says: "This was received with even less favor than I expected." Continuing, he says: "Their (Lincoln and Seward) whole object seemed to be to force reunion and an abolition of slavery." Then an "armistice" was proposed and talked about, but it "was promptly opposed by the President and Secretary of State." Then he says: "I asked him (Lincoln) to communicate the terms, if any, upon which he would negotiate with us. He said he could not treat with us with arms in our hands in rebellion, as it were, against the government." Mr. Hunter concludes his story:

> "They (Lincoln and Seward) would hint at nothing but unconditional submission, although professing to disclaim any such demand. Reunion and submission seemed their sole conditions. Upon the subject of the forfeiture of lands . . . I said that nothing was left us but absolute submission both as to rights and property. . . . Mr. Seward, it is true, disclaimed all demands for unconditional submission. But what else was the demand for reunion and abolition of slavery without any compensation for the negroes or even absolute safety for property proclaimed to have been forfeited?"

According to this story, at the Hampton Roads Conference the members talked first about "secession" and made no progress toward getting together on that theory. Then they talked about Blair's proposition, the Monroe Doctrine, and Mexico, and still made no progress. Then they conferred about an "armistice," and got nowhere. Then Mr. Hunter asked Mr. Lincoln on what terms they could have reunion, and he would "hint at nothing but unconditional submission." Then Mr. Hunter inquired what safeguards they could expect for their slaves and their property, and Mr. Lincoln referred them to his mercy. Mr. Hunter says (and he was there) "that nothing was left us but absolute submission both as to rights and property." And yet there are some (who were not there) who ask us to believe that Mr. Lincoln said something like this: "You can have union on your own terms."

Mr. Hunter says it was "reunion" that they were talking about, and what the Confederates wanted to know was the terms. Mr. Lincoln "would hint at nothing but unconditional submission." That certainly is not the same thing as saying: "Let me write 'union,' and you can write what you please after it."

CONGRESSMAN GOODE'S ACCOUNT
Mr. John Goode [Jr.] was a Virginia member of the Confederate Congress in 1865 when the Hampton Roads Conference was held.

In the March *Forum* of 1900, Volume XXIX, pages 92-103, he has published his version of this conference. It has an evidential value, because it is based upon a conversation which he had with one of the Confederate commissioners in Richmond soon after his return from Hampton Roads. His story agrees with all the other published accounts. The terms, according to his informant, were "unconditional submission." There is nothing in it which approaches "union and then what you please."

John Goode, Jr.

JUDGE REAGAN'S ACCOUNT
On the formation of the provisional government of the Confederate States at Montgomery, Ala., Mr. John H. Reagan, of Texas, was made Postmaster General in the Cabinet of Mr. Davis and continued in this office to the end of the war. Always in the confidence of his chief and loyal to him throughout the whole conflict, he was taken prisoner with him at the wind-up of it all. He published his "Memoirs" in 1906. He had all the controversies and allegations about the Hampton Roads Conference before him and devoted the thirteenth chapter of his book to the subject. He says:

> "During recent years there has been an extensive discussion through the public prints of the questions which arose at the Hampton Roads Conference. It has been asserted over and over that President Lincoln offered to pay $400,000,000 for the slaves of the South to secure an end of the war and that he held up a piece of paper to Mr. Stephens, saying: 'Let me write the word "union" on it, and you may add any other conditions you please if it will give us peace.' I am probably not using the exact words which were employed, but I am expressing the idea given to the public in the discussion. It has frequently been alleged that Mr. Stephens said these offers were made. This has been repeated by citizens of acknowledged ability and high character, and it has been said that these offers could not be acceded to because the instructions

given to the commission by President Davis prevented it. . . . I shall submit evidence that no such propositions were ever made."

The "evidence" which Judge Reagan presents is the joint report of the Confederate commissioners to Mr. Davis, the message of Mr. Davis to his Congress based upon that report, the resolutions of the Confederate Congress predicated upon the reports made to them, Mr. Lincoln's message to the Federal House on the subject, and Secretary Seward's letter to Mr. Adams, the American Minister to Great Britain. Then he says:

> "While it is true that some respectable men have asserted that Mr. Stephens told them of Mr. Lincoln's alleged offer, . . . and I have all their statements in writing or print, . . . there must have been some misunderstanding as to his language, for he was an honorable and truthful man and a man of too much good sense to have made such allegations in the face of such record as is here presented."

Then Judge Reagan names the following persons as those who have said that Mr. Stephens made the assertions about the piece of paper and union and about the $400,000,000 for the slaves: Hon. Henry Watterson, of Kentucky; Rev. E. A. Green, of Kentucky; Dr. R. J. Massey, of Georgia; and Mr. [Clark] Howell, of Georgia.

Over against these four he sets the following eight gentlemen who allege that Mr. Stephens denied to them that he ever made such statements: Rev. F. C. Boykin, of Georgia; Mr. R. F. Littig, of Mississippi; Hon. James L. Orr, of South Carolina; Hon. Frank B. Sexton and Col. Stephen W. Blount, of Texas; Mr. Charles G. Newman, of Arkansas; Gov. Augustus H. Garland, of Arkansas; and Senator [George G.] Vest, of Missouri.

Inasmuch as four reputable gentlemen affirm and eight reputable gentlemen deny, Judge Reagan disposes of the matter by saying that "there must have been some misunderstanding as to the language" which Mr. Stephens did use.

COL. HENRY WATTERSON'S ACCOUNT
Colonel Watterson is the editor of the Louisville *Courier-Journal* and the most brilliant journalist on the American continent. He has recently told the story of the Hampton Roads affair in his

newspaper. In an editorial of May 2, 1916, under the caption, "The Might-Have-Beens of History," he says:

> "There had been many epistolary and verbal exchanges between the two capitals, Washington and Richmond, before this fateful conference had come to pass. The parties to it were personally well known to each other. Mr. Lincoln and Mr. Stephens were indeed old friends. The proceedings were informal and without ceremony. At the outset it was agreed that no writing or memorandum should be made of what might be said or done. It is known, however, that at a certain point, the President of the United States and the Vice President of the Southern Confederacy sitting a little apart from the rest, Mr. Lincoln took up a sheet of paper and said byway of completing the unreserved conversation that had passed between them: 'Stephens, let me write "union" at the top of this page, and you may write below it whatever you please.' He had already committed himself, in the event that the Southern armies laid down their arms and the Southern States returned to the Union, to the payment of $400,000,000 for the slaves. That such an opportunity for the South, then on the verge of collapse, to end the war should have been refused will remain forever a mystery bordering on the supernatural."

He then characterizes President Lincoln as "the Christ-man who had thrown out a life line," wonders if it all were due to "the hand of God," moralizes about Napoleon [III], and prophesies direfully for the German Kaiser. He then introduces this paragraph:

> "It will be recalled that Mr. Jefferson Davis was wont to dwell upon the reluctance with which he quitted the Union and joined in establishing the Confederacy. Yet at the supreme moment he could not see his way clear to an advantageous peace by honorable agreement. He let the golden moment pass and went, taking with him the cause he had maintained during four years so valiantly, to precipitate and complete extinction."

Mr. Davis was not in the conference. We have seen that the report which the commissioners brought back to him informed him "that no terms or proposals of any treaty or agreement looking to an ultimate settlement would be entertained or made by him with the authorities of the Confederate States." If the commissioners told him the truth, that he could get "no terms," how did Mr. Davis "let the golden moment pass"? If Mr. Lincoln said to Mr. Stephens, "Let me write 'union,' and you can write what you please," and Mr. Stephens withheld this information until after the war was over, it would seem that it was he who "let the golden moment pass." Mr. Watterson writes like one obsessed with admiration for Mr. Lincoln, "the Christ-man," and biased against Mr. Davis, the President of the Confederacy.

When his editorial of May 2 was characterized as "fiction" by the Oklahoma City *Times* and the Macon *Telegraph*, Mr. Watterson replied in an editorial of June 20 in the *Courier-Journal*, in which he said:

Henry Watterson.

> "That Mr. Lincoln said on the occasion of the Hampton Roads Conference what is denied as 'fiction' rests upon the statement of Mr. Stephens himself made to many persons of the highest credibility. It admits of no doubt whatever. It does not appear in the official documents because it was not a part of the formal proceedings, but an aside during an interview between Mr. Lincoln and Mr. Stephens. They were warm personal friends, old Whig colleagues. Lincoln an ardent admirer of Stephens, whom he wanted to ask to become a member of his Cabinet when he was President. The two had drawn apart from the rest. 'Stephens,' said Lincoln, as Mr. Stephens reported the conversation to many of his friends, 'you know I am a fair man, and I know you to be one. Let me write "union" at the top of this page, and you may write below it whatever else you please. I am sure you will write nothing I cannot agree to.' Mr. Stephens replied that the commissioners were limited to treating upon the basis of the recognition of the independence of the Confederacy alone. 'Then, Stephens,' said Lincoln sadly, 'my hands are clean of every drop of blood spilled from this time onward.'"

Mr. Watterson says this story "does not appear in the official documents," and the reason is "because it was not part of the formal proceedings." He has told us that "no writing or memorandum was made," and so there could have been no "official documents" prepared by the conference. He has told us that "the proceedings were informal and without ceremony," and yet he says this story does not "appear" because it is "no part of the formal proceedings." He says it was "an aside," made as a kind of private remark, while Mr. Lincoln and Mr. Stephens were sitting apart from the rest. Continuing in his editorial of June 20, he says:

> "Mr. Davis did not see Mr. Stephens at all. But all that Mr. Watterson has averred in this regard was told the night of his arrival in Richmond by Mr. Stephens to Mr. Felix G. de Fontaine, with whom he lodged and who, when the facts were disputed, made oath to the truth of them, as did also Dr. Green, Mr. Stephens's pastor, and Gen. John B. Gordon and Evan P. Howell, of Atlanta, to whom later along Mr. Stephens likewise related them, as indeed he had done to Mr. Watterson himself."

Here Mr. Watterson says, "Mr. Davis did not see Mr. Stephens at all," presumably after his return from Hampton Roads. But Mr. Stephens says in his long narrative in his history:

> "We reported to him (Davis) verbally all that had occurred at the conference. . . . In this report to him I gave it as my opinion. . . . I called Mr. Davis's attention especially to the fact. . . . I gave it to him as my opinion that there should be no written report by the commissioners touching the conference. . . . I again yielded my views on that point."

Mr. Davis did not deal with Mr. Blair in the beginning of this business without making a written memorandum of what was said and submitted it to Mr. Blair. He saw the blunder of the commissioners in making no written memorandum of what was said at Hampton Roads. He wisely required that the report to him should be in black and white, so that he could be protected against misrepresentation in the matter. If Mr. Stephens may be believed, and he may be, he did see Mr. Davis after he returned from Hampton Roads and had every opportunity of telling him that Mr.

Lincoln had said: "Stephens, let me write 'union' at the top of this page, and you may write below it whatever you please." If Mr. Lincoln said it, why did not Mr. Stephens tell his President, the Confederate Congress, and all the South and change all the results?
 Did Mr. Lincoln say it? Did Mr. Stephens say he said it? Here are two questions. Let us take them up separately and see if we are not shut up to Judge Reagan's conclusion that there is a "misunderstanding" somewhere.
 1. If Mr. Lincoln said it, his message of February 10 was not frank and disingenuous. It suppressed a vital fact. At that time the newspapers had filled the atmosphere with disturbing reports, some giving it out that the President of the United States had been yielding and others that he had been uncompromising. Besides, there were two groups at Washington vexing Mr. Lincoln, the one urging that terms be made with the South and the other implacable in its attitude and urgings. Here was a context which caused the House of Representatives to ask him for the truth about the matter. He replied, saying he believed his message contained "all the information sought." That message, if our alleged story was fact, ought to have said in substance: "I offered them union on their own terms, and they declined my offer." But his message did not say that. It said: "I offered them the terms I had previously laid down to Secretary Seward—namely, (1) submission, (2) emancipation, (3) disbandment of their armies, and then such mercy as the President of the United States might be pleased to show them." If he thus kept back material fact while professing to give "all the informations ought," his admirers must think him something else than "the Christ-man." Had he made such an offer and had it refused, it is unbelievable that he would not have told the country and extinguished the peace troublers who were tormenting him. Nicolay and Hay, his heroizing biographers, do not put this story into his mouth. Why did they not tell it to illustrate his kindliness and chivalry to his foe? Moreover, why should he have made such a proposition? His game was as good as in his bag, and he knew it. Appomattox was on the 7th of April, and this conference was on the 3rd of February preceding.
 2. If Mr. Lincoln said it, why did not Messrs. Stephens, Hunter, and Campbell seize upon it, even with avariciousness, and hurry

back to Richmond with it and give it out to the President of the Confederacy and to the Southern Congress? They were the leaders of the party at Richmond who desired and believed that peace could be had by negotiation. They had been sent by their Chief Magistrate to the meeting to get the best terms they could, and the terms, according to this story, were, "Union on your own terms." Yet we are asked to believe that they came back and told Mr. Davis and the country that they found Mr. Lincoln implacable—no "terms," "conditions," "proposals," "agreements," "truce," or "armistice" except they "submitted" and threw themselves upon the mercy of the President of the United States. Did they misinform their chief? Did Messrs. Stephens and Hunter sit in Congress the next day and see that body pass resolutions frantically calling upon the country to exert itself to the last extremity because no terms could be had when they privately knew that they could have "union on their own terms"? What right had they to keep back the very heart and substance of what had been proposed at the conference? They were honorable gentlemen. Besides, they were critics of Mr. Davis. Why did they not use the information, if they had it, to triumph over Mr. Davis and save "the golden moment" and the country from "precipitate and complete extinction"? For the sake of a hearsay story lionizing Mr. Lincoln are we to blast the good name of the three Confederate commissioners?

3. If Mr. Lincoln said it only as an "aside" to Mr. Stephens for his private benefit, how was it done? They were all together during the entire time in the cabin of a small steamer. Why should Mr. Lincoln have whispered it to Mr. Stephens so that the others could not hear him? What motive could he have had in such a conference for whispering in the ear of Mr. Stephens, "Any terms you want," and then saying out loud to Messrs Hunter and Campbell, "No terms whatever"? Why should Mr. Stephens receive such an "aside" and keep it from his fellow commissioners? Why did he not get Mr. Lincoln to say it out loud? Why should he keep such a secret from his associates? Carrying such a secret in his bosom, why did he not say to Mr. Davis, "Don't send that message I have 'aside' information and will seek release from privacy"? Why did he not say to the Congress, "Don't pass those frantic resolutions I have knowledge up my sleeve"? Secret? Private? Why, Mr. Watterson

says he told it to Mr. de Fontaine and Dr. Green the first night he got to Richmond. Why could he not have told Mr. Hunter and Mr. Campbell on the way? If he did, his fellow commissioners were not ignorant of it when they reported to Mr. Davis.

4. If Mr. Lincoln said it to Mr. Stephens as an "aside" and then put him under the bonds of secrecy, why did he not write it down after the war was over and all obligations of secrecy had been removed by the death of Mr. Lincoln and the collapse of the Confederacy? He frequently wrote about the Hampton Roads Conference with the avowed purpose of telling its whole inside history. Why did he not set down this story in something that he wrote? The public was confused about it. Some were saying that it was true, and some were saying that it was false. He himself became involved in a controversy with Senator B. H. Hill about it. Why did he not put it in black and white? He was a bitter critic of Mr. Davis. In all his voluminous writing about the war after it was all over he ceaselessly put the blame for the failure upon the administration. Upon the supposition that it was fact, can we imagine that he would not have somewhere written it down and upon it made a telling point against the administration? But none can point to the story as put down by his own pen and above his own signature. The best they can do is to try to interpret his written words in such a way as to make them seem to support the story.

5. But they say that Mr. Stephens verbally told this story "to many friends." If eight men, good and true, aver that they heard Mr. Stephens tell this story, eight other men, just as good and just as true, aver that they heard Mr. Stephens say that he did not tell it. If the first eight write or print their assertion, the second eight write or print their assertion.

What conclusion shall we reach and rest in? Mr. Stephens was a Christian gentleman of the highest piety, a statesman of the highest honor, a patriot of the purest loyalty. All the records and all the circumstances are inconsistent with the story that he ever said anything like what is imputed to him. He could not have been malignant and vengeful nor yet stupid enough to have withheld from Mr. Davis, his fellow commissioners, the Confederate Congress, and the country at large information which, being known, might have saved "the cause" which Mr. Davis had maintained so "valiantly" for four years from "precipitate and complete extinction."

Judge Reagan's conclusion is the only reasonable and fair one—namely, that there must have been some "misunderstanding" of Mr. Stephens's words when he was speaking freely and conversationally with his friends about the Hampton Roads Conference.

In a recent issue the New York *Times* gave the following account of the Hampton Roads Conference:

> "At Hampton Roads he (Lincoln) refused to accept any proposal except unconditional surrender. He promised 'clemency,' but refused to define it, except to say that he individually favored compensation for slave owners and that he would execute the confiscation and other penal acts with the utmost liberality, he made it plain throughout that he was fighting for an idea and that it was useless to talk of compromise until that idea was triumphant. We are aware, of course, of the long-exploded myth telling how he offered Stephens a sheet of paper with 'Union' written on it and told the Confederate statesman to fill up the rest of the paper to suit himself. 'He offered us nothing but unconditional submission,' said Stephens on his return, and he called the conference therefore 'fruitless and inadequate.'"

The *Courier-Journal* of December 23, 1916, takes this as a text and miswrites again the "long-exploded myth" as veracious history and upon it takes occasion to reflect upon Mr. Davis and to characterize Mr. Lincoln as "a kindly, just man."

How in the name of all that is frank and fair, unbiased, and unprejudiced can the accomplished Southern editor blame Mr. Davis for not taking advantage of information obtained through the Hampton Roads Conference for the benefit of the people over whom he presided? The proposal to hold the conference came to him from Washington he appointed commissioners out of sympathy with his general administration, honest believers that something could be done by negotiating and more likely to have the favorable ear of Mr. Lincoln than any other persons in the Confederate government left them, unhampered by instructions, a free hand to do the best they could. These gentlemen brought back the report that they could get no "terms" or "agreements." The conference was a dismal failure because Mr. Lincoln was implacable.

If the Confederate commissioners, all or any one of them, had private and "aside" information that might have been used to the advantage of the Southern people, it was they who suppressed it and voided all the possible results of the conference. No one can believe that Mr. Stephens or Mr. Hunter or Judge Campbell, all or any one of them, were so unpatriotic. This story about "union on your own terms" reflects most upon Mr. Stephens, for the allegation is that it was made known to him privately, and there is no evidence that he ever communicated it to his chief who sent him.

SUMMARY
The quotations in this brief show that neither President Davis nor Vice President Stephens nor any one of the Confederate commissioners had any public or *sub rosa* information obtained through the Hampton Roads Conference which they failed to make use of to the benefit of the Southern people.

To continue to repeat this story about "union and then what you please," in view of the records presented in this monograph, is nothing short of a fabrication of history. It is based upon reports of the free conversational talks of Mr. Stephens about this meeting, and he was wont to complain with great bitterness about hearsay misrepresentations of him.

Julian S. Carr.

All the actors in that celebrated conference are now dead and gone. They were every one gentlemen of the highest reputation and honor. They were all incapable of any un-patriotic or duplicitous action. Each of them, and some of them more than once, has put on record in cold print his account of what transpired at that conference, and neither of them has intimated that there was some vital information that was not revealed or, being known, was not used.

Mr. Lincoln told Congress what he knew about it. Mr. Seward set down in black and white what he knew about it. The three Confederate commissioners, Messrs. Stephens, Hunter, and Campbell, made a formal statement of what they knew about it. These were all the members of the conference and all the persons who could have had first-hand information of what was said and done on February 3, 1863, onboard the *River Queen* at anchor in Hampton Roads. President Davis gave to the Confederate Congress his version of what occurred as it was given to him. Years after the war Mr. Stephens wrote much in books and newspapers about what did occur according to his recollection. Mr. Hunter also set down his recollections, and Judge John A. Campbell also put to record his remembrances of it. Judge John H. Reagan and other gentlemen who were present in Richmond at the time and publicly connected with administrative affairs have also written their versions, gotten from general sources.

In all fairness, these ought to constitute the veracious history of the Hampton Roads Conference, and it is altogether historically illegitimate for any man to read into this record a report founded upon the alleged free conversations of one man, who himself subsequently wrote much on the subject, but nothing which supports the alleged story and which report needlessly reflects upon the honorable participators in that conference.[70] — JULIAN S. CARR

10. THE TRUTH OF THE HAMPTON ROADS CONFERENCE

☞ One of the most important resolutions offered to the convention of United Confederate Veterans [U.C.V.] at Birmingham May 16-18, 1916, and referred to the History Committee, was the following:

> "Certain statements concerning the peace conference held at Hampton Roads on February 3, 1865, between President Lincoln and Secretary William H. Seward, for the North, and Hon. Alexander H. Stephens, Vice President C.S.A., R. M. T. Hunter, and Judge John A. Campbell, commissioners for the Confederate government, which have appeared in the press of the country from time to time and particularly in the [Louisville] *Courier-Journal* of late, have been so unjust in their reflection upon the integrity of Hon. Jefferson Davis, then President of the Southern Confederacy, and the commissioners

appointed by him to represent the Confederate government, it is deemed fitting that this convention of United Confederate Veterans take action in the following:

"Whereas in the editorial columns of the *Courier-Journal*, published in Louisville, Ky., the Hon. Henry Watterson has lately made some offensive comparisons between the Southern Confederacy and the Germany of today, in which he expressed the sentiment that 'the Southern States had no more reason to fight for their rights in the territories than Germany has to fight for a place in the sun'; and whereas Mr. Watterson repeats the old story that in the peace conference held at Hampton Roads, Va., on February 3, 1865, President Lincoln made such a proposition to Hon. Alexander Stephens, head of the commission for the Confederate government, as, 'Let me write "Union" at the top of this page, and you may write below it whatever else you please,' and, furthermore, that he offered to pay the Southern people the sum of $400,000,000 for their slaves if they would lay down their arms and return to the Union; therefore be it:

"Resolved by the United Confederate Veterans in convention assembled. That they condemn such statements as utterly false and inconsistent with the reports made by representatives of both sections in this peace conference and with Mr. Lincoln's message to Congress in December, 1864, to which he stated he would adhere; that they are unjust to the memory of President Davis and the Southern members of the peace conference, all men of the highest honor, and not only a reflection upon their integrity, but upon the whole South, since no such offers appear in the official reports of that famous peace conference; and such statements as made by Mr. Watterson in the *Courier-Journal* are denounced as utterly untrue in themselves and unworthy of the men to whom was intrusted the honor of treating for peace between the North and the South; that unconditional surrender was the only basis upon which President Lincoln would consider any peace proposals, with no assurance as to the treatment that would be accorded the Southern States on returning to the Union other than that they might expect their rights to be respected as were those of the States of other sections.

"Resolved, further. That the press of our country be asked to take particular notice of this action by the United Confederate Veterans in convention in the city of Birmingham, Ala., May 16-18, in justice to the memory of the men who gave of their best to the cause of the South, 1861-65, and that future references to that peace conference at Hampton Roads, Va., be based upon facts given in the official reports of it by representatives of both sides; and we demand of the *Courier-Journal* a correction of the statements lately repeated by Mr. Watterson in that Journal or a production of such proofs as will verify them."

The necessity for some action of this kind, and most appropriately through the Association of United Confederate Veterans, was caused by some late editorials in the *Courier-Journal*, from which we copy the following, appearing under the title of "The Might-Have-Beens of History":

"The morning of February 3, 1865, upon a steamer [the *River Queen*] lying at anchor in Hampton Roads, off Fortress Monroe, Abraham Lincoln, attended by William H. Seward, met three Confederate commissioners, Alexander H. Stephens, Robert M. T. Hunter, and John A. Campbell, appointed by Jefferson Davis 'for the purpose,' as Mr. Davis wrote, 'of securing peace to *the two countries*,' but, as Mr. Lincoln had written, 'with the view of securing peace to the people of our *one common country* [my emphasis, L.S.].'

"There had been many epistolary and verbal exchanges between the two capitals, Washington and Richmond, before this fateful conference had come to pass. The parties to it were personally well known to one another. Mr. Lincoln and Mr. Stephens were, indeed, old friends. The proceedings were informal and without ceremony. At the outset it was agreed that no writing or memorandum should be made of what might be said or done. It is known, however, that at a certain point, the President of the United States and the Vice President of the Southern Confederacy sitting a little apart from the rest, Mr. Lincoln took up a sheet of paper and said by way of completing the unreserved conversation that had passed between them: 'Stephens, let me write "Union" at the top of this page, and you may write below it whatever else you please.' He had already committed himself, in the event that the Southern armies laid down their arms and the Southern States returned to the Union, to the payment of $400,000,000 for the slaves.

"That such an opportunity for the South, then on the verge of collapse, to end the war should have been refused will remain forever a mystery bordering on the supernatural.

"Two months later Lee surrendered. Instead of achieving an honorable peace on favorable terms, the Confederacy went down in total shipwreck, vanquished, the waves of passion and plunder for ten succeeding years sweeping over the stricken survivors as they floundered in the Sea of Reconstruction, the Christ-man [Lincoln] who had thrown out a life line gone, no one left having the will and the power to stay the fury of the elements.

"Was it the hand of God? Could it have been that God deemed the South not yet sufficiently punished? Who shall tell us?"

Yankee slave ships.

Aye, who can tell us that God sends his punishments in that way? Review the history of wars in this or any other country and tell us if right has always triumphed. "God moves in a mysterious way," but the four years of war was not a punishment at his hands that the South was made to suffer. *Why call slavery the sin of the South? Did not the Constitution uphold the institution? The South was not responsible for slavery in the [early American] colonies. Those pious pilgrims of New England grew rich upon the traffic in slaves, and as long as there was a profit to them New England's conscience was dormant; but when it awoke with a "dog-in-the-manger" feeling, something had to give way. (We don't hear of them in this day worrying over the slaves in the sweatshops of the North, their surroundings far worse than were ever found on Southern plantations.) The South wanted no war; and had Mr. Lincoln acted in good faith about Fort Sumter and used conciliatory rather than coercive measures to bring the Southern States back into the Union, who can say that war might not have been averted?* [my emphasis, L.S.]

Mr. Davis has been accused of so hampering the Confederate commissioners with instructions as to the terms upon which peace would be considered that they really felt in advance their errand was futile. It is a satisfaction to bring forward a direct statement on this point from Mr. Stephens himself, who gives a chapter to the Hampton Roads conference in his book, *The War between the States*, written in the form of interrogatories and replies.

To the questions [asked of Stephens by an imaginary Yankee interrogator], "How did this celebrated conference, having these objects, originate? Who projected it, and how did it happen to fail? It has been stated that Mr. Davis again yielded to your wishes to attempt negotiations for peace, but so tied your hands with instructions that nothing could be accomplished by it, and that his object in the whole matter was to use the failure as a means more effectually to arouse the people of the Confederate States to renewed efforts and energy by showing them that there was no hope of attaining peace except by the sword. What did really occur at the interview between the Confederate commissioners and Mr. Lincoln and Mr. Seward in that conference?" he makes the following response:

> "The reports to which you refer are utterly unworthy of notice. These, as those in reference to the proposed conference in 1863, have tended only to mislead the public mind and to divert it from the truth in the case. The real objects of the Hampton Roads conference have never been made fully known to the country, so far as I am aware. It was not intended in its origin or objects to bring about direct negotiations for peace. On this point very erroneous ideas existed at the time and do yet, I believe. We had no written instructions upon that subject or any other except what were contained in the letter of our appointment, which has been published, nor any verbal instructions on that subject inconsistent with the terms of that letter. The conference, moreover, did not originate in any way with me."

LETTER OF AUTHORITY TO THE CONFEDERATE COMMISSIONERS

"City Point, Va., February 1, 1865. Thomas T. Eckert, [U.S.] Major and Aid-de-Camp—Major: Your note delivered by yourself this day has been considered. In reply we have to say that we were furnished with a copy of the letter of President Lincoln to F. P. Blair [Sr.], of the 18th of January ult., another copy of which is appended to your note. Our intentions are contained in the letter, of which the following is a copy:

> "'Richmond, January 28, 1865. In conformity with the letter of Mr. Lincoln, of which the foregoing is a copy, you are to proceed to Washington City for an informal conference with him upon the issues involved in the existing war and for the purpose of securing peace to the two countries. With great respect, your obedient servant, Jefferson Davis.'
>
> "The substantial object to be attained by the informal conference is to ascertain upon what terms the existing war can be terminated honorably. Our instructions contemplate a personal interview between President Lincoln and ourselves at Washington, but with this explanation we are ready to meet any person or persons that President Lincoln may appoint at such place as he may designate. Our earnest

desire is that a just and honorable peace may be agreed upon, and we are prepared to receive or to submit propositions which may possibly lead to the attainment of that end. Very respectfully yours, Alexander H. Stephens, Robert M. T. Hunter, John A. Campbell."

After various points had been discussed, Mr. Stephens says that Mr. Hunter went into a sort of recapitulation of the subjects talked over in the interview, and the conclusions which seemed to be logically deducible from them amounted to nothing as a basis of peace, in his judgment, but an unconditional surrender on the part of the Confederate States and their people. There could be no agreement, no treaty, nor even any stipulations as to terms—nothing but unconditional submission.

Mr. Seward promptly replied by insisting that no words like unconditional submission had been used or any importing or justly implying degradation or humiliation even to the people of the Confederate States. He wished this to be borne in mind.

Mr. Hunter repeated his view of the subject. What else could be made of it? No treaty, no stipulation, no agreement, either with the Confederate States jointly or with them separately, as to their future position or security. What was this but unconditional submission to the mercy of conquerors?

Mr. Seward said they were not conquerors further than that they required obedience to the laws. The force used was simply to maintain national authority in the execution of laws. Nor did he think that in yielding to the execution of the laws under the Constitution of the United States, with all its guarantees and securities for personal and political rights, as they might be declared to be by the courts, could be properly considered as unconditional submission to conquerors or as having anything humiliating in it. The Southern people and the Southern States would be under the Constitution of the United States, with all their rights secured thereby in the same way and through the same instrumentalities, as the similar rights of the people of the other States were.

Mr. Hunter said: "But you make no agreement that these rights will be so held and secured."

Mr. Lincoln said that, so far as the confiscation acts and other penal acts were concerned, their enforcement was left entirely with him, and on that point he was perfectly willing to be full and explicit, and on his assurance perfect reliance might be placed. He should exercise the power of the executive with the utmost liberality. He went on to say that he would be willing to be taxed to remunerate the Southern people for their slaves. *He believed the people of the North were as responsible for slavery as the people of the South* [my emphasis, L.S.], and if the war should then cease with the voluntary abolition of slavery by the States he should be in favor individually of the government paying a fair indemnity for the loss to the owners. He said he believed this feeling had an extensive existence at the North. He knew some who were in favor of an appropriation as high as four hundred millions of dollars for this purpose. "I could mention persons," said he, "whose names would astonish you who are willing to do this if the war shall now cease without further expense and with the abolition of slavery as stated." But on this subject he said he could give no assurance, enter into no stipulation. He barely expressed his own feelings and views and what he believed to be the views of others upon the subject.

The question arises, "Where does Mr. Watterson get his proofs that such offers were made by Mr. Lincoln?" Not from the official records, for in them there is no mention of any such offers. We cannot think that any of the Confederate commissioners would omit such important features of the conference from their report and then give verbal expression to such statements. They could not be true to themselves in creating a false impression by their report, and were they not honorable men? It rather seems that Mr. Watterson has placed his belief on hearsay evidence in preference to the signed statement of those who took part in the conference; that *it is an effort on his part to discredit Mr. Davis for the purpose of glorifying Mr. Lincoln* [my emphasis, L.S.]. The South can join in saying that the death of President Lincoln was its loss; but it was after the surrender at [the Battle of] Appomattox that his attitude became conciliatory, and he was then ready to give his best efforts to a quiet restoration of the South, and had he lived the South would doubtless have been spared the horrors of such Reconstruction methods as were invented by the evil genius of [Yankee socialist] Thad Stevens and his [radical Left-wing] ilk.

To show that the Confederate government was anxious for

peace between the sections, attention is called to the several efforts that were made to secure it. In his work on *The Rise and Fall of the Confederate Government* Mr. Davis gives the following account of what had been done in that direction:

> "Several efforts were made by us to communicate with the authorities at Washington without success. Commissioners were sent before hostilities were begun, and the government of the United States refused to receive them or hear what they had to say. A second time I sent a military officer with a communication addressed by myself to President Lincoln. The letter was received by General [Winfield] Scott, who did not permit the officer to see Mr. Lincoln, but promised that an answer would be sent. No answer was ever received. The third time a gentleman was sent whose position, character, and reputation were such as to insure his reception if the enemy had not been determined to receive no proposals whatever from our government. Vice President Stephens made a patriotic tender of his services in the hope of being able to promote the cause of humanity; and although little belief was entertained of his success, I cheerfully yielded to his suggestions that the experiment should be tried. The enemy refused to let him pass through their lines or to hold any conference with him. He was stopped before he reached Fortress Monroe.
>
> "If we would break up our government, dissolve the Confederacy, disband our armies, emancipate our slaves, take an oath of allegiance binding ourselves to obedience to it and to disloyalty to our own States, the government of the United States proposed to pardon us and not to deprive us of anything more than the property already robbed from us and such slaves as still remained. In order to render the proposals so insulting as to secure their rejection, the President of the United States joined to them a promise to support with his army one-tenth of the people of any State who would attempt to set up a government over the other nine-tenths, thus seeking to sow discord among the people of the several States and to excite them to civil war in furtherance of his ends."

After mentioning another movement relating to the accommodation of differences by the visit in July, 1864, of one [U.S.] Col. James F. Jacques, of the 7th Illinois Infantry, and James K. Gilmore, of Massachusetts, "the impudence of whose remarks could be extenuated only because of the ignorance displayed and the profuse avowal of the kindest motives and intentions," Mr. Davis says:

Clement C. Clay.

"The opening of the spring campaign of 1864 was deemed a favorable conjuncture tor the employment of the resources of diplomacy. To approach the government of the United States directly would have been in vain. Repeated efforts had already demonstrated its inflexible purpose—not to negotiate with the Confederate authorities. Political developments at the North, however, favored the adoption of some action that might influence popular sentiment in the hostile section. The aspect of the peace party was quite encouraging, and it seemed that the real issue to be decided in the Presidential election of that year was the continuance or cessation of the war. A commission of three persons, eminent in position and intelligence, was accordingly appointed to visit Canada with a view to negotiation with such persons in the North as might be relied upon to aid the attainment of peace. The commission was designed to facilitate such preliminary conditions as might lead to formal negotiations between the two governments, and they were expected to make judicious use of any political opportunity that might be presented.

"The commissioners—[Clement Claiborne] Clay, of Alabama, [James] Holcombe, of Virginia, and [Jacob] Thompson, of Mississippi—established themselves at Niagara Falls in July and on the 12th commenced a correspondence with Horace Greeley, of New York. Through him they sought a safe conduct to Washington. Mr. Lincoln at first appeared to favor an interview, but finally refused on the ground that the commissioners were not authorized to treat for peace. His final announcement to them was the following:

"'Executive Mansion, Washington, D.C., July 18, 1864. To Whom It May Concern: Any proposition which embraces the restoration of peace, the integrity of the whole Union, and the abandonment of slavery and which comes by and with an authority that can control the armies now at war against the United States will be received and considered by the executive government of the United States and will be met by liberal terms on other substantial and collateral points, and the bearer or bearers thereof shall have safe conduct both ways. Abraham Lincoln.'"

"This movement, like all others which had preceded it, was a failure.

"On December 30, 1864, I received a request from Mr. Francis P. Blair [Sr.], a distinguished citizen of Montgomery County, Md., for permission to visit Richmond for certain personal objects, which was conceded to him. On January 12, 1865, he visited me, and the following statement of our interview was immediately afterwards prepared:

> "'Richmond, Va., January 12, 1865. (Memorandum of a confidential conversation held this day with F. P. Blair, of Montgomery County, Md.)

"'Mr. Blair stated that, not receiving an answer to his application for permission to visit Richmond, which he had sent from the headquarters of General Grant's army, he returned to Washington and there received the reply which had been made to his application, but by some means had been withheld from him and been forwarded after having been opened; that he had originally obtained permission to visit Richmond from Mr. Lincoln after stating to him that he (Mr. Blair) had for many years held friendly relations with myself. Mr. Lincoln stopped him, though he afterwards gave him permission to visit me. He stated in explanation of his position that he, being a man of Southern blood, felt very desirous to see the war between the States terminated and hoped by an interview with me to be able to effect something to that end; that after receiving the pass which had been sent to him by my direction he sought before returning to have a conversation with Mr. Lincoln; had two appointments for that purpose, but on each occasion was disappointed and from the circumstances concluded that Mr. Lincoln avoided the interview and therefore came not only without credentials, but without such instructions from Mr. Lincoln as enabled him to speak for him. His views, therefore, were to be regarded merely as his own, and he said they were perhaps merely the dreams of an old man, etc.

"He said, despairing of being able to see me, he had determined to write me and had the rough draft of a letter which he had prepared and asked permission to read it. Soon after commencing to do so he said (pleasantly) that he found his style was marked by his old pursuit and that the paper appeared too much like an editorial. He omitted, therefore, portions of it, reading what he considered the main points of his proposition. He had recognized the difference of our positions as not entitling him to a response from me to the arguments and suggestions which he desired to offer. I therefore allowed him to read without comment on my part.

"When he had finished, I inquired as to his main proposition, the cessation of hostilities and the union of the military forces for the common purpose of maintaining the Monroe Doctrine, how that object was to be reached. He said that both the political parties of the United States asserted the Monroe Doctrine as a cardinal point of their creed; that there was a general desire to apply it to the case of Mexico. For that purpose a secret treaty might be made, etc. I called his attention to my past efforts for negotiations and my inability to see, unless Mr. Lincoln's course in that regard should be changed, how we were to take the first step.

Salmon P. Chase.

"He expressed the belief that Mr. Lincoln would now receive commissioners, but subsequently said he could not give any assurance on that point and proposed to return to Washington to explain his project to Mr. Lincoln and notify me, if his hope proved well founded, that Mr. Lincoln would now agree to a conference for the purpose of entering into negotiations.

"He affirmed that Mr. Lincoln did not sympathize with the radical men [that is, the extreme Left-wingers of the then Liberal Republican Party—in other words, Republican socialists and communists] *who desired the devastation and subjugation of the Southern States* [my emphasis, L.S.], but that he was unable to control the extreme party [that is, the [socialist-communist elements in the Republican Party], which now had great power in the Congress and would at the next session have still more, referred to the existence of two parties in the cabinet, to the reluctant nomination of Mr. [Salmon P.] Chase to be chief justice, etc. For himself he avowed an earnest desire to stop the further effusion of blood, as one every drop of whose blood was Southern. He expressed the hope that the pride, the power, and the honor of the Southern States should suffer no shock, looked to the extension of Southern territory even to the Isthmus of Darien and hoped that if his views found favor his wishes would be realized, reiterated the idea of State sovereignty with illustrations, and accepted the reference I made to explanations given in the [Washington] *Globe*, when he edited it, of the proclamation of General Jackson.

"'When his attention was called to the brutal atrocities of their armies, especially the fiendish cruelty shown to helpless women and children, as the cause of a deep-seated hostility on the part of our people and an insurmountable obstacle to an early restoration of fraternal relations, he admitted the necessity for providing a new channel for the bitter waters and another bond than that of former memories and interests. This was supposed to be contained in the proposed common effort to maintain the Monroe Doctrine on the American Continent. It was evident that he counted on the disintegration of the Confederate States if the war continued, and that in any event he regarded the institution of slavery as doomed to extinction. I thought any remark by me on the first proposition would lead to intimations in connection with public men which I preferred not more distinctly to hear than as manifested in his general remarks. On the latter point, for the reason stated, the inequality of his responsibility and mine, I preferred to have no discussion. The only difficulty which he spoke of as insurmountable was that of existing engagements between European powers and the Confederate States. This point, when referred to a second time as the dreaded obstacle to a secret treaty which would terminate the war, was met by me with a statement that we had now no such complication, were free to act as to us should seem best, and desired to keep State policy and institutions free from foreign control.'"

"'Throughout the conference Mr. Blair appeared to be animated by a sincere desire to promote a pacific solution of the existing difficulty, but claimed no other power than that of serving as a medium of communication between those who had thus far had no intercourse and were therefore without the cointelligence which might secure an adjustment of their controversy. To his hopeful anticipation in regard to the restoration of fraternal relations between the sections by the means indicated I replied that a cessation of hostilities was the first step toward the substitution of reason for passion, of sense of justice for a desire to injure, and that if the people were subsequently engaged together to maintain a principle recognized by both, if together they should bear sacrifices, share dangers, and gather common renown, new memories would take the place of those now planted by the events of this war and might in the course of time restore the feelings which preexisted. But it was for us to deal with the problems before us and leave to posterity questions which they might solve, though we could not; that in the struggle for independence by our colonial fathers, had failure instead of success attended their effort, Great Britain, instead of a commerce which has largely contributed to her prosperity, would have had the heavy expense of numerous garrisons to hold in subjection a people who deserved to be free and had resolved not to be subject.

"'Our conference ended with no other result than an agreement that he would learn whether Mr. Lincoln would adopt his (Mr. Blair's) project and send or receive commissioners to negotiate for a peaceful solution of the questions at issue; that he would report to him my readiness to enter upon negotiations, and that I knew of no insurmountable obstacle to such a treaty of peace as would secure greater advantage to both parties than any result which arms could achieve.

"'January 14, 1863. The foregoing memorandum of conversation was this day read to Mr. Blair and altered in so far as he desired, in any respect to change the expression employed. Jefferson Davis.'

"The following letter was given by me [Jefferson Davis] to Mr. Blair:

"'Richmond, Va., January 12, 1865. F. P. Blair, Esq.—Sir: I have deemed it proper and probably desirable to you to give you in this form the substance of remarks made by me to be repeated by you to President Lincoln, etc.

"'I have no disposition to find obstacles in forms and am willing now, as heretofore, to enter into negotiations for the restoration of peace, am ready to send a commission whenever I have reason to suppose it will be received or to receive a commission if the United States government shall choose to send one; that, notwithstanding the rejection of our former offers, I would, if you could promise that a commissioner, minister, or other agent would be received, appoint one immediately and renew the effort to enter into conference with a view to secure peace to the two countries. Yours, etc., Jefferson Davis.'

[Lincoln's reply to Blair:] "'Washington, January 18, 1865. P. Blair, Esq.—Sir: Having shown me Mr. Davis's letter to you of the 12th instant, you may say to him that I have constantly been, am now, and shall continue ready to receive any agent whom he or any other influential person now resisting the national authority may informally send to me with the view of securing peace to the people of our one common country. Yours, etc., A. Lincoln.'

"When Mr. Blair returned and gave me this letter of Mr. Lincoln of January 18, it being a response to my note Blair of the 12th, he said it had been a fortunate thing that I gave him that note, as it had created greater confidence in Mr. Lincoln regarding his efforts at Richmond. Further reflection, he said, had modified the views he formerly presented to me and that he wanted to have my attention for a different mode of procedure. . . . He [Blair] then unfolded to me the embarrassment of Mr. Lincoln on account of the extreme [Republican socialist and communist] men in Congress and elsewhere who wished to drive him into harsher measures than he was inclined to adopt; hence it would not be feasible for him to enter into any arrangement with us by the use of political agencies; that if anything beneficial could be effected it must be done without the intervention of the politicians. He, therefore, suggested that Generals Lee and Grant might enter into an arrangement by which hostilities would be suspended and a way paved for the restoration of peace. I responded that I would willingly intrust to General Lee such negotiation as was indicated.

"The conference then ended, and to report to Mr. Lincoln the result of his visit Mr. Blair returned to Washington. He subsequently informed me that the idea of a military convention was not favorably received at Washington, so it only remained for me to act upon the letter of Mr. Lincoln.

"I determined to send as commissioners or agents for the informal conference Messrs. Alexander H. Stephens, R. M. T. Hunter, and John A. Campbell. Some objections were made to this commission by the United States officials, because it authorized the commissioners to confer for the purpose 'of securing peace to *the two countries*'; whereas the letter of Mr. Lincoln, which was their passport, spoke of 'securing peace to the people of our *one common country* [my emphasis, L.S.].' But these objections were finally waived.

"On receiving the letter of Mr. Lincoln expressing a willingness to receive any agent I might send to Washington City, a commission was appointed to go there; but it was not allowed to proceed farther than Hampton Roads, where Mr. Lincoln accompanied by Mr. Seward, met the commissioners. *Seward craftily proposed that the conference should be confidential, and the commissioners regarded this so binding on them as to prevent them from including in their report the discussion which occurred. This enabled Mr. Seward to give his own version of it in a dispatch to the United States Minister to the French government, which was calculated to create distrust of, if not hostility to, the Confederacy on the part of the power in Europe most effectively favoring our recognition* [my emphasis, L.S.]."

The reports of the famous peace conference do not show that Mr. Lincoln was anxious for peace on any terms but his own, nor that he was willing to concede anything of his position on any question, and he was very careful as to what should go on any "piece of paper" for him to sign.

Mr. Stephens's report does show that Mr. Davis was disappointed over the result of it.

> "On the return of the commissioners to Richmond," says Mr. Stephens, "everybody was very much disappointed, and no one seemed to be more than Mr. Davis. He thought Mr. Lincoln had acted in bad faith in the matter and attributed this change in his policy to the fall of Fort Fisher, in North Carolina, which occurred on the 15th of January, after Mr. Blair's first visit to Richmond."

Had Mr. Davis himself been inclined to accept the terms of unconditional surrender, he could not have done so without the action of the Confederate Congress, which alone had the power of accepting or rejecting. So *why blame Mr. Davis for not accepting the very objectionable terms?* [my emphasis, L.S.]

[Next we shall look at material on the] Hampton Roads Conference, from [the] "Memoirs of John H. Reagan," published in 1906.

During recent years there has been an extensive discussion through the public prints of the questions which rose at the Hampton Roads conference. It has been asserted over and over that President Lincoln offered to pay $400,000,000 for the slaves of the South to secure an end of the war and that he held up a piece of paper to Mr. Stephens, saying: "Let me write the word 'Union' on it, and you may add any other conditions you please if it will give us peace." I am probably not using the exact words which were employed, but I am expressing the idea given to the public in the discussion. It has frequently been alleged that Mr. Stephens said these offers were made. This has been repeated by citizens of acknowledged ability and high character, and it has been said that these offers could not be acceded to because the instructions given to the commission by President Davis prevented it. *The purpose of urging these untrue statements seems to have been to induce the public to believe that Mr. Davis could have obtained peace on almost any terms desired and $400,000,000 for the Southern slaves if he had consented to a restoration of the Southern States to the Union, and that because of this he was responsible for the losses of life and property caused by the continuance of the war* [my emphasis, L.S.].

I shall submit evidence which will prove that no such propositions were ever made. This course is rendered necessary and just both for the truth of history and to vindicate the action of President Davis and his cabinet. For *undoubtedly one of the purposes of insisting that such offers were made is to mislead the public as to the truth* [my emphasis, L.S.].

The following is the report of the Confederate commissioners to President Davis as to what occurred at the conference:

"To the President [Davis] of the Confederate States: Under your letter of appointment of the 28th ult. we proceeded to seek an 'informal conference' with Abraham Lincoln, President of the United States, upon the subject mentioned in the letter. The conference was granted and took place on the 3rd inst. on board a steamer [the *River Queen*] anchored in Hampton Roads, where we met President Lincoln and the Honorable Mr. Seward, Secretary of State of the United States. It continued for several hours and was both full and explicit. We learned from them that the message of President Lincoln to the Congress of the United States in December last explains clearly and distinctly his sentiments as to the terms, conditions, and methods of proceeding by which peace can be secured to the people, and we are not informed that they would be modified or altered to obtain that end. We understood from him that no terms or proposals of any treaty or agreement looking to an ultimate settlement would be entertained or made by him with the authorities of the Confederate States, because that would be a recognition of their existence as a separate power, which under no circumstances would be done, and for a like reason that no such terms would be entertained by him for the States separately; that no extended truce or armistice (as at present advised) would be granted or allowed without a satisfactory assurance in advance of the complete restoration of the authority of the Constitution and laws of the United States over all places within the States of the Confederacy; that whatever consequences may follow from the reestablishment of that authority must be accepted; but that individuals subject to pains and penalties under the laws of the United States might rely upon a very liberal use of the power confided to him to remit those pains and penalties if peace be restored.

"During the conference the proposed amendment to the Constitution of the United States adopted by Congress on the 31st ultimo was brought to our notice. This amendment provides that neither slavery nor involuntary servitude except for crime should exist within the United States or any place within her jurisdiction and that Congress would have power to enforce this amendment by appropriate legislation.

Very respectfully, etc., Alexander H. Stephens, R. M. T. Hunter, John A. Campbell."

It is seen that the Confederate commissioners say that no terms or proposals of any treaty or agreement would be entertained by President Lincoln with the authorities of the Confederate States or with any of the States separately and that no truce or armistice would be allowed without satisfactory evidence in advance of the complete restoration of the authority of the Constitution and laws of the United States over all places within the States of the Confederacy. This report was signed by Mr. Stephens, Mr. Hunter, and Judge Campbell. It shows conclusively that unconditional surrender in advance of any negotiations was the only condition whereby the war could be ended. And Judge Campbell in his memoranda relating to this conference says:

> "In conclusion, Mr. Hunter summed up what seemed to be the result of the interview: that there could be no arrangements by treaty between the Confederate States and the United States or any agreement between them. There was nothing left for them but unconditional submission."

On the 6th of February, 1865, President Davis sent the report of the commissioners to the Confederate Congress with a message in which he used this language:

> "I herewith transmit for the information of Congress the report of the eminent citizens above named, showing that the enemy refused to enter into negotiations with the Confederate States or any of them separately or to give our people any other terms or guaranties than those which the conquerors may grant or to permit us to have peace on any other basis than our unconditional submission to their rule, coupled with the acceptance of their recent legislation on the subject of the relations between the black and white population of each State."

In his "History of the War between the States" (Volume II, pages 599-626) Vice President Stephens gives a carefully compiled account of what was done at the conference, and in this he shows plainly and fully the distinct refusal of President Lincoln to recognize or in any form to make or agree to any terms for peace with the government of the Confederate States or with any of the

States separately except upon the condition that they should, before any other measure should be considered, recognize and accept the Constitution and laws of the United States and trust to Congress as to what disposition was to be made of the Confederacy, their people and property. There is no word in his long account of any proposition as to the payment of $400,000,000 for the slaves or of President Lincoln's writing the word "Union" on a sheet of paper and allowing Mr. Stephens or any one else to determine the terms and conditions upon which the war should be ended.

So it is seen that we have the report of the Confederate commissioners to the President, the message of the President to Congress, the joint resolutions of the two Houses of the Confederate Congress, and the evidence of Mr. Stephens's history of what occurred at that conference to prove that no such offers were made by Mr. Lincoln.

While it may seem unnecessary, I will go farther and add to these testimonials those of President Lincoln and Secretary Seward.

Mr. Lincoln at first determined to send Secretary of State Seward to meet the Confederate commissioners and on the 31st of January, 1865, furnished him with instructions for his government, which contained these provisions:

> "You will make known to them that three things are indispensable to wit: (1) The restoration of the national authority throughout all the States; (2) no receding by the executive of the United States on the slavery question from the position assumed thereon in the late message to Congress and in preceding documents; (3) no cessation of hostilities short of an end of the war and the disbanding of all forces hostile to the government."

In Mr. Lincoln's annual message to Congress dated December 5, 1864, he says:

> "At the last session of Congress a proposed amendment of the Constitution abolishing slavery throughout the United States passed the Senate, but failed of the requisite two-thirds vote of the House of Representatives. Although the present is the same Congress and nearly the same members, and without questioning the wisdom and patriotism of those who stood in opposition, I venture to recommend the reconsideration and passage of the measure at the present session."

And the same message contained the following:

> "In presenting the abandonment of armed resistance to the national authority on the part of the insurgents as the only indispensable condition to ending the war on the part of the government I retract nothing heretofore said as to slavery. I repeat the declaration made a year ago that while I remain in my present position I shall not attempt to retract or modify the Emancipation Proclamation, nor shall I return to slavery any person who is free by the terms of that proclamation or by any of the acts of Congress. If the people should, by whatever mode or means, make it an executive duty to reenslave such persons, another, and not I, must be their instrument to perform it."

The [Final Emancipation] proclamation here referred to by President Lincoln was that of January 1, 1863, for which that of [the Preliminary Emancipation Proclamation, issued on] September 22, 1862, had prepared the way.[71] In that of the later date he declared:

> "That on the 1st day of January, 1863, all persons held as slaves within any State or designated part of a State the people whereof shall be in rebellion against the United States shall be then, thenceforward, and forever free."

In the face of his annual message of December 5, 1864, and of these two proclamations, how could President Lincoln have proposed to pay $400,000,000 for the slaves he had already set free and did not intend to return to a condition of slavery? And how could he have said that if he were allowed to write the word "Union" on a piece of blank paper the Confederate commissioners might name any terms they pleased to end the war?

On the 7th of February, 1865, Mr. Seward addressed a communication to the Hon. Charles Francis Adams [Sr.], the Minister Plenipotentiary of the United States to Great Britain, giving for his information an account of what occurred at the Hampton Roads conference. This letter, it will be observed, was written four days after that conference. In it, among other things, he said that President Lincoln announced to the Confederate commissioners:

"That we can agree to no cessation or suspension of hostilities except on the basis of the disbandment of the insurgent forces and the restoration of the national authority throughout all the States in the Union. Collaterally and in subordination to the proposition which he thus announced, the antislavery policy of the United States was reviewed in all its bearings, and the President [Lincoln] announced that he must not be expected to depart from the positions he had assumed in his Proclamation of Emancipation and other documents, as these positions were reiterated in his last annual message. It was further declared by the President that the complete restoration of national authority everywhere was an indispensable condition to any assent on our part to whatever form of peace might be proposed. The President assured the other party that, while he must adhere to these positions, he would be prepared, as far as power was lodged with the executive, to exercise it liberally. His power, however, is limited by the Constitution; and when peace should be made, Congress must necessarily act in regard to appropriations of money and the admission of representatives from the insurrectionary States. The Richmond party [the Confederate States of America] was then informed that Congress had on the 31st ultimo adopted by a constitutional majority a joint resolution submitting to the several States the proposition to abolish slavery throughout the Union and that there is every reason to expect that it will be accepted by three-fourths of the States, so as to become a part of the organic law."

While it is true that some respectable men have asserted that Mr. Stephens told them of Mr. Lincoln's alleged offer (and I have all their statements in writing or print), *there must have been some misunderstanding as to his language, for he was an honorable and truthful man and a man of too much good sense to have made such allegations in the face of such record as is here presented* [my emphasis, L.S.]. Among those who assert that Mr. Stephens made one or the other of those statements are the Hon. Henry Watterson, editor of the *Courier-Journal*; Rev. E. A. Green, of Virginia; Dr. R. J. Massey, of Georgia; and Mr. Clark Howell, of Georgia. Any impartial person who may read the statements of Mr. Green will see his gross ignorance of the matters of which he writes, and any one who will read what he says and what Dr. Massey says will see that *the main purpose with them was to throw discredit on President Davis for not making peace on terms which, as the evidence shows, were not offered and which we were fully informed could not be allowed the Confederates. And it is also clear that a prime object with Dr. Massey was to lionize Mr. Stephens, while discrediting Mr. Davis* [my emphasis, L.S.].

Among those who say Mr. Stephens denied making these statements are the Rev. F. C. Boykin, of Georgia; Mr. R. F. Littig, of Mississippi; Hon. James L. Orr, of South Carolina, who was at that time associated with Vice President Stephens as a member of the Confederate Senate; Hon. Frank B. Sexton, then a member of the Confederate Congress; Col. Stephen W. Blount, of Texas, who had been a schoolmate and was a friend to Mr. Stephens, who, in answer to Blount's inquiry, wrote that he never made any such remark; Mr. Charles G. Newman, of Arkansas; and Gov. Augustus H. Garland, of Arkansas, who was at the time of the conference a member of the Confederate Senate and the roommate of Mr. Stephens and who has been United States Senator and Attorney-General of the United States. Governor Garland says that on the return of the Confederate commissioners Mr. Stephens told him no terms of peace could be had except upon unconditional submission of the Confederates.

James L. Orr.

It is not pleasant to have to consider such a conflict of statements. It has arisen between men of ability and character in the discussion of one of the important historical questions which grew out of the great contest. And *the published statements show that there was an extensive effort being made to pervert and falsify the history of that important conference so as to cast public censure on President Davis for not terminating the war upon conditions which were not offered* [my emphasis, L.S.].

I also have a letter from Senator [George G.] Vest, of Missouri, who was then a Confederate Senator, in which he says:

"R. M. T. Hunter, who was President *pro tempore* of the Confederate Senate, told me in detail what occurred at the Fort Monroe conference, and it agrees with your statements. No more truthful and conservative man than Hunter ever lived."

The message of Mr. Lincoln of March 6, 1862, and his conference with border State representatives at that time and the statements he made to Mr. Stephens at the Hampton Roads conference and perhaps other expressions of his showed, I think, his personal willingness that compensation should have been made for the slaves of the South; but the messenger referred to and the conference which followed were in March of the second year of the war. His suggestion then was that the border States of the Confederacy should adopt a general plan of emancipation upon the basis of compensation, and that if this was done it would defeat the purpose of the Southern States. It was a bid to the border States to desert their Southern sister States. Those representing the border States declined to act on this suggestion, for it was only a suggestion. For them to have acted in advance of any move by the Northern States and with no assurance that if they should adopt such a policy it would ever be accepted by the North would have been a species of madness. This, however, had no direct relation to what occurred at Hampton Roads.

I have no doubt that Mr. Stephens recited the statement made by President Lincoln at that conference to the effect that he personally would have no objection to an arrangement for compensation for the slaves if that would end the war and that he knew persons who would be willing to pay $400,000,000 for that purpose. This is probably the basis, and the only basis, for the stories so often repeated about his [Lincoln] offering at that conference to pay $400,000,000 if it would end the war. And when Mr. Stephens spoke of these two things, his hearers, I must suppose, misunderstood him or misconstrued his words. It is better to view it thus and to assume that the stories referred to had their origin in that way than to believe that willful misstatements were made [my emphasis, L.S.].

I served with Mr. Stephens in the Congress of the United States four years before the war. We served together in the Provisional Congress of the Confederacy, were thrown together more or less during the war, and we served together in Congress for several years after the war. I always regarded him as an upright, honorable man. I was his friend and admired his genius and ability, though I thought during the war, and have not changed my opinion, that he had very impracticable views as to the methods of conducting the war. And I fear from his writings and from the statements attributed to him by others that during the latter part of the war and after it closed he allowed his great name and influence to give too much encouragement to malcontents who caused embarrassment to the Confederate government and who endeavored to cast unjust reflections on the policy, actions, and services of the President, his cabinet, and the Confederate Congress.[72] — *CONFEDERATE VETERAN*

The U.S.S. *Sabine* anchored at Hampton Roads, December 1864.

The U.S.S. *Wyoming* leading a fleet of battleships at Hampton Roads in 1917. The area's waterways are ideal for shipping and have been in use for this purpose since Colonial times.

SECTION FOUR

Personal Views & Commentary

11. WHEN GEN. LEE LOST HOPE OF SUCCESS

☛ "[Dear *Confederate Veteran*:] In answer to your request I give you what, in substance, I related to you and Mr. [Washington] Gardner [a former Union soldier from Michigan] the other day. The Hampton Roads effort at settlement, in which Messrs. Hunter, Stephens, and Campbell acted as commissioners, came about in the following manner: John B. Baldwin, of Virginia, member of the House of Representatives, and who was a Colonel under Gen. [Robert E.] Lee during the first year of the war, said to me one night in December, 1864, that he was greatly depressed, as Gen. Lee had that day informed him that the cause for which he was fighting had to fail—that he would be compelled to give up Richmond and disband his army for the want of supplies. Mr. Baldwin said he hardly felt that he had the courage to say what ought to be said in the House, as he knew Mr. [Jefferson] Davis and many members of the House still believed the war could be prosecuted to a successful termination. Before we separated it was agreed that he, Mr. Baldwin, should introduce into the House a resolution for the appointment of a committee to inquire into our ability to carry on the war. This Mr. Baldwin did the next day in secret session. The resolution was promptly passed and the committee appointed. Mr. Baldwin, perhaps the ablest man in the House, was made chairman. I, with several other members, was put on the committee. The first thing the committee did was to take the deposition of Gen. Lee. Then the evidence of other general officers was taken. Gen. Lee said in his evidence that he would be compelled to give up Richmond and disband his army for the want of supplies, and in answer to a direct question put by the chairman, he said he could devise no means of carrying on the war. The other general officers sustained him.

"The taking of this proof lasted some time; I cannot now

Robert E. Lee.

remember how long, but we were waiting on some witnesses. This evidence created in the committee a profound impression. The feeling was that another battle ought not to be fought—that the further shedding of blood was useless. The report made to the House produced a discussion that was by no means free of acrimony. It was hoped and believed that Mr. Davis would at once take some steps looking to a settlement. This was not done, and after consulting Gen. [Smith D.] Atkins and others, and alter conferring with Mr. Stephens, who was Vice-President, and getting his consent to act, I wrote the resolutions—which Mr. Stephens himself rewrote and reformed—and afterward introduced them in secret session, asking the President to appoint Stephens, Hunter, and Campbell to confer with Mr. Lincoln on the subject of bringing the war to a close. While the debate was progressing, and before a vote was taken, a member, Mr. [William] Barksdale, of Mississippi, intimated that the commission would be created if the debate was stopped, and that no vote need be taken. Thereupon Mr. Davis appointed Mr. Hunter, of Virginia, Mr. Campbell, of Louisiana, and Mr. Stephens. But as Mr. Stephens informed me when he came back, and I think he substantially states it in his book, the conditions of the authority forbade any settlement except on the basis of independence.

"Mr. Stephens was of opinion when he returned that Mr. Lincoln was willing—the Union being restored, slavery having already been abolished—that the war should end, and all Federal troops be withdrawn from the Southern States, and leaving the Southern State governments intact just as they were before the war. In other words, trusting the Southern people to keep the agreement without force, or coercion through territorial government. The specific instructions given the commissioners were not known to Congress, certainly not to the House of representatives, and when the commissioners returned and reported a failure a great effort was made by public meetings to intensify the war feeling. One great meeting was held in Richmond, where Mr. [Judah P.] Benjamin was the principal speaker."

Mr. Colyar does not report all of this conversation. [He was] asked about Mr. Davis, raising the question of his faith in final success, and he replied that Mr. Davis evidently believed that Providence would eventually overrule for the Confederacy, as was the result of [George] Washington's struggle for American independence.[73] — ARTHUR ST. CLAIR COLYAR, MEMBER OF THE CONFEDERATE CONGRESS, 1864-1865

12. POLITICS & SHENANIGANS

☛ That Mr. Lincoln's utmost wish was the restoration of the Union, as it was, (upon conditions that were the inevitable results of the conflict), is conclusively shown in the noted peace-conference at Hampton Roads, after Sherman's entry of Savannah. It was attended by Mr. Lincoln and Mr. Seward, his Secretary of State, on behalf of the United States, and by Mr. A. H. Stephens, Vice-President; John A. Campbell, Assistant Secretary of War; and R. M. T. Hunter, Senator, of the Confederate States. The last named were authorized by letter of Jefferson Davis of January 28, 1865, brought about by Francis P. Blair [Sr.]. The meeting was on board the *River Queen* February 3, 1865.

Mr. Lincoln, sustained by Mr. Seward, first stated his demands, which were substantially according to the following subdivisions:

1. As to *restoration* of the Union, it could only follow the disbanding of the armies of the insurgents and permitting the national authorities to resume their functions. He expressed it as his *opinion* that thereupon the Southern States ought to be and would be admitted to representation in the Congress of the United States, but could not enter into any *stipulations* on that subject; that when

resistance ceased the States would be immediately restored to their practical relations within the Union.

2. Upon the subject of *confiscation,* he said the confiscation acts left the control entirely to him, and he could state explicitly, that he would exercise the power with the utmost liberality.

3. The *emancipation proclamation,* he said, was a judicial question. *His opinion was, that as the proclamation was a war measure, as soon as the war ceased it would be inoperative for the future* [my emphasis, LS]. "It would be held to apply only to such slaves as had come under its operation, while it was in active exercise"—"that he would leave it to the courts to decide, and would never change its terms in the slightest particular; that he never would have interfered with slavery in the States unless he had been driven to it by a public necessity. He had always himself been in favor of emancipation, but not *immediate* emancipation, even by the States. Many evils attending this appeared to him." He went on to say, that "he would be willing to be *taxed* to *remunerate* the Southern people for *their slaves. He believed the people of the North were as responsible for slavery as the people of the South, and if the war should cease with the voluntary abolition of slavery by the States, he should be in favor himself of paying a fair indemnity to the owners* [my emphasis, L.S.]. He could mention persons whose names (Horace Greeley was one) would cause astonishment, who were willing to do this, if the war should now cease with the abolition of slavery, and were in favor of an appropriation of *four hundred millions* for that purpose." But on this subject he spoke his own mind merely; could give *no assurance.*

Mr. Secretary Seward then mentioned the proposed *Thirteenth Amendment* abolishing slavery, introduced in Congress a few days before (having been voted down by the House at the preceding session), and said, as it may be supposed that wily statesman was capable of saying, *diplomatically:* "If the South will submit and agree to immediate restoration, the *restored States might yet defeat it,"* as without some of them, the requisite three-fourths could not be obtained; intimating that the amendment had been passed by Congress "under the predominance of revolutionary passion."[74]

Gen. Grant's fidelity and magnanimity were proven on this historical occasion. He paid no heed to the proposals of the Confederate Commissioners, that he and Gen. Lee, during an

Thomas T. Eckert (seated left).

armistice, should agree upon a peace settlement. The Commissioners had been turned back by Mr. Lincoln. Maj. [Thomas T.] Eckert, the President's messenger, had reported to him that they did "not talk right." But Grant, hearing of the President's refusal to receive them, telegraphed the Secretary of War February 1, 1865, a dispatch, which was immediately seen by Mr. Lincoln, and decided him to meet the Commissioners in person. The dispatch was as follows:

> "I am convinced, upon conversation with Messrs. Hunter and Stephens, of their sincere desire to restore peace and union. I recognize the difficulty of receiving these informal Commissioners, but am sorry that Mr. Lincoln cannot have an interview with the two named, if not all three, now within our lines. U.S. Grant, Lieut.-Gen."[75]

This was about two months before the Surrender, when Grant had the Confederacy in his grasp, and he would thus forego the triumph at Appomattox.

There were four persons present at the Conference held at City Point on the 28th of March, 1865. They were Lincoln, Grant, Sherman and Admiral [David D.] Porter. It was before these men that Lincoln freely discussed the question of ending the war, and in Sherman's Memoirs he says

> "Mr. Lincoln was full and frank in his conversation, assuring me that in his mind he was all ready for the civil reorganization of affairs at the South as soon as the war was over."

Had Lincoln stopped with the general assurance of his purpose to restore the South to civil government, it might be plausible to assume that Sherman misinterpreted his expressions, but Sherman adds the following positive statement:

> "He (Lincoln) distinctly authorized me to assure Gov. [Zebulon B.] Vance and the people of North Carolina that as soon as the rebel armies laid down their arms and resumed their civil pursuits they would at once be guaranteed all their rights as citizens of a common country; and that to avoid anarchy the State Governments then in existence, with their civil functionaries, would be recognized by him as the Governments *de facto* till Congress could provide others."

There was no possibility for Sherman to mistake this expression of Lincoln. He was distinctly instructed to assure the Government of North Carolina, the State in which Sherman's army was then operating, that upon the surrender of the insurgent forces all would be guaranteed their rights as citizens, and the civil governments then in existence would be recognized by Lincoln. There was no chance for misunderstanding on this point.

He [Lincoln] refrained from emancipation for eighteen months after the war had begun, simply because he believed during that time that he might best save the Union by saving slavery, and had the development of events proved that belief to be correct he would have permitted slavery to live with the Union [my emphasis, L.S.]. When he became fully convinced that the safety of the Government demanded the destruction of slavery, he decided, after the most patient and exhaustive consideration of the subject, to proclaim his emancipation policy. *It was not founded solely, or even chiefly on the sentiment of hostility to slavery. If it had been, the proclamation would have declared slavery abolished in every State in the Union; but he excluded the slave states of Delaware, Maryland, Tennessee and Missouri, and certain parishes in Louisiana, and certain counties in Virginia, from the operation of the proclamation, declaring in the instrument that has now become immortal, "which excepted parts are for the present left precisely as if this proclamation were not issued* [my emphasis, L.S.]."

But while he was compelled to accept the issue of revolutionary emancipation, he never abandoned the idea of compensated emancipation until the final overthrow of Lee's army in 1865. He proposed it to his cabinet in February of that year, only to be unanimously rejected, and I personally know that he would have suggested it to Stephens, Campbell and Hunter at the Hampton

Roads conference in February, 1865, had not Vice President Stephens, as the immediate representative of Jefferson Davis, frankly stated at the outset that he was instructed not to entertain or discuss any proposition that did not recognize the perpetuity of the Confederacy.

In a personal interview with Jefferson Davis, when I was a visitor in his house at Beauvoir, Miss., fifteen years after the close of the war, I asked him whether he had ever received any intimation about Lincoln's desire to close the war by the payment of $400,000,000 for emancipated slaves. He said that he had not heard of it. I asked him whether he would have given such instructions to Stephens if he had possessed knowledge of the fact. He answered that he could not have given Stephens any other instructions than he did under the circumstances, because, as President of the Confederacy, he could not entertain any question involving its dissolution, that being a subject entirely for the States themselves.[76] — JOHN M. HARRELL, BRIG.-GEN. COMDG. S. DIV. ARKANSAS U.C.V.

13. YANKEE LIES NEVER CEASE

☛ A singular publication appeared recently in the New York *World*. It is dated as a telegram at Atlanta, and said, "Judge Samuel B. Herit, who is now seriously ill at Suwanee Springs, Fla., while reclining upon his bed to-day," etc. He then goes on to repeal what Mr. Stephens is reported to have said about the Hampton Roads Conference, viz., that Mr. Lincoln would agree to any terms the South would make, provided the Union was restored. How a correspondent in Atlanta could hear a conversation that day in Florida strengthens doubt concerning reports which are so resolutely denied. Of one thing all honest men must agree, that Mr. Davis believed that the cause of the South would ultimately prevail.[77] — *CONFEDERATE VETERAN*

14. ALEXANDER H. STEPHENS AT LIBERTY HALL

☛ W. H. Brooker writes from San Antonio, March 27, 1895, to the Houston, Texas, *Post*, sharp denial of the Statement over and over made, and lately embodied by Mr. Henry Watterson in one of his lectures, that Mr. Lincoln said, at the Hampton Roads

Conference, "Write Union at the top of the paper and you can put what you choose besides."

Mr. Brooker states that in 1872 he was a visitor at Crawfordsville [GA], and on that occasion several prominent statesmen of Georgia were there visiting the Sage of "Liberty Hall" [the home of A. H. Stephens]—men who espoused the cause of the Confederacy—and Mr. Stephens went back to the war to give his views at large. In the conversation he spoke of the warm personal friendship existing between Mr. Lincoln and himself, a friendship that grew strong and mutual during their sittings in the National Halls of Congress, when incidentally the Hampton Roads Conference was discussed pro and con by several present. In the course of the discussion he, being much younger than the others and perhaps retiring, said to Mr. Stephens, "Mr. Stephens, all know your warm personal friendship towards Mr. Lincoln, and your high estimation of his integrity and ability, why did you not presume on this and urge a dissolution of the war on terms honorable to your section and your people?"

"I shall never forget the breathless silence that pervaded the hall, while Mr. Stephens began his reply: "While the conference was in session some matters were discussed, but Mr. Lincoln always turned upon unconditional surrender, and he would use his good offices to ameliorate the condition of the South. . . . After the conference broke I tried to draw Mr. Lincoln into conversation on friendly terms, and when I mentioned the dissolution of the war, he grew restive and said: 'Nothing but unconditional surrender,' abruptly parted, took his cabin with Mr. Seward on his man-of-war and ordered the Captain to steam back to Washington."[78] — *CONFEDERATE VETERAN*

15. THAT HAMPTON ROADS CONFERENCE

☞ . . . I desire to say that it has been frequently asserted of late years that at the conference between President Lincoln and Secretary Seward, of the Federal side, and Messrs. Stephens, Hunter, and Campbell, of the Confederate side, at Hampton Roads, on the 3rd of January, 1865, President Lincoln offered the Confederates four hundred million dollars for the slaves if they would abandon the war and return to the Union. This story has assumed various forms to suit the rhetoric of the speakers and writers who have given it currency.

I wish to assert most solemnly that no such offer in any form was made. All the papers relating to the Hampton Roads conference are given in [Edward] McPherson's "History of the Rebellion," as he calls it. They show that the joint resolution for amending the constitution of the United States was passed by Congress, submitting to the states the question of abolishing slavery in the United States, two or three days before the date of that conference. The report of the commissioners on the part of the Confederacy, which was published at the time, shows that no such offer was made or referred to in that conference. The statements of President Davis and that of President Lincoln and of Secretary Seward show that no such offer was made or talked of at that conference.

Ulysses S. Grant.

This false statement has often been made. It is disproved by every man who was there, and by every paper which has been written by or for the men who were there. Neither President Lincoln nor any other man on the Federal side would have dared to make such an offer at that time. It was stated at the time—and I believe the statement to be true—that the Congress hurried the joint resolution above named through, so as to forestall the possibility of any such proposition. *The object of this untruthful statement was no doubt to cast odium on the Confederate President and authorities by trying to show that they would accept no terms of peace and were responsible for the continuance of the war* [my emphasis, L.S.].

President Davis appointed Vice President Stephens to go to Washington, in 1864, ostensibly to secure a renewal of the cartel for the exchange of prisoners; but the real purpose of his mission was to see President Lincoln for the purpose of ascertaining on what conditions the war could be terminated. But he was not permitted by the Federal authorities to pass through their military lines. He then appointed the commissioners to the Hampton Roads conference for the same purpose; and afterwards, in 1865, he authorized Gen. R. E. Lee to try to negotiate through Gen. Grant for the same purpose.

I mention these facts to show that it is a mistake to suppose that President Davis neglected any means in his power to end the war on honorable terms, and mention them because of the many misrepresentations which have been made on this subject [my emphasis, L.S.]. He could not have made public all he did in this respect, at the time, without discouraging our army and people. And if, at anytime, he had proposed or consented to unconditionally surrender, he would have been in danger of violence at the hands of our own people. Neither he nor they proposed or intended to surrender unconditionally unless overpowered.[79] — JOHN H. REAGAN, FORMER-POSTMASTER GENERAL, C.S.A., SPEECH BEFORE CONFEDERATE VETERANS, JUNE 1897

16. REAGAN REPLIES TO A CRITIC OF HIS SPEECH ABOVE

☛ A courteous critic in the *Nashville American* demurred to Mr. Reagan's denial that Mr. Lincoln at the Hampton Roads conference offered to pay $400,000,000 to the South for slaves if the Southern people would return to the Union. Mr. Reagan has written at length, sending copies of his reply to the *Nashville American* and also to the *Confederate Veteran*. [Here is Mr. Reagan's reply:]

Did President Lincoln, at the Hampton Roads conference, February 3, 1865, propose to Messrs. Stephens, Hunter, and Campbell that the United States would pay four hundred million dollars for the slaves, on condition that the Confederates would abandon the war and return to the Union? In my address at the reunion of ex-Confederates at Nashville, Tenn., June 22, 1897, I asserted most solemnly that no such offer in any form was made.

. . . The friendly critic reports a conversation between President Lincoln and Vice President Stephens, in which Mr. Stephens quotes President Lincoln as follows:

> "He [Lincoln] went on to say that he would be willing to be taxed to remunerate Southern people for their slaves. He believed the people

of the North were as responsible for slavery as the people of the South; and if the war should then cease with a voluntary abolition of slavery by the states, he should be in favor, individually, of the government paying a fair indemnity for the loss to the owners. He said he believed this feeling had an extensive existence in the North. He knew some who were in favor of an appropriation as high as four hundred million dollars for this purpose. 'I could mention persons,' said he, 'whose names would astonish you, who are willing to do this if the war should now cease without further expense and with the abolition of slavery as stated.' But on this subject he said he could give no assurance, enter into no stipulations. He barely expressed his own feelings and views and what he believed to be the views of others on the subject."

President Lincoln suggested that this compensation might be made if the war should cease at that time, coupled with the voluntary abolition of slavery; yet he said Congress would have to decide on such questions. To put it plainly, his suggestion was for the Confederacy to abandon their cause and free the slaves as a condition precedent, and trust to Congress for compensation.

. . . Accepting as true all that Mr. Stephens reports President Lincoln to have said, it in no wise conflicts with my declaration that no such offer was made. Mr. Lincoln merely expressed his private personal views and his opinion as to the views of others, but expressly stated that "he could give neither assurance nor enter into any stipulations" on the subject, adding that "he barely expressed his own feelings and views and what he believed to be the views of others upon the subject." This being the only authority quoted, and no doubt all that could be quoted, to prove that President Lincoln offered to pay four hundred million dollars for the slaves if the Confederates would abandon the contest and return to the Union, it would seem to be unnecessary to offer other evidence to show that no such offer was ever made.

But this false story has been so often told and repeated by persons who had been led to believe it was true that I shall, at the risk of taxing the patience of those who may read this paper, quote enough of indisputable evidence to put this story at rest and also to show the absurdity of other and kindred statements, such as that Mr. Stephens said that President Lincoln told him that if he would allow him (Lincoln) to write the word "Union" at the bottom of a sheet of paper, he (Stephens) might write any terms he pleased above it looking to terminating the war.

I prefer to call Vice President Stephens as the first witness to prove that all such statements are false. In his history of "The War between the States," Vol. II, page 602, he quotes President Lincoln as saying at the Hampton Roads conference that "the only basis on which he would entertain a proposition for a settlement was the recognition and reestablishment of the national authority throughout the land." On page 608 of the same volume Mr. Stephens quotes Mr. Lincoln as saying that he "could not entertain a proposition for an armistice on any terms while the great and vital question of reunion was undisposed of;" and on page 609 of the same volume Mr. Stephens says:

> "Judge Campbell now renewed his inquiry how restoration was to take place, supposing the Confederate States were consenting to it. Mr. Lincoln replied: 'By disbanding their armies and permitting the national authorities to resume their functions.' Mr. Seward interposed and said that Mr. Lincoln could not express himself more clearly or forcibly in reference to this question than he had done in his message to Congress in December before, and referred specially to that portion in these words: 'In presenting the abandonment of armed resistance to the national authority on the part of the insurgents as the only indispensable condition to ending the war on the part of the government, I retract nothing I said as to slavery. I repeat the declaration made a year ago, that while I remain in my present position I shall not attempt to retract or modify the Emancipation Proclamation, nor shall I return to slavery any person who is free by the terms of that proclamation or by any act of Congress. If the people should, by whatever mode or means, make it an executive duty to reenslave such persons, another, and not I, must be their instrument to perform it.'"

These quotations show that with these views Mr. Lincoln could not have offered four hundred million dollars to secure peace and that he could not have said to Mr. Stephens: "Allow me to write 'Union' at the bottom of a sheet of paper, and you may write whatever terms you please above it." Besides, and what is equally as important, Mr. Stephens never said such an offer as either of those referred to was made. He is given as authority for statements he never made, and which would be in direct conflict with what he says did occur in that conference.

Messrs. Stephens, Hunter, and Campbell, the Confederate commissioners at the Hampton Roads conference, in their report to President Davis of the result of that conference, dated February 5, 1865, said:

> ". . . We understood from him [President Lincoln] that no terms or proposals of any treaty or agreement looking to an ultimate settlement would be entertained or made by him with the Confederate States, because that would be a recognition of their existence as a separate power, which, under no circumstances, would be done; and, for the same reasons, that no such terms would be entertained by Him from the states separately; that no extended truce or armistice (as at present advised) would be granted without a satisfactory assurance of a complete restoration of the authority of the United States over all places within the states of the Confederacy."

In other words, the only terms which could be allowed was the unconditional surrender of the Confederacy.

In that report the Confederate commissioners represent President Lincoln as saying that "whatever consequences may follow from the restoration of that authority must be accepted." They also say that "during the conference the proposed amendment to the constitution of the United States, adopted by Congress on the 31st ult., was brought to our notice. This amendment declares that "neither slavery nor involuntary servitude, except for crimes, shall exist within the United States or any place within their jurisdiction."

These commissioners also say:

> "We learned from them [Lincoln and Seward] that the message of President Lincoln to the Congress of the United States, in December last [1864], explains clearly and distinctly his sentiments as to the terms, conditions, and method of proceeding by which peace can be secured to the people, and we were not informed that they would be modified or altered to obtain that end."

The report of the Confederate commissioners quoted from above is published in full in the second volume of President Davis's book, entitled "Rise and Fall of the Confederate Government," pages 619, 620, and in McPherson's history of what he calls "The Rebellion," page 571, to which attention is invited. Not one word is said in that report about any offer being made by President Lincoln of four hundred million dollars to pay for the slaves if the Confederates would cease hostilities and return to the Union, nor is anything said in that report about a proposition by President Lincoln to Mr. Stephens for an agreement that if Mr. Lincoln was allowed to write the word "Union" at the bottom of a sheet of paper Mr. Stephens might write whatever terms of adjustment he pleased above it. Our commissioners were among the most distinguished men of the Confederacy, and it cannot be supposed that if any such propositions had been made they would have omitted to state the fact in their official report of the result of that conference to President Davis.

Judge Campbell, one of the Confederate commissioners, in a memorandum submitted to President Davis in relation to what occurred at that conference, says:

> "In conclusion, Mr. Hunter summed up what seemed to be the result of this interview: that there could be no arrangement by treaty between the Confederate States and the United States or any agreement between them; that there was nothing left for them but unconditional submission."

President Lincoln informed the Confederate commissioners in the conference at Hampton Roads that in his message to Congress of the preceding December he had explained clearly and distinctly his sentiments as to the terms, conditions, and method of proceeding by which peace could be secured to the people; and the commissioners add: "We were not informed that they would be modified or altered to obtain that end."

In that message of December 5, 1864, President Lincoln said:

> "At the last session of Congress a proposed amendment of the constitution of the United States abolishing slavery throughout the United States, passed the Senate, but failed for the lack of the required two-thirds vote in the House of Representatives. Although the present is the same Congress and nearly the same members, and without questioning the wisdom or patriotism of those who stood in opposition, *I venture to recommend the reconsideration and passage of the measure at the present session.*"

This was what President Lincoln told the Confederate commissioners he adhered to, and does not agree with the statement that he, at that conference, offered four hundred million dollars for the slaves.

In that message he also said: "They [the Confederates] can at any moment have peace simply by laying down their arms and submitting to the national authority under the constitution." This also was one of the things stated in that message which he told the Confederate commissioners he adhered to: unconditional surrender, and not the purchase of peace by paying four hundred million dollars for the negroes.

In his proclamation of September 22 he says:

> "On January 1, 1863, all persons held as slaves within any state or designated part of a state, the people whereof shall then be in rebellion against the United States, shall be then, thenceforward, and forever free."

Mr. Reagan quotes from Mr. Seward, Secretary of State, after a conference with Mr. Lincoln, and he makes his position satisfactory to all except a few who won't see that his denial of the four-hundred-million dollar matter is true.

> [Seward] ". . . The foolish and false statements which I have here controverted had their origin soon after the Hampton Roads conference among the unpatriotic malcontents in the Confederacy, who were great patriots while the Confederate cause had a chance of success, but who, as misfortune and disaster fell upon the Confederacy, busied themselves in denouncing the Confederate President and authorities for not making an impossible treaty of peace; and these stories have been kept alive since, for the most part, by persons who wished to show their superior wisdom and patriotism by condemning the Confederate officials for their want of sense and patriotism and for their stubbornness in failing to accept the favorable terms offered them by President Lincoln."

The statements I am controverting, if believed, could have no other effect than to discredit President Davis and his advisers, and were no doubt invented and, for the most part, circulated for that purpose. No Northern man who had any respect for the memory of President Lincoln ever made any such statements or believed them when repeated by Southern men. How unfortunate it was that the Confederacy could not, in the days of its peril and disaster, have availed itself of the wisdom of these men who became so wise after the peril had passed! May we not hope that the attempt to impose these vicious stories on our people may henceforward be frowned down by all lovers of truth and justice?[80] — *CONFEDERATE VETERAN*

17. REPORT OF WILLIAM P. TOLLEY

☛ The following paper on the Hampton Roads Conference was prepared by Capt. William P. Tolley and presented to Camp Frank Cheatham, of Nashville, Tenn. The camp appointed a committee to investigate the paper, which submitted the report following the paper, and which report, together with the paper of Capt. Tolley, were unanimously adopted by the camp:

Rucker, Tenn., July, 1897. To Frank Cheatham Camp: All talk of the possibility of the Confederate authorities securing more favorable terms of peace at this conference, or at any other period of the war, than the unconditional surrender that finally befell our arms is the merest twaddle, were it, indeed, half so innocent as that. To give it any semblance of authority involves the stultification of some of the most renowned historical characters of the war period. Particularly does it so involve Alex H. Stephens, the Vice-President of the Confederacy, as will be seen in an investigation of the subject. Any utterance contradictory to the official report of the Confederate commissioners by either of these distinguished gentlemen makes him stultify himself, and hence such alleged utterances ought always to be taken with many grains of allowance and misgiving. The truth of what transpired on that occasion can only be learned from the official record. It is herewith submitted at once. The official report of the Confederate commissioners, made immediately on their return to Richmond, is as follows:

"Richmond, Va., February 5, 1865. 'To the President of the Confederate States: Sir: Under your letter of appointment of the 28th ult., we proceeded to seek an informal conference with Abraham Lincoln, President of the United States, upon the subject mentioned in the letter. The conference was granted, and took place on the 3rd inst., on board a steamer [the *River Queen*] in Hampton Roads, where we met President Lincoln and the Hon. Mr. Seward, Secretary of State of the United States. It continued for several hours, and was both full and explicit.

"We learned from them that the message of President Lincoln to the Congress of the United States, in December last, explains clearly and distinctly his sentiments as to the terms, conditions, and method of proceeding by which peace can be secured to the people, and we were not informed that they would be modified or altered to obtain that end. We understand from him that no terms or proposals of any treaty or agreement looking to an ultimate settlement would be entertained or made by him with the Confederate States, because that would be a recognition of their existence as a separate power, which under no circumstances would be done; and for like reasons that no such terms would be entertained by him from the states separately; that no extended truce or armistice (as at present advised) would be granted without a satisfactory assurance in advance of a complete restoration of the authority of the United States over all places within the states of the Confederacy; that whatever consequence may follow from the reestablishment of that authority must be accepted, but that individuals, subject to pains and penalties under the laws of the United States, might rely upon a very liberal use of the power confided to him to remit those pains and penalties if peace be restored.

"During the conference the proposed amendment to the Constitution of the United States, adopted by Congress on the 31st ult., was brought to our notice. This amendment declares that neither slavery nor involuntary servitude, except for crime, should exist within the United States or any place within their jurisdiction, and that Congress should have power to enforce this amendment by appropriate legislation. Of all the correspondence that preceded the conference herein mentioned and leading to the same you have heretofore been informed. Very respectfully your obedient servants, Alexander H. Stephens, Robert M. T. Hunter, John A. Campbell."

Next, as a part of the official record, comes the message of President Lincoln in answer to a resolution of Congress, with which he submitted the whole correspondence that led up to the conference:

"Executive Mansion, February 10, 1865. On the morning of the 3rd the gentlemen—Messrs. Stephens, Hunter, and Campbell—came aboard our steamer and had an interview with the Secretary of State and myself of several hours' duration. No question of preliminaries to the meeting was then and there made or mentioned. No other person was present. No papers were exchanged or produced, and it was in advance agreed that the conversation was to be informal and verbal merely. On my part the whole substance of the instructions to the Secretary of State, hereinbefore recited, was stated and insisted upon, and nothing was said inconsistent therewith, while by the other party it was not said that in any event or on any condition they ever would consent to reunion; and yet equally omitted to declare that they never would so consent. They seemed to desire a postponement of that question and the adoption of some other course first, which, as some of them seemed to argue, might or might not lead to reunion, but which course, we thought, would amount to an indefinite postponement. The conference ended without result. The foregoing, containing, as is believed, all the information sought, is respectfully submitted. Abraham Lincoln."

Next, as semiofficial at least, comes the account of the conference as given by Secretary of State Seward to Mr. [Charles Francis] Adams [Sr.], the minister of the United States to England, written four days after the conference:

"President Lincoln announced to the Confederate commissioners that we can agree to no cessation or suspension of hostilities, except on the basis of disbandment of the insurgent forces and the restoration of the national authority throughout all the states in the Union. Collaterally and in subordination to the proposition which was thus announced the antislavery policy of the United States was reviewed in all its bearings, and the President demanded that he must not be expected to depart from the positions he had heretofore assumed in his proclamations of emancipation and other documents, as these positions were reiterated in his last message."

The instructions to Mr. Seward referred to in the above special message of President Lincoln, to which he says he (Lincoln) adhered in the conference, were given before he had concluded to attend himself, and are embodied in the three following propositions:

1. The restoration of the national authority throughout all the states.
2. No receding by the Executive of the United States on the slavery question from the position assumed thereon in the late

annual message to Congress and in the preceding documents.

3. No cessation of hostilities short of an end of the war and the disbanding of all the forces hostile to the government.

The annual message of President Lincoln referred to in the above instructions to Secretary Seward and in the official report of the Confederate commissioners as containing "the terms, conditions, and method of proceeding by which peace can be secured to the people" is the message of December 6, 1864. The terms therein set forth are those of absolute and unconditional surrender, as will be seen from the following extracts:

> "They (the insurgents) can at any moment have peace simply by laying down their arms and submitting to the national authority under the constitution."
>
> "In presenting the abandonment of armed resistance to the national authority on the part of the insurgents as the only indispensable condition of ending the war on the part of the government, I retract nothing heretofore said as to slavery. I repeat the declaration made a year ago: that while I remain in my present position I shall not attempt to retract or modify the emancipation proclamation, nor shall I return to slavery any person who is free by the terms of that proclamation or by any of the acts of Congress."
>
> "In stating a single condition of peace I mean simply to say that the war will cease on the part of the government whenever it shall have ceased on the part of those who began it."

With this message before the writer, all scrutiny is challenged to find one word inconsistent with or contradictory to these extracts, from the beginning to the end of it.

Before leaving this part of the subject, special attention is called to the most significant feature of this whole record. It is that remarkable passage in the report of the Confederate commissioners to President Davis, in which the startling fact is disclosed that in no event would any sort of terms of peace be even entertained by Mr. Lincoln as coming from the commissioners; he would neither treat with the Confederate States nor any of the states thereof separately; that the whole affair was informal, and in no wise binding. It is in the following language:

"We understand from him (President Lincoln) that no terms or proposals of any treaty or agreement looking to an ultimate settlement would be entertained or made by him with the Confederate States, because that would be a recognition of their existence as a separate power, which, under no circumstances, would be done; and, for like reasons, that no such terms would be entertained by him from the states separately; that no extended truce or armistice (as at present advised) would be granted, without a satisfactory assurance in advance of a complete restoration of the authority of the United States over all places within the states of the Confederacy."

Edward O. C. Ord and family.

And the last clause of the sentence also closes the door against even a truce or armistice, a temporary suspension of hostilities, except upon the assurance, given beforehand, of an unconditional surrender of the Confederate armies; nor would they as much as grant a military convention. Overtures to this effect were made by Gen. [Edward O. C.] Ord, of the Federal army, commanding below Richmond, to Gen. [James] Longstreet, commanding on the Confederate side, soon after the Hampton Roads affair, when President Davis promptly granted to Gen. Lee the authority for holding such convention, and it was declined by Gen. Grant. The authority for this statement is found on pages 621 and 622, second volume of "The War Between the States," by Alex H. Stephens. The official report of the Confederate commissioners to President Davis is found on 792 of the same work; the special message of President Lincoln on page 802, and accompanying documents on pages 793 to 802 inclusive; the instructions given to Secretary Seward, on page 798; and Mr. Seward's letter to Minister Adams may be found on pages 570, 571 of McPherson's "History of the Rebellion," as he calls it. Mr. Stephens' account in full of the Hampton Roads Conference is on pages 576 to 622 of his "War Between the States," second volume.

Now let all these authorities, so easily accessible to everybody, be carefully read and rigidly scrutinized by every impartial inquirer for historical truth; and for every such a one, a premium is hereby offered who fails to discern the utter impossibility of there being any truth in or decent pretext for all such wild reports as that Mr. Lincoln "offered to write 'Union' at the top of the paper and allow Mr. Stephens to write his own terms of peace under it," or that $400,000,000 was offered in payment for the slaves, or could, in any event, have been secured as the price of our return to the Union, or anything, at any time, short of unconditional surrender. If there is any hypothesis or margin to predicate any of these stories on, then indeed are the most solemn averments of the most distinguished historical characters utterly worthless in establishing or ascertaining historical truth, the most authentic records are without any sort of value to the student of history, or the plainest language is without meaning.

But, going outside of the record, the authentic account, let us examine the irresponsible testimony relied on to sustain these stories designed to canonize or deify Mr. Lincoln. The most prominent of these stories is that alleged to have been told by Mr. Stephens concerning the writing at the top of the paper the word "Union," etc. The story, as they have Mr. Stephens telling it, runs:

"After we had returned to the saloon [on the *River Queen*] Mr. Lincoln was very talkative and pleasant. . . . After a while I joined him, and we went apart from the others and sat down at a small table where there was writing material," etc.

Now Mr. Stephens precludes all possibility of the truth of this statement in the very full account he gives of what transpired at the conference in his "War Between the States." He says: "The interview took place in the saloon of the steamer, on board of which were Mr. Lincoln and Mr. Seward, and which lay at anchor near Fortress Monroe. The commissioners were conducted into the saloon first. Soon after Mr. Lincoln and Mr. Seward entered." This is on page 593 of the second volume. On page 618 he says: "The parties then took formal and friendly leave of each other. Mr. Lincoln and Mr. Seward withdrawing from the saloon together. Col. [Orville E.] Babcock, our escort, soon came in to conduct us back to the steamer on which we came."

There is not the slightest intimation of any absence from the saloon of the steamer after they had assembled there so there could have been any returning thereto by any of the parties to the conference. The discussion was continuous and uninterrupted from the time it commenced until the close of the conference, except when "water, cigars, and other refreshments were occasionally brought in by a colored servant," as Mr. Stephens says. There is no time or place allowed in Mr. Stephens' account for him and Mr. Lincoln to have gone apart from the others. The actual events that occurred contradict the story, as well as the terms laid down by Mr. Lincoln at the outset.

The whole question of what took place in the conference and the possibility of securing other terms than those of absolute and unconditional surrender is concluded in the summation of Mr. Hunter, who "went into a sort of recapitulation of the subjects talked of in the interview and the conclusions which seemed to be deducible from them, which amounted to nothing as a basis of peace, in his judgment, but an unconditional surrender on the part of the Confederate States and their people. There could be no agreement, no treaty, nor even any stipulation as to terms—nothing but unconditional submission." Of course the wily Seward protested against the term "unconditional submission," but no impartial reader of the story—as told by Mr. Stephens—can escape the conclusion that they are strictly apropos.

The much-vaunted proposition to pay $400,000,000 indemnity for the slaves—which has been very late coming to light—alleged to have been made by Lincoln to his cabinet, to be submitted to Congress, but which never got any farther than the cabinet, can cut no figure in this controversy nor in any wise affect the issue, which is as to whether the "South might have obtained advantageous terms of peace within less than sixty days of the total collapse of the Confederacy," the assertion to that effect being based on the assumption that "Mr. Lincoln was eager to make peace with the Union restored and slavery abolished, and to pay $400,000,000 of indemnity," because such a proposition was never even intimated to the Confederate authorities at the Hampton Roads conference nor on any other occasion; but on this and all other occasions terms were always peremptorily demanded that precluded the possibility of any such settlement, as has been shown in the official record hereinbefore submitted. The only "intimation" of anything to the contrary in it all was in what Lincoln said, as recorded on page 617 of second volume of "War Between the States," given as his own individual views without official or other binding effect. "He went on to say that he would be willing to be taxed to remunerate the Southern people for their slaves." "He knew some who were in favor of an appropriation as high as $400,000,000 for this purpose." "But on this subject he could give no assurance, enter into no stipulation. He barely expressed his own feelings and views, and what he believed to be the views of others upon the subject." If this proposition was ever submitted by Lincoln to his cabinet, which it is not claimed ever got any farther, he changed his views very much in the four or five days between the time alleged when he made it and the 10th of February, 1865, the date of his special message to Congress, in which he informed Congress that he adhered rigidly to the three propositions contained in his instructions to Secretary Seward, both of which—special message and the instructions to Seward—are given above. Reader, turn back to them and reread them:

> "The proper conclusion of this whole matter is rendered clear when it is remembered that the conference was brought about by representations made by one Francis P. Blair, Sr., a prominent citizen on the Northern side, who stood in somewhat close personal relations to Mr. Lincoln, to the effect that at that juncture of affairs, early in 1865, a discussion between persons representing the opposing parties to the war might lead to a settlement. Mr. Davis—being ever ready to compose the trouble and bring back peace to the country, as he and the whole South had always desired peace, before, during, and after the war—readily consented to depute persons to meet those similarly authorized by Mr. Lincoln. The conference on the part of the Confederates was merely tentative to ascertain the views of the Federal authorities. There was no occasion for them to go there clothed with authority to submit propositions. We were in a situation only to hear the other side. If there had been any disposition on the part of the Federal authorities to allow any sort of terms short of a

complete surrender of all that was at issue, who doubts that Mr. Davis would have submitted the information to the Confederate Congress, so they could have acted upon it, and the country would have had the full benefit of any such disposition on the Federal side. Mr. Davis' official oath and obligation as President of the Confederacy bound him to continue the struggle for our independence as long as there was an organized army in the field. Not so with the Congress, however; they were clothed with a much larger discretion than he was. And who doubts that the information would have gone to them, with Mr. Stephens as one of our commissioners, if any had ever come to the latter, that there was a possibility of the 'South obtaining advantageous terms of peace within sixty days before the final collapse?'

"The correct position of the Confederate commissioners in these premises can be seen in the following language employed by them in a note to Maj. Eckert, aide-de-camp to Gen. Grant, of February 1, 1865, while negotiating for a passport and safe conduct within the Federal lines, for the purpose of meeting Mr. Lincoln or such persons as he might send to hold the conference with them. The substantial object to be attained by the informal conference is to ascertain upon what terms the existing war can be terminated honorably. Our instructions contemplated a personal interview between President Lincoln and ourselves at Washington; but with this explanation we are ready to meet any person or persons that President Lincoln may appoint, at such place as he may designate. Our earnest desire is that a just and honorable peace may be agreed upon, and we are prepared to receive or submit propositions which may possibly lead to that end. Alex H. Stephens, Robert M. T. Hunter, J. A. Campbell."

In a note to the same officer, of date February 2, 1865, they say:

"It is our earnest wish to ascertain, after a free interchange of ideas and information, upon what principles and terms, if any, a just and honorable peace can be established without the further effusion of blood, and to contribute our utmost efforts to accomplish such a result."

It may popularize Watterson's lecture or his proposed book on Lincoln among the people of the North, where he knows the shekels be, to twaddle this stuff to Lincoln's glorification above all contemporaries, in humanity and all the higher and nobler qualities; but the Southern people will look well to the truth of history before they shout hosannahs to his memory for sentiments of humane considerations toward them that never could find expression or any sort of manifestation in a way they ever got any benefit therefrom, notwithstanding the splendid opportunity that offered for such expression at the Hampton Roads conference; and they know from official facts in the case that there was no such expression on that occasion, and all that remained to them was to fight it out to the only honorable end left to them. William P. Tolley.

Report of Committee to Frank Cheatham Camp

To Frank Cheatham Camp No. 35, U.C.V.: We, your committee appointed to investigate the acts and doings of the Hampton Roads conference, would respectfully report that we have read all of the standard authorities on the subject and laboriously scrutinized and studied them. Among the authorities are: "The Rise and Fall of the Confederate States," by Mr. President Jefferson Davis; "The History of the United States," by Hon. Alexander H. Stephens; the address of the Hon. John H. Reagan, delivered before the convention of the United Confederate Veterans held in Nashville on June 22, 1897; the paper prepared by Hon. William P. Tolley, and more recently heard the address of Hon. A. S. Colyar. From said authorities we are fully convinced that the statement prepared by Hon. William P. Tolley is a true and correct history of the conference; that there never was submitted by Mr. Lincoln any proposition that was not coupled with the unconditional surrender of the Confederate armies; that Mr. Lincoln never offered to pay for the negroes of the South, but that he said, "If we would surrender unconditionally, a large number of people in the North would be willing to pay for them"—a proposition wholly unsustained by the record of the people of the North and utterly untenable; that he never said to Mr. Stephens, "Let me write 'Union' at the top of the page, and you can write what you please below it;" and that the Confederate commissioners at said conference did everything honorable men could have done as the representatives of a "nation that rose so white and fair and fell so free of crime."

We therefore present the following resolutions, and move their adoption:

Resolved: 1. That Camp Frank Cheatham, No. 35, fully and unequivocally endorses the statement prepared by Comrade William P. Tolley, and urges its adoption by the United Confederate Veterans.

2. That our delegates to the convention of the United Confederate Veterans to be held in Atlanta, Ga., in July next, be and they are hereby instructed to present said statement, together with this report, to said convention, and urge their adoption. The committee is composed of W. J. McMurray, Chairman; John P. Hickman, Ralph J. Neal, S. A. Cunningham.[81] — *CONFEDERATE VETERAN*

18. REAGAN ADDRESSES ANOTHER ATTACK

☞ Austin, Tex., April 3, 1901: Some one whose name is not given, in a communication dated March 18, [1901] has inclosed to me from Atlanta, Ga., what purports to be an account written by Dr. R. J. Massey of an interview between himself and Vice President Stephens, during the month of April, 1865, in which expressions are attributed to Mr. Stephens of so extraordinary a character as to make a statement as to the real facts, about which he is made to speak, necessary for two reasons: one in vindication of the truth of history, and the other to protect the good name and character for truth of Vice President Stephens.

The person who sent me Dr. Massey's paper speaks of him as a "physician of about forty years standing, and an elegant old gentleman." His high character and standing makes it the more important that the errors to which he gives publicity should be corrected.

On the 28th day of January, 1865, President Davis appointed Vice President Stephens, R. M. T. Hunter, a Confederate Senator, and Judge John A. Campbell, Assistant Secretary of War, as commissioners for an informal conference with the Federal authorities. They met President Lincoln and Secretary Seward, acting for the United States, in conference at Hampton Roads on the 3rd day of February, 1865.

In Dr. Massey's paper Mr. Stephens states:

"After the usual salutations and a few compliments, we went to business. Mr. Lincoln drew from his pocket a sheet of paper about two feet long, and held it up to the wall and said: 'Gentlemen, let me write the word "Union." The Union must be preserved, and you may fill the balance of this sheet with your own terms.'

Several points were then discussed. He proposed that all men in arms might return home unmolested, and every Southerner shall have a full and unconditional pardon for any and every crime that he may have committed against the United States; all rights shall be restored to everybody; no trials for treason, or any other crime, and that all slaves at that time in bondage shall remain so; but a bill wall be immediately introduced in Congress for the gradual emancipation, and every slaveholder shall have fair and liberal compensation for every slave so emancipated.

Did President Lincoln make such a statement at the Hampton Roads Conference? Let us see if it is possible that he could have made such a statement. In his annual message to Congress, December 5, 1864, President Lincoln said:

> "At the last session of Congress a proposed amendment of the Constitution abolishing slavery throughout the United States passed the Senate, but failed for lack of the requisite two-thirds vote in the House of Representatives. Although the present is the same Congress, and nearly the same members, and without questioning the wisdom or patriotism of those who stood in opposition, I venture to recommend the reconsideration and passage of the measure at the present session. Of course the abstract question is not changed; but an intervening election shows, almost certainly, that the next Congress will pass the measure if this does not. Hence there is only a question of time as to when the proposed amendment will go to the States for their action. And as it is to so go, at all events, may we not agree that the sooner the better?"

He thus favored abolishing slavery throughout the Union, without compensation, less than two months before the Hampton Roads Conference. In the same message he said:

> "In presenting the abandonment of armed resistance to the national authority on the part of the insurgents, as the only indispensable condition to ending the war on the part of the government, I retract nothing heretofore said as to slavery. I repeat the declaration made a

year ago, that 'while I remain in my present position I shall not attempt to retract or modify the emancipation proclamation, nor shall I return to slavery any person who is free by the terms of that proclamation, or by any of the acts of Congress.' If the people should, by whatever mode or means, make it an executive duty to reenslave such persons, another, and not I, must be their instrument to perform it."

Nothing is here said about compensation.

In his Emancipation Proclamation of September 22, 1862, President Lincoln said:

> "That, on the 1st day of January, in the year of our Lord, one thousand eight hundred and sixty-three, all persons held as slaves within any State or designated part of a State, the people whereof shall then be in rebellion against the United States, shall be then, thenceforward, and forever free; and the executive government of the United States, including the military and naval authority thereof, will recognize and maintain the freedom of such persons, and will do no act or acts to repress such persons, or any of them, in any efforts they may make for their actual freedom."

This of course covered the whole South, and nothing is said here about compensation.

In his Emancipation Proclamation of January 1, 1863, he said:

> "By virtue of the power in me vested as commander in chief of the army and navy of the United States, in time of actual armed rebellion against the authority and government of the United States, and as a fit and necessary war measure for suppressing said rebellion, I do, on this the first day of January, in the year of our Lord one thousand eight hundred and sixty-three, and in accordance with my purpose so to do, publicly proclaimed for the full period of one hundred days from the day first above mentioned, order and designate as the States and parts of States, wherein the people thereof, respectively, are this day in rebellion against the United States, the following, to wit: . . .
>
> "And by virtue of the power and for the purpose aforesaid, I do order and declare that all persons held as slaves within said designated States and parts of States are, and henceforward shall be, free; and that the executive government of the United States, including the military and naval authorities thereof, will recognize and maintain the freedom of said persons."

This covered the whole South, and nothing is said in this about compensation.

On the 31st of January, 1865, two days before the meeting of the Hampton Roads Conference, Congress finally passed the joint resolution to abolish slavery throughout the United States. No compensation.

On the 10th of February, 1865, President Lincoln, in response to a resolution adopted by the House of Representatives, calling for information about the Hampton Roads Conference, speaking for himself and Secretary Seward, said:

> "On our part, the whole substance of the instructions to the Secretary of State, herein before recited, was stated and insisted upon, and nothing was said inconsistent therewith."

In giving those instructions to Secretary Seward, to govern him in the Hampton Roads Conference, on the 21st of January, 1865, President Lincoln, among other things, said:

> "2. No receding, by the Executive of the United States, on the slavery question, from the position assumed thereon in the late annual message to Congress, and in preceding documents."

You have seen what he said in that message and in his two Emancipation Proclamations. In the face of the foregoing facts could President Lincoln have used the language attributed to him in Dr. Massey's paper?

The Confederate commissioners at the Hampton Roads Conference, making their report to President Davis on the 5th of February, 1865, as to what occurred in that conference, said in part as follows:

> "We learned from them (President Lincoln and Secretary Seward) that the message of President Lincoln to the Congress of the United States, in December last, explains clearly and distinctly his sentiments as to the terms, conditions, and methods of proceeding by which peace can be secured to the people, and we were not informed that they would be modified or altered to obtain that end. We understand from him that no terms or proposals of any treaty or agreement looking to an ultimate settlement would be entertained or made by him with the Confederate States, because that would be a recognition of their

existence as a separate power, which, under no circumstances, would be done; and for like reasons that no such terms would be entertained by him from the States separately; that no extended truce or armistice (as at present advised) would be granted, without a satisfactory assurance in advance of the complete restoration of the authority of the United States over all places within the States of the Confederacy.

"That whatever consequence may follow from the reestablishment of that authority must be accepted; but that individuals subject to pains and penalties under the laws of the United States might rely upon a very liberal use of the power confided to him to remit those pains and penalties if peace be restored.

"During the conference the proposed amendment to the Constitution of the United States, adopted by Congress on the 31st ultimo, was brought to our notice. This amendment declares that neither slavery nor involuntary servitude, except for crimes, should exist within the United States, or any place within their jurisdiction, and that Congress should have power to enforce this amendment by appropriate legislation."

This report was signed by Vice President Stephens, along with the Hon. R. M. T. Hunter and Judge Campbell.

On the 6th of February, 1865, President Davis, in communicating that report to the Confederate Congress, said:

"I herewith transmit, for the information of Congress, the report of the eminent citizens above named showing that the enemy refused to enter into negotiations with the Confederate States, or any one of them separately, or to give to our people any other terms or guarantees than those which the conqueror may grant, or permit us to have peace on any other basis than our unconditional submission to their rule."

On the 7th of February, 1865, four days after the Hampton Roads meeting, Mr. Seward, Secretary of State of the United States, wrote to the Hon. Charles Francis Adams [Sr.], the United States Minister to Great Britain, giving a detailed account of what took place at that Conference. In that paper he said:

"This suggestion, though deliberately considered, was nevertheless regarded by the President as one of armistice or truce, and he announced that we can agree to no cessation or suspension of hostilities, except on the basis of the disbandment of the insurgent forces, and the restoration of the national authority throughout all the

States in the Union. Collaterally, and in subordination to the proposition which was thus announced, the anti-slavery policy of the United States was reviewed in all its bearings, and the President announced that he must not be expected to depart from the positions he hail heretofore assumed in his proclamation of emancipation and other documents, as these positions were reiterated in his last annual message. It was further declared by the President that the complete restoration of the national authority everywhere was an indispensable condition of any assent on our part to whatever form of peace might be proposed. The President assured the other party that, while he must adhere to these positions, he would be prepared, so far is power is lodged with the Executive, to exercise liberality. His power, however, is limited by the Constitution, and when peace should be made Congress must necessarily act in regard to appropriations of money and to the admission of representatives from the insurrectionary States. The Richmond party was then informed that Congress had, on the 31st ultimo, adopted by a constitutional majority a joint resolution submitting to the several States the proposition to abolish slavery throughout the United States, and that there is every reason to expect that it will be soon accepted by three-fourths of the States, so as to become a part of the national organic law."

In the face of the foregoing official facts can any liable person believe it to be possible that President Lincoln made such a statement to Vice President Stephens as that attributed to him in Dr. Massey's paper? The whole story must be an unwarranted assumption. Mr. Lincoln would not, in the face of his own record, of the action of Congress, and of the impassioned condition of public feeling in the United States, have dared to make such a proposition.

Mr. Stephens in his book, "The War between the States," page 617 and following, gives an account of what occurred in the Hampton Roads Conference. He makes no such statement as that attributed to him by Dr. Massey, but, on the contrary, shows that the Confederates could get no terms but unconditional surrender. Can it be believed that if such an offer had been made he would, in his historical account of what occurred, have omitted it, and have, in substance, stated the opposite to it?

Judge Campbell, another member of the Confederate Commission, in giving his account of what occurred at that Conference, in a paper which was in the possession of Ex-United

States Senator [Benjamin] Fitzpatrick, of Alabama, and which was afterwards published in *The Land We Love* magazine, makes no mention of such an incident as that described in Dr. Massey's paper; but, on the contrary, he shows distinctly that nothing was promised by either President Lincoln or Secretary Seward; that no guarantees would be given, but that the South must cease hostilities and trust to clemency.

Benjamin Fitzpatrick.

On the night of the return of Mr. Stephens to Richmond from that conference, it is stated on good authority that he told the Hon. James L. Orr, a Confederate Senator from South Carolina, that the Hampton Roads Conference was "fruitless and hopeless, because Mr. Lincoln offered the Confederacy nothing but unconditional submission."

In a letter which the late Hon. Frank B. Sexton, a representative in the Confederate Congress, wrote to me he says that Mr. Stephens, on his return from Hampton Roads, told him that Mr. Lincoln offered nothing but unconditional submission.

An account of a controversy which took place between Judge Wallace, of San Augustine, Tex., and myself, a few years after the war, Judge Wallace asserting and I denying that an offer of $400,000,000 was made by President Lincoln to the Confederate Commissioners if the Confederates would abandon the war and come into the Union, attracted the attention of Col. Stephen W. Blount, who lived in the same town with Judge Wallace, and he, being an old-time friend of Mr. Stephens, wrote to him asking for the truth as to this. Mr. Stephens wrote him that "the statement was untrue;" that "the only element in reference to the slave payment was so mixed and infused with falsehood as to make the entire assertion false."

I thus offer the authentic record of what occurred at the Hampton Roads Conference, and Mr. Stephens's own several statements in signing the report of the Confederate Commissioners of the result of that Conference, in his history of the "War between the States," his statement to Senator Orr, his statement to Col. Sexton, and his letter to Col. Blount, the statement of President Lincoln, of Secretary Seward, and of Judge Campbell, formerly a justice of the Supreme Court of the United States, as evidence of the inaccuracy of the statement attributed by Dr. Massey and others to Mr. Stephens.

I add that at the last annual reunion of the Confederate Veterans Association, at Louisville, Ky., in June last, the Committee on History, with Gen. Stephen D. Lee as its Chairman, having had their attention called to the discussion of the question about the offers made by Mr. Lincoln to pay for the slaves if that would end the war and restore the Union, made

Stephen D. Lee.

a full investigation of the question, and reported that there was no shadow of foundation for any such statement. The foregoing facts dispose of the statement attributed to Vice President Stephens, in which he is made to say that President Lincoln proposed, in substance, if the Union could he preserved, "that all men in arms might return to their homes unmolested, and every Southerner shall have an unconditional pardon for any and every crime that he may have committed against the United States; all rights shall be restored to everybody, no trials for treason, or any other crime; that all slaves that at that time are in bondage shall remain so; but a bill will be immediately introduced in Congress for the gradual emancipation, and every slave- holder shall have fair and liberal compensation for every slave so emancipated." Could anything be farther from the real truth, as shown by the foregoing facts?

If any man ever needed to be protected from his supposed friends, it is Mr. Stephens. If they could induce the public to believe these representations in this respect, the effect would be to injure the character of Mr. Stephens for truth and veracity. The public will doubtless accept such facts as are herein stated, rather than the recollections of any man, however respectable, depending on his memory after the lapse of thirty-six years. I knew Vice President Stephens well, served with him four years in the House of Representatives of the United States before the war, was associated with him more or less during the war, we were fellow-prisoners in Fort Warren after the war, and we served several sessions together in the United States House of Representatives after the war. While our views were not always in accord about the conduct of the war, I always had the greatest respect for his ability, his patriotism, and his exceptionally fine character as a man and it pains me to have seen the efforts which have been made to put him in a false position, and to falsify the facts of history in a matter in which he was an actor, and all, as I believe, as a means of trying to bring discredit on the Confederate government and those who administered it.

Most of the principal actors in the war between the States have passed to their final account. So far as relates to the heroes and martyrs on the Confederate side, civil and military, in one of the greatest wars known to history, I think it can be truthfully said, as to both those in civil and military life, that braver, more patriotic, more self-sacrificing men and women never gave their services, their fortunes, and their lives to the great cause of human rights and constitutional government, and it is pitiable to see persons of later days, some of whom took no part in that struggle and made no sacrifices for that cause, busying themselves in finding fault with and in criticising the noble men who did so much and suffered so much for it. [End of Reagan's response.]

[*Confederate Veteran:*] In his letter to the *Veteran* from Austin, Gen. Reagan states: "So much has been said in Georgia and elsewhere, especially in Georgia, on the same line that I thought it necessary to put a quietus to such falsehoods and perversions of history."[82] — *CONFEDERATE VETERAN*

19. REAGAN REPLIES TO MASSEY CRITICISM

☞ [Following is the response of the Hon. John H. Reagan to "a criticism" of Dr. R. J. Massey on the paper he wrote for the *Confederate Veteran*, April 1901. See above entry.]

The object of my paper was to prove by recorded facts and the statements of a number of citizens of the highest character that at the Hampton Roads Conference no terms for the termination of the war were offered to the Confederate government by President Lincoln but the unconditional surrender of the Confederate government. I rest on that paper as absolute proof of the truth of my position, and do not care to add to what I then said, except to state that about two years ago, when this question was under discussion, Gov. [Augustus H.] Garland, of Arkansas, who at the date of that Conference was a member of the Confederate Senate, and who was the roommate of Vice President Stephens, in Richmond, in a published statement, said that on the night after Mr. Stephens's return from that Conference he told him (Garland) that no terms could be had but unconditional surrender. Garland, after the war, became Governor of Arkansas, United States Senator from that State, and then Attorney-General of the United States.

Since the war between the States a persistent effort has been made to make the public believe that President Lincoln offered the Confederate commissioners at that conference terms of peace favorable to our people, which the Confederate commissioners were prevented from accepting because President Davis insisted upon the independence of the Confederacy, for which our people had fought so long and sacrificed so much. And many of the people of the Southern States were induced to believe this was true, and that President Davis and the Confederate authorities were responsible for the continuance of the war.

Dr. Massey criticises me with much severity, and with a good deal of personal bitterness and spite, for having shown, in my paper, the utter falsehood of this assumption, and he assumes to answer me by publishing the statements of several respectable gentlemen to the effect that Mr. Stephens had told them, not of any proposed terms to the Confederate commissioners, but the substance of private conversation between President Lincoln and himself.

John H. Reagan.

He shows by the statement of Mr. Evan P. Howell that Mr. Stephens told him that Mr. Lincoln asked him into a stateroom and seated himself at a table, and said to him: "Mr. Stephens, we can settle this war and stop bloodshed. I know you well and know you can appreciate my position and feelings;" and, taking a sheet of paper, said: "I will write one word on the top of this paper, and that word is 'Union,' and you can write the terms of settlement, and I will give you my word I will use the best efforts of my life to have Congress accept the terms." I have not disputed and have no desire to dispute the fact as to whether such a private conversation occurred. I only say that no such proposition was made to the Confederate commissioners, or rejected by them, or submitted by them for the action of the Confederate government.

The same may be said as to the statement of the Hon. Clark Howell. That is not a matter in issue, so far as I am concerned, and has nothing to do with the real issue. And the same may be said as to the statements of Mr. Richardson, Mr. McBride, and Mr. Smith, whose statements he publishes. I have no controversy with the truth of these statements. They are utterly immaterial so far as relates to a proposition by President Lincoln to the Confederate commissioners for the termination of the war.

For the purpose of showing what Dr. Massey regarded as the real issues, I quote from his paper published in the Atlanta *Daily News* of February 16, 1901, to which mine of April 2 was a reply, in which he gives Mr. Stephens's statement as follows:

> "Mr. Lincoln drew from his pocket a sheet of paper about two feet long, and held it up to the wall and said: 'Gentlemen,' not privately to Mr. Stephens, but to the Confederate commissioners, 'let me write

the word "reunion," the Union must be preserved, and you may fill the balance of the sheet with your own terms.' Several points were then discussed, not with Mr. Stephens privately, but with the Confederate commissioners. He proposed that all men in arms may return home unmolested; that every Southerner shall have a full and unconditional pardon for any and every crime he may have committed against the United States; that all rights shall be restored to everybody; no trials for treason or any other crime; and all slaves at that time in bondage shall remain so; but a bill will be immediately introduced for the gradual emancipation, and every slaveholder shall have fair and liberal compensation for each slave so emancipated."

These extraordinary terms, Dr. Massey tells us, Mr. Stephens said Mr. Lincoln offered the Confederate commissioners. And extraordinarily liberal as these terms were, the Confederate commissioners could not accept them because President Davis demanded the independence of the Confederacy. In the face of the report of the Confederate commissioners, in the face of the message of President Davis transmitting that report to the Confederate Congress, in the face of what Mr. Stephens says in his book, in the face of Mr. Lincoln's two emancipation proclamations, in the face of his message of December, 1864, to Congress, in the face of his instructions to Secretary Seward for his government in those negotiations, in the face of the fact that three days before that the two Houses of Congress had passed a joint resolution submitting to the States the proposition to abolish slavery throughout the United States without compensation, in the face of the statements made by Mr. Stephens to the effect that no terms but unconditional surrender could be had, to Gov. Garland, of Arkansas, to Senator Orr, of South Carolina, to Representative Sexton, of Texas, and of his letter to his old friend, Stephen W. Blount, of Texas, in which he said the statement that President Lincoln had offered to pay $400,000,000 for the slaves of the South, can any sane person be expected to believe that any such proposition was made by President Lincoln to the Confederate commissioners, or was submitted to the Confederate government, or rejected by it?

It was such statements as these that I controverted. I had nothing to do or say about what occurred in private conversations between President Lincoln and Vice President Stephens, and I do not propose to allow Dr. Massey, or any one else, to escape from the issues they have heretofore made to the prejudice of the Confederate authorities, by saying now that they only referred to private conversation between President Lincoln and Mr. Stephens. I am not concerned about the private interviews between President Lincoln and Vice President Stephens, or about the private opinions and personal views of Mr. Lincoln. In this discussion I am concerned only with the public and official action of President Lincoln and the Confederate commissioners in the Conference at Hampton Roads, and I will see, as far as I can, that the facts as to that Conference shall go into history correctly. To this end I rest the case on the official documents and facts presented in my paper of the 3rd of April, to which Dr. Massey has replied in the Atlanta News of the 4th of May.

Lucius Q. C. Lamar.

Dr. Massey, in his last paper, passed a very high and deserved eulogy on the late Senator and Justice [Lucius Q. C.] Lamar, the late Senator [Benjamin H.] Hill, the late editor and orator [Henry W.] Grady, and upon the Hon. Clark Howell. From personal acquaintance and association with some of these gentlemen, and from a knowledge of the characters of the others, I fully concur with the Doctor in his high estimate of the ability, the genius, the patriotism and peace-loving character of each and all of them. But what has that got to do with the question as to whether President Lincoln made the offer to the Confederate commissioners al Hampton Roads, which Dr. Massey says Mr. Stephens told him was made, and which is herein above copied from Dr. Massey's letter? The Doctor might, with equal truth and with equal disregard to the rules of logic, have said that President [George] Washington was the greatest patriot and that President [Thomas] Jefferson was the greatest political philosopher of the age in which they lived. But what connection would there he between such statement and the question under consideration? Why bring such matter into this discussion of a question of history, which must at last be determined by the real facts, if not for the purpose of obscuring the real issue?[83] — JOHN H. REAGAN, FORMER POSTMASTER GENERAL, C.S.A.

20. WHAT HAPPENED AT HAMPTON ROADS?
☛ The death of the Hon. John H. Reagan [March 6, 1905], of Texas, the last member of the Confederate Cabinet, revives one of the most important and historical events of the War between the States. It relates to the conference at Hampton Roads between President Lincoln and the Confederate Commissioners, with a view of bringing the war to a close. This conference marked distinctly the positions and political views held at the time by both sections on constitutional rights. It has been so often asserted that it seems a part of the history of that great revolution that Mr. Lincoln wrote on a piece of paper "Save the Union," and, handing it to the Confederate Commissioners, said, "You can fill it up to suit yourselves." No more complete denial of this can be found than that made by the late Senator [George Graham] Vest, of Missouri, on the floor of the United States Senate. Not a word of denial or protest was entered by any of the Republican members present.[84]

Mr. Vest said the story had been denied by John H. Reagan, of Texas, who was the last surviving member of the Confederate Cabinet. He knew personally, said Mr. Vest, without having been present at that celebrated interview, that the incident was without foundation. "If true," said he, "it would place the government and officers of the Confederacy in the category of criminals, because it offered the Confederacy all that it ever demanded in the wildest hope of the most extreme partisans of that cause if they would only return to the Union."

A deep silence had fallen upon the chamber, and every Senator on the floor listened to him with rapt attention. With great deliberation Senator Vest continued: "If true, it would mean that the Confederates could have placed on that sheet of paper the perpetual establishment of slavery and the right of secession, the most extreme demand that had ever taken shape even in the dream of any Confederate."

From the lips of Stephens and Hunter had come to him, he said, the details of what had taken place. Upon the return of the Commissioners of the Confederacy he heard their official report as Mr. Reagan [the Confederacy's postmaster general] heard it, the latter being a member of the Cabinet and the speaker (Mr. Vest) a member of the Senate of the Confederacy. "I am to-day the only survivor of the twenty-six gentlemen who were the Confederate Senators," he said.

Mr. Vest then stated that what did happen at Hampton Roads, beyond question, was this: "When President Lincoln and Secretary Seward met the Commissioners of the Confederacy, Mr. Lincoln, addressing himself to Mr. Hunter, whom he knew well, said, 'In the first place, gentlemen, I desire to know what are your powers and instructions from the Richmond government,' avoiding," said Mr. Vest, as Mr. Hunter told him himself, the words "Confederate States." "Mr. Hunter, to whom the inquiry was addressed, said: 'Mr. President, we are instructed to consider no proposition that does not involve the independence of the Confederate States of America.' 'Then,' said Mr. Lincoln, 'the interview had as well terminate now; for I must say to you, gentlemen, frankly and honestly, that nothing will be accepted from the government at Richmond except absolute and unconditional surrender.'"

Mr. Vest said that this terminated the interview, and as the Confederate Commissioners retired President Lincoln, addressing Stephens, who was the last to go out, said: "Stephens, you are making a great mistake. Your government is a failure; and when the crash comes, as it soon must come, there will be chaos and disasters, which we cannot now foresee, which must come to your people."

"This account of that meeting," continued Mr. Vest, "substantially and almost word for word as I have given it, came to me from Mr. Stephens and Mr. Hunter."

Mr. Vest said that he considered it his duty to make his statement in order that history may not be falsified, in order that the men who were said to have refused this offer at the hands of President Lincoln should not be made to suffer in their graves, adding: "For if they had refused what was said to have been tendered them by the President, they would have been accessories to the murder of every man who fell from that time in defense of the Confederacy, and they should have given the intentions which they risked everything, everything that is held dear amongst men, in defense of the Confederate cause."

While the deep silence still reigned in the chamber as he spoke, and with every eye directed toward him, Mr. Vest closed as follows: "It may be but a very short time until I shall join the twenty-five colleagues I had in the Confederate Senate, and I did not want this statement to go on the record of this country without my statement of those facts and my solemn denial that there is a shadow of truth in this assertion which has been going the rounds of the newspapers of the country for the last few years."[85] — CONFEDERATE VETERAN

21. THE BITTER TIDE OF LIBERALISM AT HAMPTON ROADS

☛ The article in your June issue entitled "What Happened at Hampton Roads" induces me to call the attention of Confederates once more to the matter involved. Many intelligent old soldiers seem to be still laboring under the impression that at the Hampton Roads conference, which occurred February 3, 1865, between Vice President Alex H. Stephens, R. M. T. Hunter, and Judge Campbell, on our side, and Mr. Lincoln and Mr. Seward, Mr. Lincoln agreed to give them what they pleased if they would only write Union at the head of the agreement.

Another error which I have several times heard old soldiers express is that at that conference Mr. Lincoln agreed to pay the South for her slaves, provided the war was then stopped.

Mr. Vest's statement on the floor of the United States Senate as to what Mr. Stephens said on that occasion will, of course, be accepted by all reasonable and unprejudiced people; but some may say that after so long an interval of time the worthy Senator's memory may have been at fault.

The written report of the commissioners to the Confederate Senate does not go into details of the occurrences of the conference; but fortunately the whole thing, or at least enough of it for our purpose, was carefully and accurately recorded shortly after the conference, by Mr. Stephens himself, in his "War between the States." On page 599, Volume II, Mr. Stephens said, in opening the conference at Hampton Roads: "Mr. President, is there no way of putting an end to the present trouble?"

. . . Mr. Lincoln replied that there was but one way that he knew of, and that was for those who were resisting the laws of the Union to cease that resistance. . . . The restoration of the Union is a *sine qua non* with me," etc. (See page 601.)

"Judge Campbell now renewed his inquiry as to how restoration was to take place." (Page 609.)

"Mr. Lincoln replied: 'By disbanding their armies and permitting the national authorities to resume their functions.' (Page 609.) "Mr. Lincoln further declared that he never would change or modify the terms of the emancipation proclamation in the slightest degree." (Page 611.)

"After some four hours' discussion, Mr. Hunter said that in his opinion Mr. Lincoln's propositions amounted to nothing but unconditional surrender on the part of the Confederates. There could be no treaty nor even any stipulation as to terms—only unconditional submission." (Page 616.)

"Mr. Lincoln said he believed the people of the North were as responsible for slavery as the people of the South, and if the war should then cease, with the voluntary abolition of slavery by the States, he should be in favor, individually, of the government paying a fair indemnity for the loss to the owners. . . . But on this subject he said he could give no assurance—enter into no stipulation." (Page 617.)

On pages 622, 623 Mr. Stephens says, after his return to Richmond and report to Mr. Davis: "Mr. Davis's position was that inasmuch as it was now settled beyond question by the decided and pointed declaration of Mr. Lincoln that there could be no peace short of unconditional submission the part of the people of the Confederate States, . . . he himself seemed more determined than ever to fight it out on that line."

The above extracts from Mr. Stephens's admirable work show positively that Mr. Lincoln would agree to nothing but unconditional surrender; and that there is no foundation whatever in fact for the statement that Mr. Lincoln said, "Agree to come back into the Union, and you can have what else you please," nor for the assertion that Mr. Lincoln agreed that his government would pay for the slaves. He did say that individually he was in favor of paying for them, but distinctly stated that he did not know that his government would agree to it. It is said to be a fact that he afterwards brought the matter before his Cabinet, and that no member of it agreed with him.

Although the assassination of Mr. Lincoln was a sad misfortune to the South, it is doubtful whether he could have stayed the pernicious and malignant hand of the [then Left-wing radically-run Republican] government. The passage of various offensive bills, originated by cowardly skulkers for the purpose of persecuting the prostrate South, over Mr. [Andrew] Johnson's repeated vetoes, indicates that even Mr. Lincoln could not have stayed the bitter tide.[86] — DR. CHALMERS DEADERICK, KNOXVILLE, TENN.

22. ONE REASON JEFFERSON DAVIS BELIEVED THE SOUTH WOULD WIN

☛ Mr. Davis was thoroughly honest and sincere. He had become so imbued with the [Revolutionary] history of [George] Washington and his struggling compatriots and so accustomed to seeing analogies in the Confederate situation that he believed Providence would in some way bring relief, and that Confederacy would succeed in its efforts to establish a permanent government.[87] — WASHINGTON GARDNER

23. THE CONFEDERACY AFTER JULY 4, 1863

☛ A Memorial Day address under the above caption by C. P. J. Mooney appeared in the *Confederate Veteran* for March. The following is quoted from it:

> "By all the rules of war, Vicksburg and Gettysburg should have marked the collapse of the aggressive fighting strength of the South. . . . Jefferson Davis, the head of the Confederacy, might have said: 'We have fought a good fight. The fortunes of war are against us. What have you to offer?'"

In *The Rise and Fall of the Confederate Government*, Volume II, page 609, President Davis uses this language:

> "When Major [John] Pitcairn marched the British soldiers upon the common at Lexington, Mass., exclaiming, 'Disperse, ye rebels, disperse,' he expressed the same conditions which were offered to us in all our negotiations with the President of the United States. Several efforts were made by us to communicate with the authorities at Washington without success. Commissioners were sent before hostilities began, and the government of the United States refused to receive them or hear what they had to say. A second time I sent a military officer with a communication addressed by myself to President Lincoln. The letter was received by General [Winfield] Scott, who promised that an answer would be sent. No answer was ever received. Vice President Stephens made a patriotic tender of his services. The enemy refused to let him pass through their lines or to hold any conference with him."

Page 611:

> "The opening of the spring campaign of 1864 was deemed a favorable conjuncture for the employment of the resources of diplomacy. To approach the government of the United States directly would have been vain. Repeated efforts had already demonstrated its inflexible purpose not to negotiate with the Confederate authorities. A commission of three persons, eminent in position and intelligence, was accordingly appointed to visit Canada with a view to negotiation with such persons in the North as might be relied upon to aid in the attainment of peace. The commission Messrs. [Clement Claiborne] Clay, of Alabama, [James] Holcombe, of Virginia, and [Jacob] Thompson, of Mississippi—established themselves at Niagara Falls [known as the Niagara Peace Talks] in July and on the 12th commenced a correspondence with Horace Greeley, of New York. Through him they sought a safe conduct to Washington. Mr. Lincoln at first appeared to favor an interview, but finally refused on the ground that the commissioners were not authorized to treat for peace. This movement, like all others which preceded it, was a failure."

(Here Mr. Davis gives an account of the visit to Richmond of Francis P. Blair [Sr.], who had gone to Washington and brought a letter from Mr. Lincoln addressed to himself which stated that he would receive an agent of Mr. Davis "or any other influential person" with the view of securing peace.)

Then Mr. Davis says:

"I determined to send as commissioners or agents for the informal conference Messrs. Alexander H. Stephens, R. M. T. Hunter, and John A. Campbell. The letter of Mr. Lincoln expressing a willingness to receive any agent I might send to Washington City, a commission was appointed to go there; but it was not allowed to proceed farther than Hampton Roads, where Mr. Lincoln, accompanied by Mr. Seward, met the commissioners. Seward craftily proposed that the conference be confidential, and the commissioners regarded this so binding on them as to prevent them from including in their report the discussions which occurred."

The following is an extract from the report made by the commission to President Davis:

"We understood from him [Lincoln] that no terms or proposals of any treaty would be entertained or made by him with the authorities of the Confederate States; that no extended truce or armistice (as at present advised) would be granted or allowed without satisfactory assurance in advance of the complete restoration of the Constitution and laws of the United States over all places in the Confederacy. During the conference the proposed amendment to the Constitution of the United States was brought to our notice. This amendment provides that neither slavery nor involuntary servitude should exist within the United States."

Says Judge Campbell in his memoranda:

"In conclusion, Mr. Hunter summed up what seemed to be the result of the interview—'that there was nothing left for them [Confederates] but unconditional submission.'"

The report was signed by the commissioners and is given in A. H. Stephens's "History of the United States" and in *The Rise and Fall of the Confederate Government*, by Mr. Davis.

In sending his message to the Confederate Congress on February 6, 1865, President Davis said:

"I herewith transmit for the information of Congress the report of the eminent citizens above named, showing that the enemy refused to enter into negotiations with the Confederate States or any one of them or to give our people any other terms or guarantees than that which the conqueror may grant or permit us to have peace on any other basis than our unconditional submission to their rule."

Horace Greeley.

In the *Confederate Veteran* of April, 1901, Hon. John H. Reagan, ex-Postmaster General C.S.A., replies to a published account of what purported to be an interview of one Dr. R. J. Massey with Vice President Stephens in April, 1865. The supposed statement of Mr. Stephens in this interview was to the effect that at the Hampton Roads conference Mr. Lincoln proposed that all the Confederates lay down their arms and come into the Union as they were before hostilities commenced; that there should be no prosecutions of any for their supposed "crimes" against the Union; and that he would immediately cause to be introduced into the Congress of the United States measures providing for gradual emancipation with remuneration to every owner for the slaves so emancipated. Mr. Reagan pronounces this story "an unwarranted assumption," and writes as follows:

"On the night of the return of Mr. Stephens from that conference it was stated on good authority that he told Hon. James L. Orr, Confederate Senator from South Carolina, that the Hampton Roads conference was fruitless and hopeless, because Mr. Lincoln offered the Confederacy nothing but unconditional submission."

Mr. Reagan further says:

"In a letter which the late Hon. F. B. Sexton, a representative in the Confederate Congress, wrote me he says that Mr. Stephens on his return from Hampton Roads told him that Mr. Lincoln offered nothing but unconditional submission."

Mr. Reagan next refers to a letter of Col. Stephen W. Blount, of San Antonio, Tex., an old-time friend of Vice President Stephens. Colonel Blount wrote Mr. Stephens "asking for the truth as to this. Mr. Stephens wrote him that the statement was untrue"; that "the only element in reference to the slave payment was so mixed and infused with falsehood as to make the entire assertion false."

Mr. Reagan refers to the report of the Historical Committee of the Veterans' Association, Gen. Stephen D. Lee, Chairman (Louisville, 1900), which made a full investigation of the question about the offers made by Mr. Lincoln to pay for the slaves if that would restore the Union and end the war, and reported that there was no shadow of a foundation for any such statement.

Dr. Massey having made some reply, Mr. Reagan later wrote the following to the *Veteran*:

> "I rest upon that paper (in the *Veteran* for April, 1901) as absolute proof of the truth of my position and do not care to add to what I then said except to state that about two years ago, when this question was under discussion, Governor Garland, of Arkansas, who at the time of that conference was a member of the Confederate Senate, and who was the roommate of Vice President Stephens in Richmond, in a published statement said that on the night after Mr. Stephens's return from that conference he told him [Garland] that no terms could be had but unconditional surrender. Garland after the war became Governor of Arkansas, United States Senator from that State, and then Attorney-General of the United States."

And, finally, Mr. Reagan says:

> "Since the War between the States a persistent effort has been made to make the public believe that President Lincoln offered the Confederate commissioners at that conference terms of peace favorable to our people which the commissioners were prevented from accepting because President Davis insisted upon the independence of the Confederacy, for which our people had fought so long and sacrificed so much. Many of the people of the Southern States were induced to believe that this was true and that the President and the Confederate authorities were responsible for the continuance of the war. . . . I will see as far as I can that the facts as to that conference shall go into history correctly. Most of the principal actors in the War between the States have passed to their final account, and it is pitiable

to see persons of later days, some of whom took no part in the struggle and made no sacrifices for that cause, busying themselves in finding fault with and criticizing the noble men who did and suffered so much for it."[88] — R. M. HOUSTON, MERIDIAN, MISS.

24. TREATMENT OF SOUTHERN COMMISSIONERS
☛ [The lies and scheming of the Lincoln administration at the beginning of the War, particularly in relation to Fort Sumter in April 1861] . . . put an end to further negotiations [between South and North—temporarily], and the [Confederate] commissioners returned to their homes about April 22, utterly disgusted at the insincerity and duplicity of the United States government.

The crooked path of diplomacy of modern times can scarcely furnish an example as lacking in candor, truth, and honor as was manifested by the highest officials of the United States government toward the excellent gentlemen who composed the last commission [at Hampton Roads]. Some of the best, most intelligent and patriotic of Northerners, including members of the Senate and House of Representatives, were much mortified and blushed with shame at the disgraceful conduct of their own government. [Yankee] Major [Robert] Anderson, who was in command of the garrison at Sumter, was one of those who heartily disapproved of the bad faith of his government, and, except for the rules of the soldier's code of ethics, he would have expressed his disgust in unmeasured terms.

Including all of the different sets or boards of commissioners sent to Washington in behalf of the South, they were a fine body of men. Perhaps no nation on earth could have produced their superiors. They were able, honorable, sincere, and patriotic. They asked for and wanted nothing except justice and equity. With intense earnestness of purpose and with admirable patience, courage, and forbearance they submitted to the provoking discourtesies, the tedious delays, the violation of promises, and the disgusting want of truth and honor displayed by the highest officials of the United States government. It was not their fault that they failed to accomplish their object.

In your perusal of the pages of modern history did you ever find the record of the ermine of a civilized nation so besmirched, stained, and blotted by ugly black spots of insincerity, broken pledges, and want of honor? Can you possibly imagine even for a moment President Davis and his Secretary of State stooping to the level of such disgusting machinations and duplicity as marked the course of similar officials [namely William H. Seward] on the other side?

During the long series of years since the war all effort to find damaging evidence against the acts of the Confederate officials by their war-time enemies has failed entirely. The record of their conduct of both State and military affairs contains no pages marred by ugly stains of dishonor. The Confederate ensign of honor has been folded and laid aside about fifty years; but, having never been allowed to drag in mud or dust, it is still as white as the driven snow. Look on this picture and then on that.

The last commission appointed by the Confederacy was composed of Alexander H. Stephens, Mr. Hunter, and Judge Campbell. These gentlemen met Mr. Lincoln and Mr. Seward at Hampton Roads in February, 1865. Inasmuch as that conference has been misunderstood by many, including a number of ex-Confederate soldiers, I shall make a very brief statement of what really occurred. I have talked with several Confederates and other Southerners who honestly believed Mr. Lincoln assured the commissioners that all they had to do was to come back into the Union, and if they would write "Union" in an agreement they could have pay for their slaves and anything else they pleased.

As a matter of fact, Mr. Lincoln said no such thing. He gave them no assurance of anything. At the very beginning of the conference Mr. Seward announced that the interview was to be informal. There was no clerk or secretary, no writing or record of anything that was said. Then Mr. Stephens asked Mr. Lincoln if there was any way of putting an end to the war and bringing about general good feeling and harmony between the South and the North.

Mr. Lincoln replied that there was but one way that he knew of, and that was for those who were resisting the laws of the Union to cease that resistance. A discussion followed that lasted four hours. Upon a number of questions raised by the commissioners, Mr. Lincoln said be could give only his own individual opinion. He said he would be willing to be taxed to remunerate the Southern people for their slaves; that he knew some Northern people who were in favor of paying as high as four hundred million dollars for this purpose, provided the war should cease at once; but of this he could give no assurance, nor could he enter into any stipulation.

When Mr. Lincoln returned to Washington he sounded his Cabinet on the matter of paying for the slaves, and not a single one of them would agree to it.

Toward the last interview Mr. Hunter recapitulated the matters talked over and stated that the South had been offered nothing but an unconditional surrender.[89] — DR. CHALMERS DEADERICK, KNOXVILLE, TENN.

25. THE AMAZING JEFFERSON DAVIS

☞ . . . The Confederacy at first victorious [in the War], events followed rapidly tending to its final collapse. Yet Mr. Davis did not once despair, and stood a rampart of strength and courage which was liberally imparted to all who came to him, and as the days grew darker and the clamor arose for a peace compromise, Mr. Davis (distrusting the outcome) sent commissioners to Hampton Roads to confer with Mr. Lincoln, but nothing was accomplished.

Some have said that Mr. Lincoln was very liberal, writing at the head of the page, "The Union shall and must be preserved," and saying, "You gentlemen of the South may write the terms." This sounds liberal to those not in the strife, but to us of the South who were fighting for self-preservation and for constitutional government

Richard Taylor.

to surrender this vital point was to surrender all for which our armies were still in the field—[Robert. E] Lee before Richmond and [Joseph Eggleston] Johnston in Georgia, [Richard] Taylor in Mississippi and [Sterling] Price and [Edmund Kirby] Smith in the trans-Mississippi.

We claimed to be a separate government from that of the United States. For Mr. Davis to surrender our nationality would have been treason, notwithstanding the liberality of the terms. But Mr. Stephens and his associates made no such report to President Davis. If Mr. Lincoln made such overtures they were not conveyed to our President. . . .[90] — COL. B. W. GREEN, JUNE 1915

26. THE LEFT WILL NOT STOP LYING ABOUT THE HAMPTON ROADS CONFERENCE

☞ The article in the *Confederate Veteran* for June on "The Truth of the Hampton Roads Conference" evidently provoked the seer [Henry Watterson] of the [Louisville] *Courier-Journal* to another eruption on the subject, though he quotes from an editorial in a daily paper of a Western State as the reason for the outbreak. As he made no response to a letter of protest by the *Veteran* upon the appearance of his first objectionable editorials nor gave it place in the columns of his journal, it is evident that he considers the official organ of the United Confederate Veterans as beneath his notice. Nevertheless, in an indirect way he is now giving it attention.

Under date of June 20 Mr. Watterson holds forth on "The Truth of History" and proceeds to pervert it. He continues to assert that President Lincoln made the wonderful offer of everything for "Union" in the informal conference he had with Alexander Stephens and other Confederate commissioners at Hampton Roads, Va., in February, 1865—this not-withstanding *the inconsistent position in which he places the man of his idolatry, the "Christ-man" [Lincoln], who countenanced such severe measures as the cessation of the cartel of exchange, so that prisoners of war continued to suffer and die by the thousands in order that the ranks of the Confederate army might not be swelled by its returned soldiers, and who allowed the ravaging of a country already desolated by a war of invasion, so that the old men, women, and children should also suffer in the extreme for their connection with the Confederacy; yea, the "Christ-man" who made no effort at the beginning of hostilities to bring about a peaceful settlement of differences between the sections, but showed bad faith in not keeping the promise as to Fort Sumter and upon its fall sent out his call for troops to invade the South* [my emphasis, L.S.]. What might not have been the outcome if "faith as to Sumter" had been fully kept?

In his book on "The War between the States" Mr. Stephens concludes his report of this famous conference by saying:

> "This is as full and accurate an account as I can now give of the origin, the objects, and the conduct of this conference from its beginning to its end. In giving it, as stated before, I have not undertaken to do more than to present substantially what verbally passed between all the parties therein mentioned."

That is, we take it, he touched upon every phase of the discussion; yet he nowhere intimates that he and Mr. Lincoln had any conference apart from the others in which Mr. Lincoln made the very inconsistent offer credited to him. He was already pledged to his position on slavery, for had he not said in his message to Congress in December before: "If the people should, by whatever mode or means, make it an executive duty to reenslave such persons, another, and not I, must be their instrument to perform it"? Under such a declaration could he have offered to concede everything else for the restoration of the Union? And what reason could Mr. Stephens have had for withholding mention of that offer to his chief at Richmond? Why should Mr. Lincoln have made such an offer if he had not intended it to have the consideration of the Confederate authorities? He knew that Mr. Stephens's mission was simply to secure terms of peace for submitting to Mr. Davis and the Confederate Congress, and any proposition he made should have gone before them. Judging Mr. Stephens by the light thrown on his character by the editor of the *Courier-Journal*, he was a traitor, indeed, to himself as well as to those who had intrusted him with a high mission. What could have been his object in writing one thing and stating verbally another? If he divulged such an advantageous offer to Mr. Felix G. de Fontaine, the noted Southern war correspondent, the night after his return to Richmond, as Mr. Watterson says he did, why should he not have reported it to Mr. Davis, who was entitled to know everything that had transpired?

Mr. Watterson says this wonderfully liberal offer "does not appear in the official documents because it was not a part of the formal proceedings, but an aside during an interview between Mr. Lincoln and Mr. Stephens"; yet the latter says this conference was strictly informal, and he makes no reference to any conference with Mr. Lincoln in which the other commissioners did not participate. Why should Mr. Lincoln have made such an offer to Mr. Stephens alone, knowing he had no power to accept it? If he really made it, Mr. Stephens evidently considered it an idle expression—a "talking through his hat" on the part of Mr. Lincoln—not to have passed it on to his superiors at Richmond for consideration.

Mr. Watterson says:

> "The Hampton Roads conference came to naught because the restoration of the Union was a *sine qua non* of one party and the recognition of the Confederacy a *sine qua non* of the other; but when the words 'unconditional surrender' are used in this connection as the Lincoln ultimatum, they are, to say the least, misleading."

Since Mr. Stephens's report shows conclusively that unconditional submission to the power of the Federal government was the only basis upon which there would be a cessation of war upon the South, one wonders upon what Mr. Watterson bases his counter assertion. Did Mr. Lincoln make any formal offer of peace other than upon the surrender of the Confederate army unconditionally—that is, did he give any assurance as to what was in store for the people of the South in case of surrender? Mr. Stephens says he did not, and surely Mr. Stephens knew.

Mr. Watterson further says:

> "Mr. Lincoln's proposal that the Southern armies should disband and go home, that the Southern States should assemble conventions in each of the several capitals and repeal the ordinances of secession, and, this done, that they should send their Senators and Representatives to Washington to be accepted and received by Congress, was, under the circumstances, a generous offer, not a demand for 'unconditional surrender.'"

Was this an offer or a mere suggestion? If an offer, it should have carried a promise that the Southern States would again be admitted to participation in government affairs without question; but nothing was promised. Mr. Stephens brings this out merely as a suggestion to him in the case of Georgia, and with it went the condition of ratifying the constitutional amendment abolishing slavery; and *when*

Mr. Stephens mentioned that *suffering among the old and infirm and children would necessarily attend emancipation in that way, as they could not support themselves,* and asked Mr. Lincoln his plan for protecting them, the latter responded with an anecdote about the man who saved time and labor by turning his hogs on the ungathered crops to feed themselves, and to a neighbor's inquiry as to what he expected them to do when winter came and the ground was frozen he said: "Well, let 'em root [my emphasis, L.S.]."[91] And that is just about the spirit of a majority of those who were so anxious to free the slaves.

Mr. Watterson says, "The South has no reason to falsify history or to misread it," yet he deliberately does both. He misreads the written record in giving credence to oral statements at variance with such written record, and he falsifies history in publishing his belief is as proper evidence. He makes Mr. Stephens appear guilty of double-dealing to have withheld from his report the one and only offer worth considering. He actually says that Mr. Davis did not see Mr. Stephens at all after the conference at Hampton Roads; that they were not on friendly or even speaking relations. In view of that, it is strange indeed that Mr. Stephens should put on record that he and the other commissioners made a verbal report of the conference to Mr. Davis and upon the latter's insistence put it in writing to lay before the Confederate Congress, that he should later speak of his "last interview with Mr. Davis before leaving Richmond," and that he "left Richmond in no ill humor with Mr. Davis." We prefer to believe this written testimony of the state of their relations rather than the assertions of one who had no connection with the principals in this affair and who seems to have sought only to bring discredit upon them for the purpose of placing the other, the "Christ-man," in the Godlike attitude of offering "peace at any price" for Union.

But if proof of this can be shown then indeed may we, in the name of justice, let the proof be shown! Burdened and harassed by the responsibilities of the office and betrayed by one in whom he had placed high trust, not on the President of the Confederacy should fall the blame for this failure to arrange terms of peace, but on the trusted lieutenant who failed to report the only terms that could have been accepted.[92] — *CONFEDERATE VETERAN*

27. THE TRUTH WILL RISE AGAIN

☛ I had read Mr. [Henry] Watterson's version of the Hampton Roads conference, copied in one of our local papers some time ago, and am gratified to find the "Truth of the Hampton Roads Conference" in the June number of the *Confederate Veteran* and for the steps taken at the [Confederate Veterans] Reunion in Birmingham.

While time in its power of adjustment rights all wrongs, we cannot feel that we have been loyal or just if we let an untruth go by unnoticed, though we well know that "truth crushed to earth will rise again." Mr. Watterson has been the tool in the hands of justice to unearth these truths, and they shine out all the brighter because the sordid earth of untruth has been washed away, as has been done in many cases.

Another fifty years, perhaps more or less, will place all the wreaths of honor where they justly belong, and the world will know that the same motive that forced secession is the same that has prompted the war [World War I] in Europe. In His own good time and in His own good way justice is meted out. Nothing is hidden from His all-seeing eyes and His just hand. He was before and at Fort Sumter, Gettysburg, and Appomattox. "God chasteneth whom he loveth." As a reward for this love we have the field of his vineyard, Africa and its people, for ours in which to labor; we have paid its price in blood.

The hero worship of Mr. Lincoln will in time pass, and the world will know that he was flesh and blood, with hopes and ambitions, passions and faults, just as the rest of us weak mortals, though a wonderful and unusual man. Truth and honor do not need defense.

We of the South fought for principle, and they of the North because of jealousy. Had Harriet Beecher Stowe, Mr. Lincoln, and the abolitionists of the North been prompted by a true, pure motive of "all people being equal," they would have made it possible to abolish slavery without a Fort Sumter, an Appomattox, or a Reconstruction period.

If the United States government could pay $400,000,000 for the freedom of the slaves on February 3, 1865, at the Hampton Roads conference, after the heavy cost of millions of dollars and the appalling loss of life and injured, what could it not have paid before the secession of South

Carolina! [my emphasis, L.S.] Many of the abolitionists of the South, as well as those of the North, had freed their slaves and stood the criticism of those who did not believe as they did, and yet those same abolitionists took up their arms in defense of the right of secession. I know whereof I speak. My husband's father and mine both trod the road of battle, sons of Southern abolitionists who did not believe in slavery because their Christian consciences would not permit it. I say again that the freedom of the slaves could have been bought, just their slavery was bought, with money instead of with blood.

Could we cleanse our minds and hearts of all animosity and live the principle of true Christianity taught us by our leader, Robert E. Lee, the greatest leader that the world has ever known, how soon would truth shine out as the "Star of the East" did to the wise men![93] — MRS. STEPHEN D. KNOX, LITTLE ROCK, ARK.

28. MORE FALSEHOODS OF NORTHERN MYTHOLOGY

☞ In the name of the Confederate soldiers who followed General Lee in the War between the States and knew that they were right in fighting for their rights under the Constitution of the United States, let me thank you for your just and noble defense of the main object of the Committee's report at [the] Richmond [Confederate Veterans] Reunion: to open the eyes of all men regarding the open and secret endeavors of Northern fanatics [that is, Yankee socialists and communists] to instill in the minds of our children, by textbooks and teachers, the false and pernicious doctrine that their fathers and kinsmen who followed Lee were traitors.

As to the part of the report stigmatizing Lincoln as being "personally responsible for forcing the war upon the South," there is room for difference of opinion. I agree with you that "to put the blame on Lincoln alone for having conceived and inaugurated the War between the States, will need strong proof to sustain."

With you, I would respectfully ask, why the protest of Generals [Julian S.] Carr and Howry against that part of the report which they repudiated in the public press was not made in the meeting that adopted the report. Had I been present at the meeting, I would have sustained the purpose of the report, and have thanked the Committee for their labor of love in exposing the efforts of those

people in the North to teach our children that our sacred cause was the cause of traitors; but would have suggested a change in the phraseology of a part of the report, something like this: That the War between the States was indorsed and commended by Mr. Lincoln because he made no effort to prevent it when the opportunity was offered him by the Peace Conference; and that he was responsible for the secession of Virginia by calling out 75,000 armed men to coerce the Southern States. More than that, he had it in his power at the Hampton Roads Conference in February, 1865, to end the cruel war, and thus prevent further suffering to our soldiers in the field, in the prisons, and to their loved ones at home. The handing to Mr. Stephens a blank sheet of paper by Mr. Lincoln and saying to him, "Mr. Stephens, let me write 'Union' at the top of that sheet, and you may write anything you please under it," is sheer fiction, widely disseminated by the late Henry Watterson.

On its face it is absurd to suppose that Mr. Lincoln would have committed himself to the retention in the Southern States of slavery, which he professed to abominate. Mr. Stephens says (on page 550-9, Vol. I, "Confederate Military History") that the President's first and only proposition was "unconditional surrender of the States and their people." And he adds:

> "The conference reached the line where it seems the Southern Commissioners would have taken a step committing their government to dissolution without another battle, provided only they had been fully and frankly assured by authority to be trusted that the Union, even without slavery, would be at once reestablished, the States with all their rightful relations restored, the people of the South protected, the Constitution respected, and sectionalism ended forever."

Had these concessions of the Committee been accepted by Mr. Lincoln, ratified by President Jefferson Davis and the Confederate Congress, the awful and unequal conflict, with its terrible suffering of all concerned—North as well as South—would have been brought to an end; the horrors of the never-to-be-forgotten period of reconstruction would never have disgraced the [then Liberal] Republican Party nor have humiliated the people of the South; and the glorious Union, founded by our Fathers "for, with, and by the consent of the people," would have been cemented by the cords of perpetual love. Then, we could, with commendable pride, have taught our children to reverence the name of Abraham Lincoln and acclaim him "a great and good man."

But no; judging him by his actions—advising the Republicans in Congress to vote against the Crittenden resolutions, the part he played at the Peace Conference, approving Seward's deception in conferring with the committee from the Virginia convention, driving Virginia out of the Union by his proclamation for 75,000 men to coerce the Southern States, and not accepting the concessions made by the Committee at the Hampton Roads Conference—are we to be considered uncharitable in thinking that Mr. Lincoln had but one idea from the beginning to the end of the unhappy struggle, and that idea was the subjugation of the Southern people?

And are Confederate veterans to be censured for resenting the false charge of being traitors, because we fought—under the leadership of our great and good President Jefferson Davis and the peerless Robert E. Lee—to defend our homes, and our Constitutional rights?[94] — REV. GILES B. COOKE, MATHEWS, VA.

29. THE HALLUCINATION

☛ In July, 1864, President Lincoln wrote [Yankee socialist] Horace Greeley to produce a man, or men, who had a proposition from Jefferson Davis (in writing) for peace, embracing the restoration of the Union and the abandonment of slavery, and no matter what else it embraced, that he, or they, might come to him with it, and from this extremely elastic letter there has been promulgated a myth which, like the proverbial ghost, is hard to down.

Even quite recently it has been publicly stated that during the famous peace conference at Hampton Roads, in February, 1865, Mr. Lincoln told our commissioners to let him write Union at the top of the page, and they could write anything they wished below. There is nothing in the "Official Records" to substantiate any such assertion.

Mr. Lincoln certainly told the United States Congress of no such plan, for in his annual message of 1864, he says that the only terms of peace possible to our people was to lay down their arms, and closes by saying that the war would cease when it would be stopped by those who started it.

Mr. Davis told our Congress that the enemy would give us no terms other than a complete submission to their rule, and as our commissioners reported that they were not informed of any modification or alteration whatever of the terms as stated in Mr. Lincoln's message it is proper for the spreaders of this seeming hallucination to either give proof of their assertion or acknowledge their error.[95] — COL. JOHN C. STILES, BRUNSWICK, GA.

30. THE ABSURDITY OF THE HAMPTON ROADS MYTH

☞ Those who have helped to spread such a report [as cited in the previous entry] —and the late Henry Watterson was prominent among them—evidently did not realize its absurdity or gave Lincoln credit for less common sense than is rightfully his due. Many things could have been written under the heading of "Union" that would have nullified it, as he well knew. Even ministers are given to quoting the absurd statement. Sensible people should realize its absurdity.[96] — *CONFEDERATE VETERAN*

31. THE SOUTH'S SIXTH & FINAL ATTEMPT AT PEACE

☞ The Hampton Roads Conference is perhaps the best known of [the six major efforts] made by the South for peace during the War between the States. Events in the opening of 1865 came thick and fast. It was evident now that nothing short of remarkable good fortune could save the Confederates from defeat. Still they held out, believing so sincerely in the justice of their cause that they refused to look defeat in the face; or to even think it possible. About this time various efforts were made toward effecting a peace.

The Hampton Roads Conference was held February 3, 1865, at this place in Virginia. Its object was to find, if possible, some terms for ending the war between the North and South. The conference was brought about by Francis P. Blair, Sr., an influential journalist of Washington. He was a native of Abingdon, Va., and lived in Kentucky, but was at this time a citizen of Maryland. He was a Democrat [at that time a Conservative], and had been a personal friend of President [Jefferson] Davis, but had supported [Abraham] Lincoln for President, and "fellowshiped" with the North during the war.

Blair thought peace might be brought about by getting the two Governments to suspend hostilities and join their forces in a common campaign against Maximilian and the French in Mexico, in an application of the Monroe Doctrine. He felt that by the time this task should be finished, and because it would have been jointly done, the animosities between the two sections would be so assuaged that North and South could settle their differences without further bloodshed.

Blair presented his idea first of all to President Lincoln, who gave him a passport to Richmond. There he laid his project before President Davis, in a private interview. Mr. Davis first satisfied himself that he was an informal, though unofficial, representative of President Lincoln; made a written memorandum of the interview; submitted the same to Blair for his approval of its correctness; and, on January 12, 1865, gave him a note, in which he said: "I am willing now, as heretofore, to enter into negotiations for the restoration of peace."

Mr. Lincoln asked Mr. Blair to reply that he was ready to receive any agent or influential person that Mr. Davis would informally send him,"with a view of securing peace to the people of our common country." President Davis appointed three commissioners. Vice President Alexander H. Stephens, Senator R. M. T. Hunter, and Assistant Secretary of War John A. Campbell, men of the highest integrity, who were the most likely to succeed. These three men believed that the war could be settled by negotiations if only a fair trial were made. They were in as good favor at Washington as any men Mr. Davis could have selected, who would most likely get favorable terms.

President Lincoln would not allow the Conference to be held in Washington, as that would be to acknowledge the Confederate States as another Nation, though he had said in his reply to President Davis, "Peace to the people of our common country."

The message came that Mr. Seward, Secretary of State, would meet the Southern Commissioners at Hampton Roads, or Fortress Monroe, Va., and Lincoln instructed Seward what to say in a most explicit way:

> "You will make it known to them that three things are indispensable, to wit:
> "First. The restoration of the national authority throughout the States; second, no receding by the Executive of the United States on the slavery questions; third, no cessation of hostilities short of an end of the war, and the disbanding of all the forces hostile to the government.
> "You will inform them that all propositions of theirs not inconsistent with the above will be considered and passed upon in a spirit of sincere liberality. Do not assume to consummate anything."

Then Mr. Lincoln telegraphed to General Grant: "Let nothing hinder or delay your military plans."

When General Grant learned that President Lincoln would not see the members of the commission, he telegraphed Hon. E. M. Stanton, [U.S.] Secretary of War, that he was convinced from a conversation with these gentlemen that they were sincere in their expressed desire to have peace and union restored, and that the action of the President had placed him in a very awkward position, and he was very sorry that Mr. Lincoln would not have an interview with Mr. Stephens and Mr. Hunter. When Mr. Stanton repeated this telegram to the President, he wired Seward that he would meet him at Fortress Monroe.

After many difficulties and much dispatching, the conference was held on February 3 [1865], on the *River Queen*, a small steamer anchored out in the river, for the sake of greater privacy. This meeting lasted four hours behind closed doors, with only the three Southern Commissioners, Lincoln, and Seward present. President Davis left his representatives untrammeled, their object being to secure peace between the two countries.

At the outset of the conference, the wily Seward proposed that there be no secretary and nothing like minutes. So no written memorandum of anything said or done was made at the time. What then did transpire at this Conference?

It would seem to be easy to answer this question, because every member of the conference—the only ones who could possibly know—has written and printed and given to the public each his own account of what did occur. And every one of these accounts agree. There is no variation as to substantive terms that were proposed. What, then, did transpire at this Conference?

And yet there has been much discussion, down to the present day, as to what was precisely proposed to the South at that Conference. Some contend that the only terms offered were "unconditional surrender." Others contend that President Lincoln said to Mr. Stephens, the chairman for the Confederate representatives, words to this effect: "Stephens, let me write Union, and you can write after it what you please." So these think that Lincoln offered the Southern men reconciliation and peace on their own terms. What he himself substantively says he demanded at this Conference was equal to "unconditional surrender." He gave a report to the House of Representatives to this effect, on February 10 [1865].

On the return of the three Confederate Commissioners from the Hampton Roads Conference, they made a unanimous report of what took place at the meeting. They formally and officially informed President Davis that President Lincoln would entertain no "terms" or "conditions," or "methods of proceeding," or "proposals," or "agreement," or "truths," or "armistice," "without a satisfactory assurance in advance of a complete restoration of the authority of the United States over all places within the States of the Confederacy." This report stated that Lincoln gave the commissioners to understand that "no terms or proposals of any treaty looking toward an ultimate settlement would be made by Lincoln with the authorities of the Confederate States, as that would be a recognition of their existence as a separate power, which under no circumstances would be done."

The report also stated that Mr. Lincoln had shut out all other possible results than the disbandment of the armies and the restoration of the authority of the United States government in such manner as he might indicate or Congress might require. It was submission to whatever might come. So this Conference was closed and all negotiations with the government of the United States for the establishment of peace.

The conclusion of the report of these Confederate commissioners was that the result of this Hampton Roads Conference showed there could be no agreements between the warring factions, as there was nothing left to the South but "unconditional surrender."

At the request of Mr. Davis, Mr. Stephens submitted to the Confederate Congress a written report of this Conference. The president himself, had no power to accept or reject any terms offered, and *the conference was not for the purpose of making peace terms, but to ascertain terms on which peace might be procured*, and, of course, the Confederate Congress had the decision in its hands. Yet *Mr. Davis has been blamed for not accepting peace terms which were never offered* [my emphasis, L.S.].

In his "War between the States," Alexander Stephens says of this conference (in conclusion): "This is as full and accurate an account as I can give from beginning to end." There was no reason why Vice President Stephens could not have there verified the statement that others said he made in regard to Lincoln's words, had they been true.

Many years after the war, the New York *Times* gave the following account of the Hampton Roads Conference:

> "At Hampton Roads, Lincoln refused to accept any proposal except unconditional surrender. He promised clemency, but refused to define it, except to say that he individually favored compensation for slave owners, and that he would execute the confiscation and other penal acts with the utmost liberality. He made it plain, though, that he was

fighting for an idea, and that it was useless to talk of compromise until that idea was triumphant. We are aware, of course, of the long exploded myth, telling how he offered Stephens a sheet of paper with Union written on it, and told the Confederate statesman to fill up the rest of the paper to suit himself."

"He offered us nothing but unconditional surrender," said Stephens on his return, and he called the Conference 'fruitless and inadequate.'"

When the commissioners returned to Richmond, President Davis and all the South were disappointed over the failure of the Conference. All hopes of peace having now vanished from the minds of the South, there was no alternative left save continuation of the war. The Confederate Congress passed resolutions accepting the issue, calling upon the army and the people to redouble their efforts, and invoking the help of Almighty God.

The peace conference of 1865 had come to naught after five other attempts to restore peace with honor, this was of no avail.

Much of this history has been rewritten within the last few years; more remains to be done on the vexed question of the South's part in this war and of her many efforts to secure peace.[97]
— MRS. JOHN H. ANDERSON, RALEIGH, N.C.

32. DISSEMINATING UNTRUTH

☞ The Southern Society of New York City, "organized for the purpose, among other things, of perpetuating the history and traditions of the South," has recently sponsored a series of addresses on Southern Statesmen by radio, the last of this series being on Abraham Lincoln, as presented by Mr. Hugh Gordon Miller. The why of including Lincoln in this series is not apparent other than his having been born in Kentucky.

Aside from that, Mr. Miller saw fit to revive that story of Lincoln and Alexander Stephens at the Hampton Roads Conference in February, 1865—a conference called for the purpose of considering terms by which peace could be secured. The story is refuted by its own weakness as well as by the statements of the Southerners taking part in that dramatic meeting. Mr. Miller tells that Mr. Lincoln "took the Vice-President of the Confederacy aside and, pointing to a sheet of paper he held in his hand, said to him,

'Stephens, let me write "Union" at the top of that piece of paper, and you and your fellow-commissioners may write below that word any other condition you please,'" implying that all Lincoln thought or cared for was Union. Even though it had been all he was fighting for, such a proposition could have entangled him in so many ways that there would have been no peace in union for him.

According to Lincoln's own statement, which those who tell this story lose sight of, he was irrevocably committed to the abolition of slavery, yet this offer made no provision for that. Nothing more ridiculous than this could be accredited to the astute Lincoln, and his admirers do not glorify him in repeating this old story, revived and exploited *ad nauseam* by the late Henry Watterson, who became a Lincoln worshiper in his late years, and thus made and held a large Northern audience for his lectures.

Mr. Stephens' report to President Davis, and later to the Confederate Congress, and which was corroborated by the other Confederate Commissioners to the Hampton Roads Conference, was that unconditional surrender was the only things brought out, so matters were left just where they were before the conference was planned. The late victories of the Union army had encouraged the hope of the Federal Government for an early cessation of hostilities, and Lincoln was in no mind to make any concessions for peace, however much the North wanted it. All that is brought out in Mr. Stephens work on "The War Between the States" and Mr. Davis' "Rise and Fall of the Confederate Government."

President Davis was blamed at the time and through the years following, by the uninformed, for not accepting the terms for peace, when no terms were offered. That he was anxious for peace is shown by the several efforts that were made by the Southern Confederacy to bring that about.

Another statement by Mr. Miller in this address was that Gen. R. E. Lee said that "duty is the sublimest word in our language." General Lee made duty sublime, but he did not so express it in any letters known to have been written by him. The letter containing that expression, which is known as the "Duty letter," first appeared in print in the New York *Sun* in November, 1864, and was repeated in a Richmond paper in December, followed by a repudiation in the same Richmond paper on December 16, 1864. This repudiation could have come from General Lee only—or was written after consultation with him. All this is brought out in a pamphlet published by Professor A. C. Graves, of the University of Virginia, in 1913, and was reproduced in the *Veteran* for November, 1915; yet it seems as difficult to down it as the story of General Lee's having tendered his sword to Grant at Appomattox.

Facts are needed, not sentiment, to establish history, and Mr. Miller should take the first occasion possible and the same means to correct these untruths of Southern history which he has broadcast to millions of listeners.[98] — EDITH DRAKE POPE, EDITOR, *CONFEDERATE VETERAN*

The End

Jefferson Davis.

APPENDIX A

- ADDITIONAL COMMENTARY -
CONCERNING THE HAMPTON ROADS CONFERENCE

• "1865 (February).—Hampton Roads peace conference. Several informal attempts at opening negotiations for the termination of hostilities were made in the course of this Winter—Hon. Francis P. Blair [Sr.], of Maryland, visiting Richmond twice on the subject, with the consent, though not by the request, of President Lincoln. At length, upon their direct application, Messrs. Alex. H. Stephens, John A. Campbell, and Robert M. T. Hunter, were permitted to pass General Grant's lines before Petersburg, and proceed to Fortress Monroe; where [on board a steamer in Hampton Roads] they were met by Governor Seward, followed by President Lincoln; and a free, full conference was had."[99] — HORACE GREELEY, SOCIALIST FOUNDER OF THE NEW YORK *TRIBUNE*

• "Mr. [Alex. H.] Stephens, with clearness and precision, stated the conditions we had been instructed to place before President Lincoln and the dispositions we had in respect to them, and which we had supposed [based on communications with Francis P. Blair, Sr.] were more or less settled upon.
"President Lincoln [however] disclaimed all knowledge of any such proposed conditions, denied having given any sort of authority to any one to hold out any expectations of any arrangements of the kind being made, and declared that he would listen to no proposition which did not include an immediate recognition of the National [U.S.] authority in all the States and the abandonment of resistance to it.
"I confess that these answers did not surprise me, and that any other would have filled me with amazement."[100] — JOHN A. CAMPBELL, C.S. ASSISTANT SECRETARY OF WAR, 1887

Last meeting of Jefferson Davis and his cabinet, at the home of Amstead Burt, May 4, 1865. Left to right: Basil W. Duke, John C. Breckinridge, W. C. P. Breckinridge, Jefferson Davis, Judah P. Benjamin, S. W. Ferguson, Braxton Bragg, J. C. Vaughn, G. C. Dibrell.

APPENDIX B

HISTORICAL DATA ON THE U.S. STEAMER *RIVER QUEEN*

By Harry B. Turner, 1910

The U.S.S. *River Queen*, whose decks hosted the Hampton Roads Conference on February 3, 1865. In attendance were Alexander H. Stephens, John A. Campbell, Robert. M. T. Hunter, Abraham Lincoln, and William H. Seward.

Service of the *River Queen*: The steamer *River Queen* (one of the oldest side-wheelers now in service) was built at Keyport, N.J., in 1864, is 181 feet long, 28 1-2 feet beam, and of 587 tons. She was used by General [Ulysses S.] Grant as his private dispatch boat on the Potomac river during the last year of the Civil War, was later operated by the Newport Steamboat Company between Providence and Newport, and was in service across Nantucket sound as the running mate to the *Island Home* from 1873 to 1880—about eight years. The *River Queen* was first placed in service about the Vineyard and Nantucket sounds by the Vineyard company, which bought and operated her in 1871-2 (when the railroad was extended to Woods Hole) to replace the *Monohansett*, which had been chartered to the Old Colony railroad to run in connection with its Woods Hole branch. The *River Queen* was maintained by the Vineyard company about two years and was then sold for $60,000 to the Nantucket & Cape Cod Steamboat company, making her first trip to Nantucket on May 26, 1873—when she was nine years old—under command of Captain Cromwell.

It was the next year (1874) that the third radical change in the island steamboat service occurred, for that summer chronicled three noteworthy events—the inauguration of a two-boats-a-day schedule for the first time, the reconstruction of the steamboat wharf at Nantucket, and the erection of the restaurant building on the north side of the wharf (where the building remained until a few years ago, when it was purchased by Capt. John Killen and removed to a site on Pine street and converted into a dwelling). The fact that the island company had, through the purchase of the *River Queen*, two steamers available for its service to and from Nantucket, caused the directors to try the experiment of running "two-boats-a-day," in response to the earnest efforts made by the late Joseph S. Barney and others, in that direction, and the experiment proved so successful that the following summer (1875) the company commenced operating its first Sunday boat in connection with the two-boats-a-day service.

The *River Queen* was commanded by the late Captain George H. Brock of Nantucket, and continued in service until the autumn of 1881, when she was removed from the island service and for several years was chartered to various parties around New York and farther south. She returned to New Bedford in the early fall of 1891, and took the place of steamer *Nantucket* upon one occasion, while the latter boat was overhauling her boiler. During the following winter she was sold to the Mount Vernon & Marshall Hall Steamboat company, of Washington, D.C., and for nineteen years has been in service on the Potomac river.

It was on one of the passages across the sound on the *River Queen* with Captain Brock at the helm, that Miss Anna C. Starbuck (Mrs. A. E. Jenks) penned the following poem, which was published in the Rochester, N.Y., *Democrat*, early in July, 1878:

On board the steamer *River Queen*,
   In sight of my dear old island home,
My heart leaps forth to the perfect scene,

As I sip the spray of the ocean foam.

Good-bye to the heat and the city's din,
    Good-bye to prose with its leaden fold;
Come rhythmic dreams on the surf-bound shore,
    With peace and health and joy untold!

The winds shall sing a lullaby
    To all the past of grief and pain;
The ripple of the wavelet's laugh
    Shall soothe me with its low refrain.

O, perfect heart of a perfect God,
    That beats through the flow and the ebb o' the tide,
Thanks to Thy grace that brings me back,
    Back to the home of my love and pride!

Oh, happy isle on the ocean's breast,
    Thy ships are idle, thy commerce dead;
But the angel of health "sits up aloft"
    And sheds a halo o'er thy head!

    The *River Queen*, besides gaining fame as General Grant's dispatch boat, has considerable notoriety from the fact that it was on board her that the celebrated conference between President Lincoln of the United States and A. H. Stephens, the Vice President of the Southern Confederacy, took place, and a room on the upper deck is still shown as the one in which this noteworthy event occurred, Capt. Nathan B. Saunders, the veteran captain of the Fall River Line steamers (now retired), being in command of the *River Queen* at that period. Captain Saunders has a distinct recollection of President Lincoln, and states that the great emancipator frequently took passages on the steamer, returning from one of these trips on the boat barely forty-eight hours before he was assassinated.
    The *River Queen* is, at this late date, one of the most popular excursion boats on the Potomac river, and is a serviceable craft, although now forty-six years old. The accompanying picture of the steamer was taken as she lay at her pier on the Potomac a short time ago, and the model of the boat appears to have been changed but little since she left the Nantucket service.[101]

Deck and turret of the ironclad U.S.S. *Monitor*, July 1862.

"The First Battle Between Iron Ships of War": The ironclad frigate C.S.S. *Virginia* (right) vs. the ironclad warship U.S.S. *Monitor* (left), Hampton Roads, Virginia, March 8-9, 1862.

NOTES

1. Tarbell, Vol. 2, p. 144.
2. Rutherford, *Miss Rutherford's Scrap Book*, pp. 12-13.
3. Seabrook, *Abraham Lincoln Was a Liberal, Jefferson Davis Was a Conservative: The Missing Key to Understanding the American Civil War*, p. 55.
4. Schlüter, p. 23.
5. Woods, p. 47.
6. On Lincoln's socialistic, Marxist, and communist thoughts, ideas, and tendencies, see my books: 1) *Lincoln's War: The Real Cause, The Real Winner, the Real Loser*; 2) *Abraham Lincoln Was a Liberal, Jefferson Davis Was a Conservative: The Missing Key to Understanding the American Civil War*; 3) *Abraham Lincoln: The Southern View*. Also see McCarty, passim; Browder, passim; Benson and Kennedy, passim.
7. See J. W. Jones, TDMV, pp. 144, 200-201, 273.
8. Schlüter, p. 23.
9. Nichols, p. 59. (I have paraphrased this quote. L.S.)
10. *The Independent*, Vol. 102, No. 3724, June 5, 1920, p. 309. For more on this topic see my appendix, "Commies in the White House," in my book *Twelve Years in Hell: Victorian Southerners Expose the Myth of Reconstruction, 1865-1877*.
11. See Seabrook, *The Alexander H. Stephens Reader*, passim. See also, Pollard, LC, p. 178; J. H. Franklin, pp. 101, 111, 130, 149; Nicolay and Hay, ALCW, Vol. 1, p. 627.
12. *Confederate Veteran*, Vol. 12, 1904, p. 442.
13. *Confederate Veteran*, Vol. 35, 1927, p. 288.
14. Seabrook (ed.), *A Short History of the Confederate States of America* (J. Davis), p. 59.
15. Seabrook (ed.), *A Short History of the Confederate States of America* (J. Davis), pp. 55-56.
16. For more on this specific topic, see my book *Everything You Were Taught About the Civil War is Wrong, Ask a Southerner!*, pp. 34-39.
17. BISG (the "Book Industry Study Group"), for example—a Left-wing organization which describes itself as "the leading book trade association for standardized best practices, research and information, and events"—gives its BISAC ("Book Industry Standards and Communications") listing for works on the War for Southern Independence under the heading "Civil War Period, 1850-1877." Nearly all books published in the U.S.A. today are under the categorizational control of this progressive group located in New York City.
18. See e.g., Seabrook, *The Quotable Jefferson Davis*, pp. 30, 38, 76.
19. See e.g., Seabrook (ed.) *The Rise and Fall of the Confederate Government* (J. Davis), Vol. 1, pp. 55, 422; Vol. 2, pp. 4, 161, 454, 610. Besides using the term "Civil War" himself, President Davis cites numerous other individuals who use it as well.
20. See e.g., *Confederate Veteran*, Vol. 20, 1912, p. 122.
21. Minutes of the Eighth Annual Meeting, July 1898, p. 87.
22. See e.g., Fitzhugh, pp. 154, 287, 324; see also, e.g., Messer-Kruse, p. 103.
23. See Marx and Engels, passim.
24. For more on the nihilistic, atheistic, anti-life, anti-tradition, anti-American, anti-Constitution, anti-capitalism, anti-South agenda of the Victorian Republican Party (then the Liberal Party) and the modern Democratic Party (now the Liberal Party), otherwise known as "The Communist/Socialist Rules for Revolution," see Hasselberg, pp. 2350-2351; Lenin, passim; Marx and Engels, passim; B. Dodd, passim. Also see my book *What the Confederate Flag Means to Me: Americans Speak Out in Defense of Southern Honor, Heritage, and History*.
25. *Confederate Veteran*, Vol. 9, 1901, p. 318.
26. *Minutes U.C.V., Vol. 2. Proceedings of the Tenth Annual Meeting and Reunion of the United Confederate Veterans*, held at Louisville, Kentucky, May 30-June 3; 1900, New Orleans, LA: United Confederate Veterans, p. 25.

27. Gaslighting, one of the primary weapons of the Left, is defined as "deceiving a person or group of people through repetition of a constructed false narrative." Medically speaking it is defined as "a form of emotional abuse or psychological manipulation involving distorting the truth in order to confuse or create doubt in another person to the point where they begin to question their sanity or reality."
28. Bullock, p. 66.
29. *Vide supra*, pp. 15-16.
30. Seabrook, *Lincoln's War: The Real Cause, The Real Winner, the Real Loser*, p. 191.
31. Seabrook, *Twelve Years in Hell: Victorian Southerners Debunk the Myth of Reconstruction, 1865-1877*, p. 26.
32. For more on these topics see my book, *The Great Yankee Coverup: What the North Doesn't Want You to Know About Lincoln's War!*
33. For more on these topics see my books, *Abraham Lincoln Was a Liberal, Jefferson Davis Was a Conservative: The Missing Key to Understanding the American Civil War*, and *Lincoln's War: The Real Cause, the Real Winner, the Real Loser*.
34. *Vide infra*, p. 255.
35. *Vide infra*, p. 90.
36. *Vide infra*, p. 112.
37. Seabrook, *Abraham Lincoln: The Southern View* (4th edition), p. 244.
38. Seabrook, *Abraham Lincoln: The Southern View* (4th edition), p. 245.
39. Seabrook, *Abraham Lincoln: The Southern View* (4th edition), p. 252.
40. Seabrook, *Abraham Lincoln: The Southern View* (4th edition), p. 111.
41. Seabrook, *Abraham Lincoln: The Southern View* (4th edition), pp. 111-112.
42. *Vide infra*, p. 82.
43. For more on this topic see my book, *All We Ask is to be Let Alone: The Southern Secession Fact Book*.
44. Seabrook, *Abraham Lincoln: The Southern View* (4th edition), p. 62.
45. For more on these topics see my book, *Confederacy 101: Amazing Facts You Never Knew About America's Oldest Political Tradition*.
46. For more on this topic see my book, *Everything You Were Taught About African-Americans and the Civil War is Wrong, Ask a Southerner!*
47. *Recollections of Alexander H. Stephens: His Diary Kept When a Prisoner at Fort Warren, Boston Harbour, 1865*, pp. 148, 165-170, 326-332. [Kirkland's note.]
48. This statement is not entirely accurate. Toward the end of the War Lincoln was losing control of the Republican Party to its radical wing, the Republican socialist and communist element, which took over after Lincoln's assassination and was the primary instigator, implementor, and enforcer of the horrors of so-called "Reconstruction." For more on this topic see my book: *Twelve Years in Hell: Victorian Southerners Debunk the Myth of Reconstruction, 1865-1877*.
49. For a full discussion of this incident see my book, *Abraham Lincoln: The Southern View*.
50. Kirkland, pp. 196-258. Note: It might seem odd that I would begin a Southern-oriented book on the Hampton Roads Conference with an essay by a Yankee historian, Charles C. Kirkland of Vermont. However, Kirkland was not only a Southern supporter, and a true Copperhead, his work, cited here, received the grudging approval of *Confederate Veteran*—despite "falling into error at times." (See *Confederate Veteran*, Vol. 35, 1927, p. 288.) Yes, Kirkland's writing contains a number of historical errors and, of course, an overt Yankee point of view. Despite these shortcomings, he provides one of the most elaborate, well-researched, and well-written overviews of the Hampton Roads Conference I have come across, perfectly setting the stage for the many far less detailed essays, articles, and commentaries that I have included afterward. L.S.
51. My research has indeed uncovered what President Davis refers to as a "cabal" infecting the Lincoln administration. Although facts are scarce due to them having been ignored, suppressed, and even destroyed by the mainstream (one of the many participants), it is obvious that the numerous socialists and communists entrenched in both the then Left-wing Republican Party and U.S. military, had as one of their primary goals the sabotage, subversion, and overthrow of Lincoln's presidency *and* the U.S. Constitution, with the ultimate objective being to socialize then communize the United States of America. This is no mere conspiracy theory. This Left-wing campaign of evil continues today, stronger than ever, as any current observer of American sociopolitics can easily see. For more on these topics, see my entire catalog of books on American history, listed on pages 2 and 3 of this work.
52. Seabrook (editor), *The Rise and Fall of the Confederate States of America*, Vol. 2, pp. 617-625.
53. Reagan, pp. 166-179.

54. There are a number of important points to be raised here regarding Lincoln, his attitude toward blacks and slavery, and the Emancipation Proclamation. He states that: 1). He only issued the Emancipation Proclamation as a "war measure," not for the benefit of enslaved blacks. 2). Because of this, the proclamation would become "inoperative" when the War ended. Finally, 3). Only blacks who came under the proclamation's jurisdiction would remain free after the War, thus excluding enslaved blacks in various areas of the South (itemized in the proclamation) and *all* enslaved blacks in the North. For more on these topics see my book, *Abraham Lincoln: The Southern View*.
55. For a full discussion of this incident see my book, *Abraham Lincoln: The Southern View*.
56. For more on this topic see my book, *All We Ask is to be Let Alone: The Southern Secession Fact Book*.
57. Stephens, *A Constitutional View of the Late War Between the States: Its Causes, Character, Conduct and Results*, Vol. 2, pp. 598-623. For more on the thoughts and words of Stephens, see my books: *The Alexander H. Stephens Reader: Excerpts From the Works of a Confederate Founding Father*; and *The Quotable Alexander H. Stephens: Selections From the Writings and Speeches of the Confederacy's First Vice President*.
58. *Transactions of the Southern Historical Society*, Vols. 1-2, January-December 1874 and 1875, pp. 190-194.
59. *Southern Historical Society Papers*, Vol. 3, January-June 1877, pp. 173-176.
60. E. McPherson, p. 569.
61. E. McPherson, p. 570.
62. "War of the Rebellion," Series I, Volume XLVL, pages 505-513. [Carr's note.]
63. "War of the Rebellion," Series I, Volume XLVL, page 446; Stephens's "War Between the States," Volume II, page792. [Carr's note.]
64. "War of the Rebellion," Series I, Volume XLVL, page 446; Stephens's "War Between the States," Volume II, pages 621, 792, 623. [Carr's note.]
65. "Rise and Fall of the Confederate Government," Volume II, page 6. [Carr's note.]
66. Page 619. [Carr's note.]
67. Stephens's "War Between the States," Volume III, pages 576-624. [Carr's note.]
68. Page 264. [Carr's note.]
69. "Letters and Speeches," pages 198, 199. [Carr's note.]
70. *Confederate Veteran*, Vol. 25, 1917, pp. 57-66.
71. For a detailed and factual discussion on all three versions of the Emancipation Proclamation see my book, *Abraham Lincoln: The Southern View*.
72. *Confederate Veteran*, Vol. 24, 1916, pp. 249-256.
73. *Confederate Veteran*, Vol. 1, 1893, pp. 324-325.
74. Stephen's War Between the States; Campbell's Recollections. [Harrell's note.]
75. House Proceedings, Second Session, 38th Congress. [Harrell's note.]
76. A. K. McClure in the St. Louis *Globe Democrat*. [Harrell's note.] This entire entry: Harrell, pp. 104-106. Note: The title of this entry is mine. LS.
77. *Confederate Veteran*, Vol. 2, 1894, p. 124. Note: The title of this entry is mine. L.S.
78. *Confederate Veteran*, Vol. 3, 1895, p. 109. Note: The title of this entry is mine. L.S.
79. *Confederate Veteran*, Vol. 5, 1897, pp. 345-346.
80. *Confederate Veteran*, Vol. 5, 1897, pp. 347-349. Note: The title of this entry is mine. L.S.
81. *Confederate Veteran*, Vol. 6, 1898, pp. 328-332. Note: The title of this entry is mine. L.S.
82. *Confederate Veteran*, Vol. 9, 1901, pp. 168-170. Note: The title of this entry is mine. L.S.
83. *Confederate Veteran*, Vol. 9, 1901, pp. 228-229. Note: The title of this entry is mine. L.S.
84. This sentence may confuse those who are not aware of the great party platform switch that occurred during the 1896 presidential election, the year the then Conservative Democratic Party became the Conservative Republican Party and the then Liberal Republican Party became the Liberal Democratic Party. Thus by the time of Vest's death in 1904 and Reagan's death in 1905, Republicans had been Conservatives for eight and nine years respectively. The writer, quite probably Sumner A. Cunningham, the editor of *Confederate Veteran* at the time, seemed unaware of this massive change between America's two main political parties, and so wrote: "Not a word of denial or protest was entered by any of the *Republican* members present." However, by this date, 1904, this sentence should have read: "Not a word of denial or protest was entered by any of the *Democrat* members present." This confusion concerning the great party switch has dragged on for many decades, which is why a number of right-leaning Southern politicians were members of the Democratic Party well into late 20th Century—and even into the early 21st Century. As of this writing, early 2024, American bewilderment surrounding the history of the two parties continues. For a full

treatment of this important topic see my book, *Abraham Lincoln Was a Liberal, Jefferson Davis Was a Conservative: The Missing Key to Understanding the American Civil War*.

85. *Confederate Veteran*, Vol. 13, 1905, p. 268.
86. *Confederate Veteran*, Vol. 13, 1905, pp. 325-326. Note: The title of this entry is mine. L.S.
87. *Confederate Veteran*, Vol. 21, 1913, p. 470. Note: The title of this entry is mine. L.S.
88. *Confederate Veteran*, Vol. 22, 1914, pp. 263-264.
89. *Confederate Veteran*, Vol. 22, 1914, p. 451.
90. *Confederate Veteran*, Vol. 23, 1915, pp. 7-8, part of the insert of "Speech on Jefferson Davis." Note: The title of this entry is mine. L.S.
91. For more details surrounding this story, and more specifically Lincoln's *true* attitude toward blacks, see my book, *Abraham Lincoln: The Southern View*.
92. *Confederate Veteran*, Vol. 24, 1916, pp. 292-293. Note: The title of this entry is mine. L.S.
93. *Confederate Veteran*, Vol. 24, 1916, p. 388. Note: The title of this entry is mine. L.S.
94. *Confederate Veteran*, Vol. 30, 1922, p. 437. Note: The title of this entry is mine. L.S.
95. *Confederate Veteran*, Vol. 32, 1924, p. 334. Note: The title of this entry is mine. L.S.
96. *Confederate Veteran*, Vol. 32, 1924, p. 334. Note: The title of this entry is mine. L.S.
97. *Confederate Veteran*, Vol. 39, 1931, pp. 338-340. Note: The title of this entry is mine. L.S.
98. *Confederate Veteran*, Vol. 40, 1932, p. 324.
99. Larned, Vol. 11, p. 8961.
100. Campbell, p. 10.
101. Turner, pp. 66-68.

BIBLIOGRAPHY

And Suggested Reading

Alexander, Edward Porter. *Military Memoirs of a Confederate.* New York: Charles Scribner's Sons, 1907
Anderson, Mabel Washbourne. *Life of General Stand Watie: The Only Indian Brigadier General of the Confederate Army and the Last General to Surrender.* Pryor, OK: self-published, 1915.
Armstrong, J. M. *The Biographical Encyclopedia of Kentucky of the Dead and Living Men of the Nineteenth Century.* Cincinnati, OH: J. M. Armstrong and Co., 1878.
Ashe, Samuel A'Court. *History of North Carolina.* 2 vols. Greensboro, NC: Charles L. Van Noppen, 1908.
Benson, Al, Jr., and Walter Donald Kennedy. *Lincoln's Marxists.* Gretna, LA: Pelican, 2011.
Bond, P. S. (ed.). *Military Science and Tactics: A Text and Reference for the Reserve Officers' Training Corps.* Washington, D.C.: P. S. Bond Publishing Co., 1938.
Boyd, James P. *Parties, Problems, and Leaders of 1896: An Impartial Presentation of Living National Questions.* Chicago, IL: Publishers' Union, 1896.
Brock, Robert Alonzo (ed.). *Southern Historical Society Papers.* 52 vols. Richmond, VA: Southern Historical Society, 1876-1943.
Browder, Earl. *Lincoln and the Communists.* New York, NY: Workers Library Publishers, Inc., 1936.
Bryan, William Jennings. *The First Battle: A Story of the Campaign of 1896.* Chicago, IL: W. B. Conkey Co., 1896.
Bullock, Alonzo Mansfield. *Lincoln.* Appleton, WI: self-published, 1913.
Burns, James MacGregor. *The Vineyard of Liberty.* New York, NY: Alfred A. Knopf, 1982.
Campbell, John Archibald. *Reminiscences and Documents Relating to the Civil War During the Year 1865.* Baltimore, MD: John Murphy and Co., 1887.
Carpenter, Stephen D. *Logic of History - Five Hundred Political Texts: Being Concentrated Extracts of Abolitionism Also Results of Slavery Agitation and Emancipation Together With Sundry Chapters on Despotism, Usurpations and Frauds.* Madison, WI: self-published, 1864.
Christian, George Llewellyn. *Abraham Lincoln: An Address Delivered Before R. E. Lee Camp, No. 1 Confederate Veterans at Richmond, VA, October 29, 1909.* Richmond, VA: L. H. Jenkins, 1909.
———. *A Capitol Disaster: A Chapter of Reconstruction in Virginia.* Richmond, VA: self-published, 1915.
———. *Confederate Memories and Experiences.* Richmond, VA: self-published, 1915.
Commons, John R., David J. Saposs, Helen L. Sumner, E. B. Mittelman, H. E. Hoagland, John B. Andrews, Selig Perlman. *History of Labour in the United States.* New York: Macmillan Co., 1918.

Confederate Veteran (Sumner Archibald Cunningham, ed.). 40 vols (original forty year run). Nashville, TN: Confederate Veteran, 1893-1932.

Dean, Henry Clay. *Crimes of the Civil War, and Curse of the Funding System*. Baltimore, MD: self-published, 1869.

Dodd, Bella. *School of Darkness*. New York, NY: P. J. Kennedy and Sons, 1954.

Early, Jubal Anderson. *A Memoir of the Last Year of the War for Independence, in the Confederate States of America*. Lynchburg, VA: Charles W. Button, 1867.

Edmonds, George. *Facts and Falsehoods Concerning the War on the South, 1861-1865*. Memphis, TN: self-published, 1904.

Evans, Clement Anselm (ed.). *Confederate Military History*. 12 vols. Atlanta, GA: Confederate Publishing Co., 1899.

Ewing, E. W. R. *Northern Rebellion, Southern Secession*. Philadelphia, PA: The John C. Winston Co., 1904.

Fitzhugh, George. *Cannibals All! Or, Slaves Without Masters*. Richmond, VA: A. Morris, 1857.

Franklin, John Hope. *Reconstruction After the Civil War*. Chicago, IL: University of Chicago Press, 1961.

Gardiner, C. *Acts of the Republican Party as Seen by History*. Washington, D.C.: self-published, 1906.

Harrell, John M. *The Brooks and Baxter War: A History of the Reconstruction Period in Arkansas*. St. Louis, MO: self-published, 1893.

Hasselberg, P. D. (ed.). *Parliamentary Debates: First Session, Fortieth Parliament, 1982, House of Representatives* (Vol. 445). Wellington, New Zealand: Government Printer, 1982.

Hill, Benjamin Harvey. *The Union and Its Enemies: Speech of Hon. Benjamin H. Hill, of Georgia*. Washington, D.C.: Globe Printing and Publishing House, 1879.

Johnson, Robert Underwood, and Clarence Clough Buel (eds.). *Battles and Leaders of the Civil War*. 4 vols. New York, NY: The Century Co., 1884-1888.

Johnstone, Huger William. *Truth of War Conspiracy, 1861*. Idylwild, GA: H. W. Johnstone, 1921.

Jones, John William. *The Davis Memorial Volume Or Our Dead President, Jefferson Davis and the World's Tribute to His Memory*. Richmond, VA: B. F. Johnson, 1889.

Kamman, William F. *Socialism in German American Literature*. Philadelphia, PA: Americana Germanica Press, 1917.

Kirkland, Edward Chase. *The Peacemakers of 1864*. New York: Macmillan Co., 1927.

Larned, Josephus Nelson. *The New Larned History for Ready Reference, Reading, and Research*. 12 vols. Springfield, MA: C. A. Nichols, 1924.

Lenin, Vladimir. *"Left Wing" Communism: An Infantile Disorder*. Detroit, MI: The Marxian Educational Society, 1921.

Livermore, Thomas L. *Numbers and Losses in the Civil War in America, 1861-65*. 1900. Carlisle, PA: John Kallmann, 1996 ed.

Magliocca, Gerard N. *The Tragedy of William Jennings Bryan: Constitutional Law and the Politics of Backlash*. New Haven, CT: Yale University Press, 2011.

Marx, Karl, and Frederick Engels. *Manifesto of the Communist Party*. Chicago, IL: Charles H. Kerr and Co., 1906.

McCarty, Burke (ed.). *Little Sermons in Socialism by Abraham Lincoln*. Chicago, IL:

The Chicago Daily Socialist, 1910.
McPherson, Edward. *The Political History of the United States of America During the Period of Reconstruction*. Washington, D.C.: James J. Chapman, 1880.
McPherson, James M. *Abraham Lincoln and the Second American Revolution*. New York, NY: Oxford University Press, 1991.
Meriwether, Elizabeth Avery (pseudonym, "George Edmonds"). *Facts and Falsehoods Concerning the War on the South, 1861-1865*. Memphis, TN: A. R. Taylor and Co., 1904.
Messer-Kruse, Timothy. *The Yankee International: Marxism and the American Reform Tradition, 1848-1876*. Chapel Hill. NC: University of North Carolina Press, 1998.
Miller, Francis Trevelyan, and Robert S. Lanier (eds.). *The Photographic History of the Civil War*. 10 vols. New York, NY: The Review of Reviews Co., 1911.
Minutes of the Eighth Annual Meeting and Reunion of the United Confederate Veterans, Atlanta, GA, July 20-23, 1898. New Orleans, LA: United Confederate Veterans, 1907.
Minutes of the Ninth Annual Meeting and Reunion of the United Confederate Veterans, Charleston, SC, May 10-13, 1899. New Orleans, LA: United Confederate Veterans, 1907.
Minutes of the Twelfth Annual Meeting and Reunion of the United Confederate Veterans, Dallas, TX, April 22-25, 1902. New Orleans, LA: United Confederate Veterans, 1907.
Muzzey, David Saville. *The United States of America: Vol. 1, To the Civil War*. Boston, MA: Ginn and Co., 1922.
——. *The American Adventure: Vol. 2, From the Civil War*. 1924. New York, NY: Harper and Brothers, 1927 ed.
Nicolay, John G., and John Hay (eds.). *Abraham Lincoln: A History*. 10 vols. New York, NY: The Century Co., 1890.
——. *Complete Works of Abraham Lincoln*. 12 vols. 1894. New York, NY: Francis D. Tandy Co., 1905 ed.
——. *Abraham Lincoln: Complete Works*. 12 vols. 1894. New York, NY: The Century Co., 1907 ed.
ORA (full title: *The War of the Rebellion: A Compilation of the Official Records of the Union and Confederate Armies*). 128 vols. Washington, DC: Government Printing Office, 1880.
ORN (full title: *Official Records of the Union and Confederate Navies in the War of the Rebellion*). 30 vols. Washington, DC: Government Printing Office, 1894.
Pierson, Israel Coriell. *Zeta Psi Fraternity of North America, Semicentennial Biographical Catalogue*. New York: John C. Rankin, 1900.
Pollard, Edward Alfred. *The Lost Cause*. New York, NY: E. B. Treat and Co., 1867.
——. *Life of Jefferson Davis: With a Short History of the Southern Confederacy, Gathered Behind the Scenes in Richmond*. Philadelphia, PA: National Publishing Co., 1869.
Reagan, John Henniger. *Memoirs, with Special Reference to Secession and the Civil War*. New York: Neale Publishing Co., 1906.
Rhodes, James Ford. *History of the United States from the Compromise of 1850 to the Final Restoration of Home Rule at the South in 1877*. New York: Macmillan Co.,

1916.

Richardson, John Anderson. *Richardson's Defense of the South*. Atlanta, GA: A. B. Caldwell, 1914.

Rogers, William P. *The Three Secession Movements in the United States: Samuel J. Tilden, the Democratic Candidate for Presidency the Advisor, Aider and Abettor of the Great Secession Movement of 1860 and One of the Authors of the Infamous Resolution of 1864 His Claims as a Statesman and Reformer Considered*. Boston, MA: John Wilson and Son, 1876.

Ross, Earle Dudley. *The Liberal Republican Movement*. New York: Henry Holt and Co., 1919.

Rove, Karl. *The Triumph of William McKinley: Why the Election of 1896 Still Matters*. New York, NY: Simon and Schuster, 2015.

Rutherford, Mildred Lewis. *Truths of History: A Fair, Unbiased, Impartial, Unprejudiced and Conscientious Study of History*. Athens, GA: n.p., 1920.

——. *Miss Rutherford's Scrap Book: Valuable Information About the South*. Vol. 1, January 1923. Athens, GA: self-published, 1923.

Schlüter, Herman. *Lincoln, Labor and Slavery: A Chapter From the Social History of America*. New York: Socialist Literature Co., 1913.

Seabrook, Lochlainn. *Carnton Plantation Ghost Stories: True Tales of the Unexplained from Tennessee's Most Haunted Civil War House!* 2005. Franklin, TN, 2016 ed.

——. *Nathan Bedford Forrest: Southern Hero, American Patriot*. 2007. Franklin, TN, 2010 ed.

——. *Abraham Lincoln: The Southern View*. 2007. Franklin, TN: Sea Raven Press, 2013 ed.

——. *The McGavocks of Carnton Plantation: A Southern History - Celebrating One of Dixie's Most Noble Confederate Families and Their Tennessee Home*. 2008. Franklin, TN, 2011 ed.

——. *A Rebel Born: A Defense of Nathan Bedford Forrest*. 2010. Franklin, TN: Sea Raven Press, 2011 ed.

——. *Everything You Were Taught About the Civil War is Wrong, Ask a Southerner!* 2010. Franklin, TN: Sea Raven Press, revised 2019 ed.

——. *The Quotable Jefferson Davis: Selections From the Writings and Speeches of the Confederacy's First President*. Franklin, TN: Sea Raven Press, 2011.

——. *The Quotable Robert E. Lee: Selections From the Writings and Speeches of the South's Most Beloved Civil War General*. Franklin, TN: Sea Raven Press, 2011 Sesquicentennial Civil War Edition.

——. *Lincolnology: The Real Abraham Lincoln Revealed In His Own Words*. Franklin, TN: Sea Raven Press, 2011.

——. *The Unquotable Abraham Lincoln: The President's Quotes They Don't Want You To Know!* Franklin, TN: Sea Raven Press, 2011.

——. *Honest Jeff and Dishonest Abe: A Southern Children's Guide to the Civil War*. Franklin, TN: Sea Raven Press, 2012.

——. *Encyclopedia of the Battle of Franklin - A Comprehensive Guide to the Conflict that Changed the Civil War*. Franklin, TN: Sea Raven Press, 2012.

——. *The Quotable Nathan Bedford Forrest: Selections From the Writings and Speeches of the Confederacy's Most Brilliant Cavalryman*. Spring Hill, TN: Sea Raven Press, 2012.

———. *Forrest! 99 Reasons to Love Nathan Bedford Forrest*. Spring Hill, TN: Sea Raven Press, 2012.
———. *Give 'Em Hell Boys! The Complete Military Correspondence of Nathan Bedford Forrest*. Spring Hill, TN: Sea Raven Press, 2012.
———. *The Constitution of the Confederate States of America Explained: A Clause-by-Clause Study of the South's Magna Carta*. Spring Hill, TN: Sea Raven Press, 2012 Sesquicentennial Civil War Edition.
———. *The Great Impersonator: 99 Reasons to Dislike Abraham Lincoln*. Spring Hill, TN: Sea Raven Press, 2012.
———. *The Old Rebel: Robert E. Lee As He Was Seen By His Contemporaries*. Spring Hill, TN: Sea Raven Press, 2012 Sesquicentennial Civil War Edition.
———. *The Quotable Stonewall Jackson: Selections From the Writings and Speeches of the South's Most Famous General*. Spring Hill, TN: Sea Raven Press, 2012 Sesquicentennial Civil War Edition.
———. *Saddle, Sword, and Gun: A Biography of Nathan Bedford Forrest for Teens*. Spring Hill, TN: Sea Raven Press, 2013.
———. *The Alexander H. Stephens Reader: Excerpts From the Works of a Confederate Founding Father*. Spring Hill, TN: Sea Raven Press, 2013.
———. *The Quotable Alexander H. Stephens: Selections From the Writings and Speeches of the Confederacy's First Vice President*. Spring Hill, TN: Sea Raven Press, 2013 Sesquicentennial Civil War Edition.
———. *Give This Book to a Yankee! A Southern Guide to the Civil War for Northerners*. Spring Hill, TN: Sea Raven Press, 2014.
———. *The Articles of Confederation Explained: A Clause-by-Clause Study of America's First Constitution*. Spring Hill, TN: Sea Raven Press, 2014.
———. *Confederate Blood and Treasure: An Interview With Lochlainn Seabrook*. Spring Hill, TN: Sea Raven Press, 2015.
———. *Nathan Bedford Forrest and the Battle of Fort Pillow: Yankee Myth, Confederate Fact*. Spring Hill, TN: Sea Raven Press, 2015.
———. *Everything You Were Taught About American Slavery War is Wrong, Ask a Southerner!* Spring Hill, TN: Sea Raven Press, 2015.
———. *Confederacy 101: Amazing Facts You Never Knew About America's Oldest Political Tradition*. Spring Hill, TN: Sea Raven Press, 2015.
———. *The Great Yankee Coverup: What the North Doesn't Want You to Know About Lincoln's War!* Spring Hill, TN: Sea Raven Press, 2015.
———. *Slavery 101: Amazing Facts You Never Knew About America's "Peculiar Institution."* Spring Hill, TN: Sea Raven Press, 2015.
———. *Confederate Flag Facts: What Every American Should Know About Dixie's Southern Cross*. Spring Hill, TN: Sea Raven Press, 2016.
———. *Nathan Bedford Forrest and the Ku Klux Klan: Yankee Myth, Confederate Fact*. Spring Hill, TN: Sea Raven Press, 2016.
———. *Seabrook's Bible Dictionary of Traditional and Mystical Christian Doctrines*. Spring Hill, TN: Sea Raven Press, 2016.
———. *Everything You Were Taught About African-Americans and the Civil War is Wrong, Ask a Southerner!* Spring Hill, TN: Sea Raven Press, 2016.
———. *Nathan Bedford Forrest and African-Americans: Yankee Myth, Confederate Fact*. Spring Hill, TN: Sea Raven Press, 2016.

———. *Women in Gray: A Tribute to the Ladies Who Supported the Southern Confederacy*. Spring Hill, TN: Sea Raven Press, 2016.

———. *Lincoln's War: The Real Cause, the Real Winner, the Real Loser*. Spring Hill, TN: Sea Raven Press, 2016.

———. *The Unholy Crusade: Lincoln's Legacy of Destruction in the American South*. Spring Hill, TN: Sea Raven Press, 2017.

———. *Abraham Lincoln Was a Liberal, Jefferson Davis Was a Conservative: The Missing Key to Understanding the American Civil War*. Spring Hill, TN: Sea Raven Press, 2017.

———. *All We Ask is to be Let Alone: The Southern Secession Fact Book*. Spring Hill, TN: Sea Raven Press, 2017.

———. *The Ultimate Civil War Quiz Book: How Much Do You Really Know About America's Most Misunderstood Conflict?* Spring Hill, TN: Sea Raven Press, 2017.

———. *Rise Up and Call Them Blessed: Victorian Tributes to the Confederate Soldier, 1861-1901*. Spring Hill, TN: Sea Raven Press, 2017.

———. *Victorian Confederate Poetry: The Southern Cause in Verse, 1861-1901*. Spring Hill, TN: Sea Raven Press, 2018.

———. *Confederate Monuments: Why Every American Should Honor Confederate Soldiers and Their Memorials*. Spring Hill, TN: Sea Raven Press, 2018.

———. *The God of War: Nathan Bedford Forrest as He Was Seen by His Contemporaries*. Spring Hill, TN: Sea Raven Press, 2018.

———. *The Battle of Spring Hill: Recollections of Confederate and Union Soldiers*. Spring Hill, TN: Sea Raven Press, 2018.

———. *I Rode With Forrest! Confederate Soldiers Who Served With the World's Greatest Cavalry Leader*. Spring Hill, TN: Sea Raven Press, 2018.

———. *The Battle of Nashville: Recollections of Confederate and Union Soldiers*. Spring Hill, TN: Sea Raven Press, 2018.

———. *The Battle of Franklin: Recollections of Confederate and Union Soldiers*. Spring Hill, TN: Sea Raven Press, 2018.

———. *A Rebel Born: The Screenplay* (for the film). Written 2011. Franklin, TN: Sea Raven Press, 2020.

———. (ed.) *A Short History of the Confederate States of America* (Jefferson Davis, Belford Company, NY, 1890). A Sea Raven Press Reprint. Spring Hill, TN: Sea Raven Press, 2020.

———. (ed.) *Prison Life of Jefferson Davis: Embracing Details and Incidents in his Captivity, With Conversations on Topics of Public Interest* (John J. Craven, Sampson, Low, Son, and Marston, London, UK, 1866). A Sea Raven Press Reprint. Spring Hill, TN: Sea Raven Press, 2020.

———. *What the Confederate Flag Means to Me: Americans Speak Out in Defense of Southern Honor, Heritage, and History*. Spring Hill, TN: Sea Raven Press, 2021.

———. *Heroes of the Southern Confederacy: The Illustrated Book of Confederate Officials, Soldiers, and Civilians*. Spring Hill, TN: Sea Raven Press, 2021.

———. *Support Your Local Confederate: Wit and Humor in the Southern Confederacy*. Spring Hill, TN: Sea Raven Press, 2021.

———. *America's Three Constitutions: Complete Texts of the Articles of Confederation, Constitution of the United States of America, and Constitution of the Confederate States of America*. Spring Hill, TN: Sea Raven Press, 2021.

——. *Vintage Southern Cookbook: 2,000 Delicious Dishes From Dixie.* Spring Hill, TN: Sea Raven Press, 2021.

——. *The Bittersweet Bond: Race Relations in the Old South as Described by White and Black Southerners.* Spring Hill, TN: Sea Raven Press, 2022.

——. (ed.) *The Rise and Fall of the Confederate Government* (Jefferson Davis, D. Appleton, New York, 1881). 2 vols. A Sea Raven Press Facsimile Reprint. Spring Hill, TN: Sea Raven Press, 2022.

——. *I, Confederate: Why Dixie Seceded and Fought in the Words of Southern Soldiers.* Spring Hill, TN: Sea Raven Press, 2023.

——. *Twelve Years in Hell: Victorian Southerners Expose the Myth of Reconstruction, 1865-1877.* Cody, WY: Sea Raven Press, 2023.

——. *Seabrook's Complete Battle Book: The War Between the States, 1861-1865.* Cody, WY: Sea Raven Press, 2023.

Southern Historical Society Papers. Richmond, VA: Rev. J. William Jones.

Steel, Samuel Augustus. *The South Was Right.* Columbia, SC: R. L. Bryan Co., 1914.

Stephens, Alexander Hamilton. *Speech of Mr. Stephens, of Georgia, on the War and Taxation.* Washington, D.C.: J & G. Gideon, 1848.

——. *A Constitutional View of the Late War Between the States: Its Causes, Character, Conduct and Results.* 2 vols. Philadelphia, PA: National Publishing, Co., 1870.

——. *Recollections of Alexander H. Stephens: His Diary Kept When a Prisoner at Fort Warren, Boston Harbour, 1865.* New York, NY: Doubleday, Page, and Co., 1910.

Tarbell, Ida Minerva. *The Life of Abraham Lincoln: Drawn From Original Sources and Containing Many Speeches, Letters, and Telegrams Hitherto Unpublished.* 2 vols. 1895. New York: Lincoln History Society, 1924 ed.

Thompson, Holland. *The New South: A Chronicle of Social and Industrial Evolution.* New Haven, CT: Yale University Press, 1920.

Transactions of the Southern Historical Society. Baltimore, MD: Turnbull Brothers.

Turner, Harry B. *The Story of the Island Steamers.* Nantucket, MA: The Inquirer and Mirror Press, 1910.

Warner, Ezra J. *Generals in Gray: Lives of the Confederate Commanders.* 1959. Baton Rouge, LA: Louisiana State University Press, 1989 ed.

——. *Generals in Blue: Lives of the Union Commanders.* 1964. Baton Rouge, LA: Louisiana State University Press, 2006 ed.

Woods, Thomas E., Jr. *The Politically Incorrect Guide to American History.* Washington, D.C.: Regnery, 2004.

Naval operating base, Hampton Roads, Virginia.

INDEX

Abingdon, VA, 141, 252
abolition, 39, 61, 70, 110, 114, 115, 126, 127, 129, 154, 155, 172, 196, 203, 234, 257
abolition of slavery, 110, 114, 115, 126, 127, 129, 154, 155, 172, 196, 203, 234, 257
abolitionism, 269
abolitionist, 15
abolitionists, 15, 247, 248
account, 9, 54, 59, 62, 79, 87, 88, 93, 97, 100, 116, 117, 119, 125, 130, 131, 144-146, 148, 150, 152-157, 164, 165, 173, 179, 183-185, 210, 213, 214, 218, 222-224, 226, 232, 236, 238, 239, 244, 254, 255
action, 43-45, 49, 51, 53, 61, 63, 70, 90, 151, 165, 167, 168, 174, 181, 182, 219, 223, 228, 230, 253
Adams, Charles F., Sr., 96, 97, 130, 140, 146, 157, 185, 210, 212, 222
affair, 131, 151, 157, 211, 212, 246
Africa, 247
African Church, 72, 73, 150
agitators, 131
Alabama, 58, 174, 224, 236
alternative health, 291
amalgamation, 30, 38
America, 2, 3, 6, 12, 14, 16, 21, 23-25, 43, 81, 87, 93, 94, 119, 125, 130, 154, 232, 270-274
American Colonization Society, 29
American Party, 27
American Revolutionary War, 12, 13
American slavery, 2, 273, 293
Americans, 2, 15-17, 30, 42, 125, 273, 274
anarchy, 198
Anderson, Mrs. John H., 256
Anderson, Robert, 240
Annapolis, MD, 66, 70, 73

Antarctica, 291
Appalachia, 291
Appomattox Court House, 21, 75
Appomattox, VA, 258
Arkansas, 98, 157, 187, 199, 227, 229, 239, 270
armies, 33, 38, 43, 49, 51, 63, 72, 89, 92, 108, 134, 144, 146, 152, 158, 161, 168, 173, 175, 177, 195, 198, 204, 212, 217, 234, 242, 245, 254, 271
army, 15, 21, 38, 40, 42, 48, 51, 59-62, 87, 92, 94, 95, 108, 109, 121, 122, 151, 173, 175, 193, 198, 202, 212, 216, 220, 243, 245, 256, 257, 269
Articles of Confederation, 2, 273, 274
astronomy, 291
Atkins, Chet, 291
Atkins, John C. D., 52
Atkins, Smith D., 194
Atlanta Daily News, 228
Atlanta, GA, 48, 199, 218
Atlantic Ocean, 41
attack, 10, 48, 56, 218
Augusta Constitutionalist, 49
Augusta, GA, 49
Babcock, Orville E., 63, 70, 115, 214
Baldwin, John B., 52, 193
Baltimore, MD, 73
Barksdale, William, 194
Barney, Joseph S., 262
battle, 2, 13, 32, 41, 63, 76, 88, 172, 194, 248, 249, 264, 269, 272-275
Battle of Appomattox, 172, 247
Battle of Atlanta, 116
Battle of Bull Run, 41
Battle of Chattanooga, 47
Battle of Fort Sumter, 247
Battle of Fort Sumter, First, 13
Battle of Gettysburg, 47, 88, 247
Battle of Hampton Roads, 76
Battle of Missionary Ridge, 47

Battle of Vicksburg, 47, 88, 116
Beauvoir, MS, 199
Beecher, Henry W., 73
Benjamin, Judah P., 58, 60, 195, 260
Benning, Henry L., 56
Bible, 3, 273, 291
big government, 13
biography, 2, 3, 273, 291
Birmingham, AL, 167
black enlistment, 59
black population, 110
blacks, 29, 40, 110, 246
Blair family, 37, 61, 64, 65
Blair, Elizabeth, 38
Blair, Francis P., Jr., 41
Blair, Francis P., Sr., 37-43, 53, 54, 56, 58, 61, 62, 64, 65, 67, 73, 79, 89, 102, 107, 116, 117, 123, 126, 128, 131, 141-143, 151, 160, 170, 175, 178-181, 195, 236, 252, 259
Blair, Montgomery, 38, 40
blockade, 116, 117
Blount, Stephen W., 98, 157, 187, 224, 229, 239
Bocock, T. S., 95
Bolling, Edith, 291
Bolshevik Period, 27
bondage, 219, 225, 229
Boone, Pat, 291
border states, 37, 99, 188
Boston, MA, 8, 38
Boykin, F. C., 98, 157, 187
Bragg, Braxton, 260
Breckinridge, John C., 58, 260
Breckinridge, W. C. P., 260
Britain, 13, 97, 123, 124, 157, 178, 185, 222
British Empire, 13
British Parliament, 129
British soldiers, 236
Brock, George H., 262
Brooker, W. H., 199
Brown, Joseph E., 45, 48
Buchanan, Patrick J., 291
Buckner, Simon B., 86
Burt, Amstead, 260
C. S. House of Representatives, 150
C.S.A., 13, 21, 166, 202, 231, 238
Caesar, 128

Calhoun, John C., 58
Campbell, John A., 19, 21, 23, 32, 56, 59, 60, 65, 67-69, 71, 73, 79, 82, 90-92, 94, 104, 108, 109, 113, 117, 119, 120, 125, 130, 132, 133, 139, 141-145, 148-150, 152, 154, 161, 162, 165, 166, 168, 171, 180, 183, 193-195, 198, 200, 202, 204-206, 209, 216, 218, 222, 223, 233, 234, 237, 241, 252, 259, 261
Campbell, Joseph, 291
Canada, 174, 236
Candine forks, 129
Cape Fear River, 116
capital, 43, 52, 53, 72, 81
capitalism, 16
Carnton Plantation, 3, 272
Carr, Julian S., 139, 165, 248
Carson, Martha, 291
Cash, Johnny, 291
cattle, 59
cavalry, 2, 274
central government, 12, 44, 48
centralists, 11
centralization, 16
Charles I, King, 70, 111, 123, 129
Charleston, SC, 117
Chase, Salmon P., 176, 177
Cherokee, 21
Chicago Tribune, 8
Chicago, IL, 8
Chief Magistrate, 139, 145, 162
children, 3, 32, 113, 122, 177, 243, 246, 248-250
Christ, 3, 158, 159, 161, 168
Christian, 3, 16, 163, 248, 269, 273
Christianity, 3, 248
Christmas, 3
church, 72, 73, 150
cigars, 116, 214
citizens, 8, 13, 26, 28, 90, 93, 94, 131, 150, 156, 181, 183, 198, 222, 227, 237
City Point, VA, 47, 63, 66, 70, 115, 117, 170
civil rights, 45
Civil War, 2, 3, 11, 13, 14, 16, 27, 39, 42, 44, 51, 56, 58, 75, 128,

129, 131, 173, 231, 261, 269-274, 291, 293
clay, 174, 236, 270
Clay, Clement C., 174, 236
Cleveland, Henry, 141
colonization, 29
Colyar, Arthur S. C., 52, 195, 217
Combs, Bertram T., 291
commerce, 106, 116, 117, 178, 263
Committee on the Conduct of the War, 73
communism, 15, 270
communist, 11, 15, 16, 27, 37, 55, 62, 73, 127, 177, 270
communist revolution, 27
communists, 13, 24, 42, 81, 269
compensated emancipation, 198
Confederacy, 2, 3, 10, 29, 31, 33, 37, 39, 41-49, 53, 55-60, 67, 68, 72-75, 80-82, 91-93, 99, 100, 117, 120, 121, 124, 140, 147, 148, 151, 152, 158, 159, 162, 163, 166-168, 173, 180, 182-184, 188, 195, 197, 199, 201, 203, 205-209, 212, 214, 216, 222, 224, 227, 229, 231-233, 235, 237-239, 241-243, 245, 246, 254, 256, 257, 263, 271, 273, 274
Confederate, 2, 3, 9, 11, 12, 14, 16, 17, 19, 21-23, 28, 31, 32, 37, 38, 41-43, 45, 47, 49-55, 58-64, 66, 71, 75, 81, 82, 84, 86, 87, 89-100, 104, 107-111, 113, 114, 117-121, 123, 139, 140, 142, 144, 146-152, 154-158, 161-174, 177, 178, 181-189, 193, 195, 196, 199-202, 204-212, 214-218, 221-248, 250, 251, 253-258, 269-275, 291, 293
Confederate army, 21, 38, 243, 245, 269
Confederate authorities, 89, 92, 119, 174, 208, 215, 227, 230, 236, 239, 244
Confederate Cabinet, 231
Confederate capitol, 148
Confederate Cause, 47, 49, 207, 233
Confederate commissioners, 28, 31,

32, 61-64, 66, 75, 90-92, 95-98, 139, 140, 144, 147, 149, 156, 157, 162, 165, 166, 168-170, 172, 182-185, 187, 196, 205-208, 210-212, 216, 217, 221, 224, 225, 227-232, 239, 243, 254, 255, 257
Confederate Congress, 28, 51, 52, 81, 93, 95, 98, 100, 150, 155, 157, 161, 163, 166, 181, 183, 184, 187, 189, 195, 216, 222, 224, 229, 237, 238, 244, 246, 250, 255-257
Confederate flag, 2, 16, 273, 274, 293
Confederate forces, 61
Confederate generals, 14
Confederate government, 3, 14, 92, 100, 140, 148, 149, 151, 164, 166, 167, 172, 173, 189, 205, 226-229, 236, 237, 257, 275
Confederate military, 52, 270
Confederate navy, 47
confederate republic, 41
Confederate States, 2, 3, 9, 12, 19, 21, 23, 41, 43, 47, 51, 52, 71, 81, 82, 84, 86, 87, 89, 91-94, 104, 107-111, 113, 114, 117-121, 123, 147, 150-152, 154, 156, 158, 169, 171, 177, 178, 182, 183, 186, 195, 204-206, 208, 209, 211, 212, 214, 217, 221, 222, 232, 234, 237, 253, 254, 270, 273, 274
Confederate States of America, 2, 3, 12, 21, 23, 41, 43, 87, 93, 94, 119, 232, 270, 273, 274
Confederate veterans, 14, 17, 139, 166-168, 202, 217, 218, 243, 250, 269, 271
Confederate war, 45
Confederates, 14, 33, 38, 44, 62, 63, 70, 73, 81, 98, 106-108, 155, 186, 187, 200, 202, 203, 206, 215, 223, 224, 232-234, 238, 241, 251
confederation, 2, 106, 273, 274
confiscation, 38, 41, 55, 68, 70, 74, 109, 114, 121, 123, 164, 171, 196, 255

Confiscation Acts, 109, 114, 121, 171, 196
conformity, 79, 90, 143, 170
Congress, 6, 28, 31, 51, 52, 55, 58, 63, 67, 68, 70, 71, 74, 81-85, 88, 91, 93-100, 109-112, 119, 121-123, 134, 140, 143, 147, 148, 150, 151, 155, 157, 161-163, 166, 167, 177, 179, 181-189, 195-198, 200, 201, 203-206, 209, 211, 214-216, 219-225, 228, 229, 237, 238, 244-246, 250, 251, 255-257
Congressional Taylor Club, 101
Connecticut, 101
conservatism, 27
Conservatives, 11, 12, 27, 42, 231
consolidation, 12
Constitution, 2, 7, 14, 16, 17, 23, 25, 27, 30, 31, 39, 45, 70, 71, 81-87, 91-93, 96, 97, 110, 112, 114, 122, 134, 147, 169, 171, 182-184, 186, 201, 205-207, 209, 211, 219, 222, 223, 237, 248, 249, 273, 274
Constitution of the Confederate States, 2, 273, 274
constitutional law, 270
constitutional rights, 231, 250
conventions, 6, 245
Cook County, IL, 8
Cooke, Giles B., 250
copperhead, 75
cotton, 58, 116
Crawford, Cindy, 291
Crawfordsville, GA, 150, 200
crime, 55, 82, 182, 209, 217, 219, 225, 229
criminals, 73, 231
Crittenden Resolutions, 250
croakers, 49, 51
Cromwell, Oliver, 128
Cruise, Tom, 291
Cunningham, Sumner A., 218
Curtis, Judge, 58
Cyrus, Miley, 291
Davis, Jefferson, 7, 11, 12, 14, 23, 27, 28, 31-33, 37-39, 41-49, 51, 53, 54, 56, 58, 60, 61, 64, 71, 72, 74, 79, 80, 87-90, 92, 93, 95, 98, 100, 102, 116-119, 125, 130, 131, 139-142, 147-151, 156-158, 160, 162-166, 168-170, 172, 173, 179, 181-183, 186, 193-195, 199, 201, 202, 205-208, 211, 212, 215, 217, 218, 221, 227, 229, 234-237, 239, 241-244, 246, 250-255, 257, 258, 260
de Fontaine, Felix G., 140, 160, 163, 244
Deaderick, Chalmers, 235, 242
death, 3, 37, 42, 163, 172, 231
Debs, Eugene V., 11
debt, 70
debunk, 2, 27, 62
Declaration of Independence, 13, 48
Delaware, 198
Democratic Party, 11, 12, 16, 231
Demosthenes, 150
Dent, Julia B., 64, 65
Depression, 24
despotism, 45, 46, 53, 269
Dibrell, G. C., 260
disaster, 40, 43, 81, 207, 208, 269
discrimination, 26
disloyalty, 173
disorder, 24, 270
disunion, 43, 59
Dixie, 3, 275
Doaksville, OK, 21
Don (U.S. steamer), 43, 54
Duke, Basil W., 260
Duvall, Robert, 291
Earl of Oxford, 291
Early, Jubal A., 38
Eckert, Thomas T., 62, 64-66, 132, 133, 170, 197, 216
education, 16, 17, 26
educators, 291
election of 1896, 12
Emancipation Proclamation, 29, 69, 83, 96, 109, 110, 185, 196, 204, 211, 220, 234
empire, 13, 103, 120
employment, 174, 236
England, 8, 111, 124, 128, 169, 210
English, 11, 13, 15, 127
entertainment, 291
equal rights, 47

Europe, 55, 80, 180, 247
European royalty, 291
Fall River Line Steamers, 263
farmer, 69, 113
federal government, 109, 245, 257
Federals, 88
Ferguson, S. W., 260
Final Emancipation Proclamation, 185
Fitzpatrick, Benjamin, 224
Florida, 199
Flournoy, Thomas S., 57, 101
Floyd, John B., 38
Foote, Henry S., 51, 52
Foote, Shelby, 291
Forbes, John M., 38
Ford's Theater, 75
foreign commerce, 116
foreigners, 120
Forrest, Nathan B., 14, 21
Fort Caswell, 116
Fort Fisher, 70, 116, 181
Fort Gaines, 117
Fort Jackson, 117
Fort Macon, 117
Fort Morgan, 117
Fort Powell, 117
Fort Pulaski, 117
Fort St. Philip, 117
Fort Sumter, 13, 117, 169, 240, 243, 247
Fort Warren, 46, 140, 153, 226, 275
Fortress Monroe, 47, 65, 66, 100, 117, 132, 133, 143, 168, 173, 213, 253, 259
Founders, 41
Founding Fathers, 11, 31
Founding Generation, 27
Fourteenth Amendment, 24
France, 103, 104, 124
Frank Cheatham Camp, 208, 217
freedom, 25, 40, 55, 110, 220, 247, 248
Frémont, John C., 11
Fry, James B., 8
Gardner, Washington, 193, 235
Garland, Augustus H., 98, 157, 187, 227, 229, 239
garrisons, 178
gas, 51
gaslighting, 17, 24
gastronomy, 291
Gayheart, Rebecca, 291
genealogy, 291
George III, King, 13
Georgia, 45, 47-50, 57, 73, 98, 112, 140, 148, 157, 186, 187, 200, 226, 242, 245, 270, 275
Germany, 167
Gettysburg, PA, 47, 235
Gibson, Randall L., 38
Gilmore, James K., 173
God, 2, 3, 72, 95, 151, 158, 168, 169, 256, 263, 274
gold, 2, 5, 291
Goode, John, Jr., 141, 155, 156
Gordon, John B., 14, 17, 141, 160
government, 3, 12-14, 16, 27, 29, 30, 32, 41-44, 48, 51, 54, 60, 63, 68, 69, 80, 82, 83, 85, 87-89, 92-96, 100, 103-109, 111, 112, 114, 116, 120-122, 126-129, 131-134, 140, 142, 143, 148, 149, 151, 155, 156, 164, 166, 167, 172-175, 179, 180, 183-185, 189, 195, 197, 198, 203-205, 211, 219, 220, 226-229, 231, 232, 234-237, 240, 242, 243, 245, 247, 249, 253-255, 257, 270, 271, 275
Grady, Henry W., 230
Grant, Ulysses S., 21, 27, 55, 61-66, 74, 87, 100, 115, 116, 127, 132, 133, 175, 180, 196, 201, 202, 212, 216, 253, 258, 259, 261, 263
graves, 233, 258, 291
Graves, A. C., 258
Graves, Robert, 291
Great Britain, 13, 97, 123, 124, 157, 178, 185, 222
Great Emancipator, 263
Greeley, Horace, 60, 174, 196, 236, 238, 250
Green, B. W., 243
Green, Dr., 163
Green, E. A., 98, 140, 157, 186
Griffith, Andy, 291
Guadalupe Hidalgo, Treaty of, 131
Gulf of Mexico, 40, 41
habeas corpus, 45, 48, 50, 52, 53

Hampton Roads commissioners, 150
Hampton Roads Conference, 1, 2, 5, 6, 8-10, 15, 21, 23, 26, 27, 30-33, 37, 66, 70, 71, 73-75, 88, 90, 92, 97, 99, 136, 139-141, 147, 148, 150, 152, 153, 155, 156, 159, 163-166, 169, 170, 181, 185, 188, 199-202, 204, 205, 207, 208, 213, 215, 217, 219, 221, 223-225, 227, 233, 238, 243, 245, 247, 249, 251, 252, 254-257, 259, 261
Hampton Roads, VA, 66, 140, 145, 149, 156, 160, 166, 167, 195, 243
happiness, 3, 42, 51, 85
Harding, William G., 291
Harrell, John M., 199
Harrison, Burton M., 37
Hatch, William H., 61
hate, 26
hay, 12, 97, 140, 161, 271
Hay, John, 97
Herit, Samuel B., 199
Hickman, John P., 218
Hill, Benjamin H., 45, 141, 163, 230
history, 2, 3, 6, 8, 9, 12, 13, 15-17, 22-26, 28-31, 33, 35, 45, 70, 81, 87, 88, 90, 92, 93, 95, 98, 111, 123, 140, 141, 151, 152, 154, 158, 160, 163-166, 169, 182, 184, 187, 204, 205, 213, 216-218, 225, 226, 230-232, 235, 239, 240, 246, 256, 258, 269-272, 274, 275, 291
History of the War Between the States (Stephens), 87
hogs, 69, 113, 122, 246
Holcombe, James, 174, 236
Holden, William W., 44
home rule, 271
horses, 59
House of Representatives, 30, 31, 49-52, 71, 95, 96, 145, 149-151, 161, 184, 193, 195, 206, 219, 221, 226, 240, 254, 270
Houston Texas Post, 199
Houston, R. M., 240
Howell, Clark, 98, 140, 157, 186, 230
Howell, Evan P., 160, 228
humor, 3, 43, 246, 274, 291
Hunter, Robert M. T., 19, 21, 23, 31, 57-60, 64, 65, 67-69, 73, 79, 81, 82, 89, 91, 92, 94, 95, 107, 111, 113, 117, 119, 122-126, 130, 132, 133, 139, 141-145, 148-150, 152, 154, 155, 161, 162, 165, 166, 168, 171, 180, 183, 188, 193-195, 197, 198, 200, 202, 205, 206, 209, 214, 216, 218, 222, 232-234, 237, 241, 242, 252, 253, 259, 261
ignorance, 17, 18, 98, 123, 173, 186
Illinois, 69, 113, 173
India, 127
industry, 13
intelligence, 84, 174, 236
intolerance, 26
Ireland, 3
iron, 264
Island Home (steamer), 261
Jackson, Andrew, 41, 43
Jacques, James F., 173
James River, 133
jealousy, 68, 247
Jefferson Davis Historical Gold Medal, 2, 5, 291
Jefferson, Thomas, 11, 41, 43, 231
Jenks, Mrs. A. E., 262
Jesus, 3
Johnson, Andrew, 235
Johnston, Albert S., 38
Johnston, Joseph E., 14, 51, 87, 242
Jones, John, 270
Juarez, Benito, 40
Judd, Ashley, 291
Judd, Naomi, 291
Judd, Wynonna, 291
Kentucky, 17, 140, 141, 157, 252, 256, 269, 291
Keough, Riley, 291
kerosene, 63
Keyport, NJ, 261
Killen, John, 262
Kirkland, Edward C., 45, 75
Knox, Mrs. Stephen D., 248
Knoxville, TN, 235, 242

Ku Klux Klan, 2, 273
labor, 83, 246-248, 272
Lamar, Lucius Q. C., 230
Lane, Joseph, 58
law, 3, 6, 40, 45, 67, 68, 83, 84, 97, 105-107, 134, 186, 223, 270
Lee family, 37
Lee, Robert E., 21, 38, 46, 51, 55, 64, 87, 128, 168, 180, 193, 196, 198, 202, 212, 242, 248, 250, 257
Lee, Samuel P., 38, 47
Lee, Stephen D., 225, 239
Left-wing history-destroying tactics, 24-26, 28
Left-wing, 12, 13, 15, 16, 24, 26, 27, 30-32, 81, 127, 235
Left-wing party, 27
legislation, 49, 82, 91, 93, 147, 182, 183, 209, 222
Lexington, MA, 236
Liberal party, 16
liberalism, 10, 233
liberalization, 16
liberals, 11-13, 24, 26
libertarian, 11
liberty, 10, 41, 62, 87, 95, 128, 131, 153, 199, 269
Liberty Hall, 200
Lincoln administration, 48, 53, 81, 117, 240
Lincoln, Abraham, 8, 11, 13, 15-17, 20, 21, 23, 28, 29, 31, 33, 37, 38, 42, 46-49, 53, 56-58, 61-69, 71-74, 79-81, 83, 86, 88-97, 99, 100, 102, 104, 105, 108, 110-119, 121-126, 128-131, 133, 134, 139-152, 154-158, 160-164, 166-168, 170-172, 174, 175, 178-186, 188, 194, 195, 197, 199-209, 211-216, 218-221, 223, 224, 227-229, 231-239, 241-245, 247, 248, 250-254, 256, 257, 259, 261, 263
Lincoln's War, 2, 3, 11, 13, 16, 17, 27, 273, 274, 293
Lincoln's War (Seabrook), 16
Littig, R. F., 98, 157, 187
Little Rock, AR, 248

Longstreet, James, 14, 212
Lost Cause, 271
Louisiana, 68, 106, 194, 198, 275
Louisiana State University, 275
Louisville Courier-Journal, 140, 157, 167, 243
Louisville Democrat, 139, 140, 145
Louisville, KY, 167, 225
Loveless, Patty, 291
magic, 43
Magna Carta, 2, 273
malice, 17
Malvern (U.S.S. steamer), 136
martial law, 45
Marvin, Lee, 291
Marx, Karl, 15
Marxism, 271
Mary Martin (U.S. boat), 66
Maryland, 64, 122, 131, 141, 198, 252, 259
Massachusetts, 173
Massey, R. J., 98, 140, 157, 186, 218, 221, 223, 227, 229, 230, 238
Mathews, VA, 250
Maximilian I, 39, 89, 141, 148, 252
McBride, Mr., 228
McClellan, George B., 49, 62
McGavocks, 3, 272
McGraw, Tim, 291
McPherson, Edward, 201, 205, 213
Meade, George G., 64
Medill, Joseph, 8
memorial, 235, 270
memories, 15, 17, 177, 178, 269
men, 8, 21, 23, 37, 41, 43, 48, 57, 58, 60, 66, 86, 95, 97, 98, 103, 113, 122, 127, 142, 157, 163, 167, 172, 177, 179, 186, 187, 197, 199, 201, 206, 208, 217, 219, 225, 226, 229, 233, 240, 243, 248-250, 252, 254, 269
Menees, Thomas, 52
Meridian, MS, 240
Merrimack (U.S.S. vessel), 76
Mexico, 39-41, 56, 59, 68, 89, 103, 104, 108, 119, 120, 123, 124, 126, 141, 148, 155, 176, 252
military, 2, 14, 17, 21, 38, 45-47, 51-56, 59, 61, 64, 67, 68, 70,

71, 74, 75, 81, 83, 86, 88, 89,
  103, 107, 108, 115, 118, 120,
  121, 128, 131, 148, 150, 173,
  176, 180, 202, 212, 220, 226,
  236, 241, 249, 253, 269, 270,
  273, 291
military authorities, 52, 89
military despotism, 45, 46, 53
Miller, Hugh G., 256-258
Missionary Ridge, 47
Mississippi, 51, 52, 68, 98, 106, 117,
  157, 187, 194, 242, 243
Mississippi River, 117
Missouri, 99, 122, 157, 187, 198, 231
Mobile, AL, 117
monarchy, 13, 39
money, 59, 97, 126, 127, 134, 186,
  223, 248
Monitor (U.S.S. ironclad), 76, 264
Monohansett (U.S. steamer), 261
Monroe Doctrine, 53, 67, 71, 103,
  104, 108, 120, 125, 128, 141,
  148, 154, 155, 176, 177, 252
Montgomery County, MD, 175
Montgomery, AL, 93
Mooney, C. P. J., 235
Mosby, John S., 291
Mount Vernon & Marshall Hall
  Steamboat Company, 262
music, 291
musicians, 291
Mussolini, Benito, 12
Nantucket (steamer), 262
Nantucket & Cape Cod Steamboat
  Company, 262
Nantucket, MA, 261
Napoleon III, 39, 40, 43, 104, 128,
  158
Nashville American, 202
Nashville, TN, 208
national government, 16, 107, 108
nationalism, 12
nature, 3, 52, 55, 64, 71, 73, 106,
  151, 291
naval siege, 116
navies, 271
navy, 47, 220
Neal, Ralph J., 218
negro, 144
negroes, 59, 128, 129, 146, 155, 207,
  217
Nelson, Judge, 58
New England, 8, 169
New Jersey, 21
New Orleans, LA, 117
New South, 275
New Testament, 3
New York, 13, 62, 85, 86, 139, 164,
  174, 199, 236, 255-257, 259,
  262, 269-272, 275
New York Sun, 257
New York Times, 39, 164, 255
New York Tribune, 259
New York World, 39, 199
Newman, Charles G., 98, 157, 187
Newport Steamboat Company, 261
Newport, RI, 261
Nicolay, John G., 97
Ninth Amendment, 31
North, 2, 3, 8, 17, 27, 28, 31, 32, 37,
  39-41, 43, 44, 46-48, 50-55, 58,
  62, 67, 69-75, 99, 103, 108,
  110, 114, 116, 117, 120, 124,
  125, 127, 141, 151, 166, 167,
  169, 172, 174, 181, 188, 196,
  198, 203, 216, 217, 234, 236,
  241, 247-249, 252, 257, 262,
  269, 271, 273, 291
North Carolina, 39, 44, 50, 51, 116,
  117, 181, 198, 269, 271, 291
Northern abolitionists, 15
Northern capital, 52
Northern mythology, 10, 248
Northern states, 31, 99, 124, 188
Northerners, 2, 240, 273
Northernization, 16
Northwest, 8
Oath of Allegiance, 173
occupation, 120
Official Records, 172, 271
Ohio, 58
Oklahoma, 21, 159
Old Dominion Line, 76
Old South, 2, 3, 16, 275
onomastics, 291
Ord, Edward O. C., 61, 212
Ordinances of Secession, 245
Orr, James L., 98, 157, 187, 224,
  229, 238
Orr, John A., 52

Ould, Robert, 56, 116
Pacific Ocean, 41
parades, 135
paranormal, 3, 291
Parton, Dolly, 291
party, 11, 12, 15, 16, 26, 27, 33, 42, 44, 48, 49, 51, 62, 66, 73, 80, 81, 83, 84, 97, 121, 126, 127, 130, 132-134, 162, 174, 177, 186, 210, 223, 231, 245, 250, 270
patriotism, 96, 184, 206, 207, 219, 226, 230
patriots, 17, 207
peace, 8, 10, 23, 27, 28, 32, 37-40, 42, 44-46, 48-65, 67, 69-75, 79-82, 87-94, 97, 98, 102, 105, 109, 113, 115, 118, 126, 131, 132, 134, 141-147, 149, 151, 156, 158, 161, 162, 166-171, 173, 174, 178-183, 186, 187, 195, 197, 201, 204-209, 211, 213-216, 221-223, 227, 230, 234, 236, 238, 239, 242, 244-246, 249-257, 259, 263
peace negotiations, 44, 53, 59, 62, 118
peace party, 48, 49, 80, 174
peculiar institution, 41
Pendleton, Louis, 141
Pennsylvania, 46
Petersburg, VA, 61, 63, 259
Pilgrims, 169
Pitcairn, John, 236
plantation, 3, 59, 272
plantations, 169
plunder, 168
political parties, 11, 12, 176, 231
political party, 15
politically incorrect, 275
politics, 10, 50, 195, 270, 291
Pope, Edith D., 258
population, 93, 110, 122, 183
Porter, David D., 21, 197
potatoes, 122
Potomac River, 261-263
Preliminary Emancipation Proclamation, 185
presentism, 16
preservationist, 291

Presley, Elvis, 291
Presley, Lisa M., 291
Preston, William B., 38, 101
Price, Sterling, 242
pride, 94, 177, 250, 263
prisoners, 46, 56, 70, 88, 115, 116, 201, 226, 243
Prohibition, 85
prosperity, 42, 178
prostitution, 3
Providence, 195, 235, 261
Providence, RI, 261
Provisional Congress, 100, 188
provisions, 41, 95, 184
public meetings, 95, 195
racism, 25, 26
Radicals, 37, 73, 74
Raleigh Standard, 44
Raleigh, NC, 256
Reagan, John H., 28, 32, 89, 100, 139, 141, 156, 157, 161, 164, 166, 181, 202, 207, 217, 218, 226-228, 231, 232, 238, 239
rebellion, 40, 68, 96, 129, 140, 145, 146, 148, 149, 155, 185, 201, 205, 207, 213, 220, 270, 271
Rebels, 70, 236
Reconstruction, 2, 11, 27, 37, 62, 67, 68, 75, 119, 124, 168, 172, 247, 250, 262, 269-271, 275
refreshments, 66, 116, 214
religion, 291
Republican Party, 11, 12, 16, 27, 33, 42, 62, 73, 81, 231, 250, 270
restoration of the Union, 67, 102-104, 111, 113, 195, 234, 244, 245, 250
reunion, 14, 17, 32, 56, 60, 61, 67, 74, 124-126, 129, 154, 155, 202, 204, 210, 225, 247, 248, 271
revolution, 15, 16, 27, 53, 122, 231, 271
Revolutionary history, 235
Revolutionary War, 12, 13, 291
Rhode Island, 86
Richardson, John, 272
Richardson, Mr., 228
Richmond Examiner, 55
Richmond, VA, 39, 43, 49, 50,

53-55, 65, 70, 79, 89, 90, 102, 107, 116, 126, 131, 132, 140-142, 148, 149, 156, 158, 162, 168, 175, 181, 193, 195, 208, 212, 236, 239, 244-246, 252, 256, 257, 259
River Queen (U.S. steamer), 21, 23, 66, 100, 133, 144, 166, 168, 182, 195, 209, 213, 253, 261-263
Rocky Mountains, 18, 291
Roman Senate, 128
Romero, Matias, 40
Rucker, Edmund W., 291
Rucker, TN, 208
Rutherford, Mildred L., 8
Sabine (U.S.S. sailing frigate), 190
San Antonio, TX, 199, 239
San Augustine, TX, 224
Saunders, Nathan B., 263
Savannah River, 117
Savannah, GA, 195
school, 270
science, 269, 291
Scott, George C., 291
Scott, Winfield, 173, 236
Scylla, 128
Sea Raven Press, 3, 5, 6, 14, 18, 272-275, 293
Seabrook, Lochlainn, 33, 291, 293
secession, 2, 13, 30, 31, 44, 45, 48, 85, 116, 125, 142, 154, 232, 245, 247-249, 270-272, 274, 293
sectionalism, 249
securities, 114, 171
Seddon, James A., 51, 58
self-government, 32
servant, 66, 116, 135, 143, 144, 170, 214
servants, 91, 148, 209
servitude, 82, 91, 147, 182, 205, 209, 222, 237
Seward, William H., 20, 21, 23, 33, 42, 63, 65-68, 70, 74, 80, 81, 90, 94, 95, 97, 100, 105, 107-111, 113-115, 119-126, 129, 130, 132, 135, 140, 143, 144, 146, 152, 154, 157, 166, 168, 170, 171, 180, 182, 184, 185, 195, 196, 200, 204, 205, 207, 209, 210, 212, 218, 221, 222, 224, 232, 233, 237, 241, 250, 253, 259, 261
Sexton, Frank B., 98, 157, 187, 224, 229, 238
Shelby, Joseph O., 38
Sherman, William T., 21, 48, 87, 195, 197
ship displays, 135
shipping, 190
ships, 117, 169, 263, 264
siege, 88, 116
Silver Spring, MD, 37
Skaggs, Ricky, 291
slave, 69, 83, 110, 122, 127, 164, 169, 198, 219, 224, 225, 229, 239, 255
slave states, 198
slave trade, 127
slavery, 2, 15, 29, 32, 40, 63, 69, 70, 74, 82-84, 91, 95-97, 109, 110, 112-115, 122, 125-127, 129, 134, 143, 147, 154, 155, 169, 172, 174, 177, 182, 184-186, 194, 196, 198, 201, 203-206, 209-211, 214, 219-223, 229, 232, 234, 237, 244, 245, 247-250, 253, 257, 269, 272, 273, 293
slaves, 28, 29, 40, 42, 69, 70, 73, 90, 93, 96, 99, 110, 114, 115, 125, 127, 155-158, 167-169, 172, 173, 181, 184, 185, 188, 196, 199, 200, 202, 203, 206, 207, 213, 215, 219, 220, 225, 229, 233, 235, 238, 239, 241, 242, 246-248, 270
Smith, Edmund K., 242
Smith, Freeman, 119
Smith, Mr., 228
Smith, Truman, 101
Smith, William, 72
socialism, 12, 15, 270
socialist, 11, 15, 16, 37, 55, 62, 73, 127, 179, 259, 271, 272
socialists, 13, 24, 26, 42, 61, 69, 73-75, 81, 177, 248
soldiers, 2, 3, 28, 32, 63, 86, 94, 95, 233, 236, 241, 243, 248, 249,

274, 275, 291
Sons of Confederate Veterans, 14, 291
South, 2, 3, 5, 8, 10, 13, 14, 16, 17, 24, 25, 27-29, 31, 32, 37, 39-41, 43, 45-48, 50, 53-55, 67, 68, 70-72, 74, 87, 90, 98, 99, 107, 110, 114, 118, 121, 125, 127, 141-144, 151-153, 156-158, 161, 167-169, 172, 181, 187, 188, 196, 197, 199, 200, 202, 203, 215, 217, 220, 221, 224, 229, 233-235, 238, 240-243, 245-252, 254-256, 262, 270-272, 274, 275, 290, 291
South Carolina, 98, 157, 187, 224, 229, 238, 248
Southern abolitionists, 248
Southern capital, 43
Southern Cause, 3, 27, 43, 73, 274
Southern Confederacy, 2, 3, 31, 39, 158, 166-168, 257, 263, 271, 274
Southern Magazine, 154
Southern plantations, 169
Southern society, 256
Southern states, 29, 31, 41-43, 51, 69, 90, 99, 114, 124, 141, 149, 158, 167-169, 171, 177, 181, 188, 195, 227, 239, 245, 249, 250
Southerners, 2, 3, 11, 13, 14, 16, 27, 55, 62, 70, 71, 74, 241, 256, 275
Spottswood Hotel, 39
Stanton, Edwin M., 8, 47, 58, 61, 62, 65, 73, 74, 133, 253
Starbuck, Anna C., 262
State Department, 59
state sovereignty, 177
statesmen, 37, 127, 200, 256
states' rights, 11, 12
steamboat, 261, 262
Stephens, Alexander H., 11, 14, 19, 21, 23, 28, 29, 31, 45-49, 53, 56, 57, 59, 60, 64, 65, 67-70, 72, 79, 82, 87, 89, 91-94, 97-101, 119, 120, 123-125, 128, 130, 132, 133, 140, 142-145, 148-150, 152, 153, 156, 158,

160-166, 168, 169, 171, 173, 180, 181, 183, 184, 186-188, 193-195, 197, 198, 200, 202-206, 208, 209, 212-214, 216-218, 222-225, 227, 229, 230, 232-234, 236-239, 241, 243-245, 249, 252, 253, 255-257, 259, 261, 263, 291
Stephens, Linton, 45, 48, 49
Stevens, Thaddeus, 172
Stiles, John C., 251
Stowe, Harriet B., 247
Stubbs, William, 11
Sunshine Sisters, the, 291
Supreme Court, 56, 57, 90, 225
Suwanee Springs, FL, 199
Taylor, Richard, 14, 242
Taylor, Zachary, 67, 101, 119
telegraph, 62, 65, 133, 159
Tennessee, 3, 51, 52, 198, 272, 291
Tenth Amendment, 31, 86
Texas, 98, 156, 157, 187, 199, 229, 231
The Bittersweet Bond (Seabrook), 16
The Democrat, 231
the East, 37
The Hampton Roads Conference: The Southern View (Seabrook), 15, 33
The Herald, 145
The Land We Love, 224
the Left, 10, 16, 17, 24, 26, 27, 33, 243
The New York World, 199
the North, 2, 8, 27, 28, 31, 32, 37, 39-41, 43, 46-48, 50, 52-55, 58, 62, 67, 69-75, 99, 103, 108, 110, 114, 120, 124, 125, 127, 141, 151, 166, 167, 169, 172, 174, 188, 196, 203, 216, 217, 234, 236, 241, 247-249, 252, 257, 262, 273
The Rise and Fall of the Confederate Government (Davis), 14, 173
The Sentinel, 53, 55
The South, 8, 10, 13, 14, 17, 25, 28, 29, 31, 32, 39-41, 43, 45-48, 50, 55, 67, 68, 70-72, 74, 87, 90, 99, 107, 110, 114, 118, 121, 125, 127, 142-144, 151-153,

156, 158, 161, 167-169, 172, 181, 188, 196, 197, 199, 200, 202, 203, 217, 224, 229, 233-235, 240-243, 245, 247-251, 254-256, 270-272, 275, 290
Thirteenth Amendment, 29, 69, 110, 112, 134, 196
Thomas Colyar (U.S. boat), 66
Thomas, George H., 62
Thompson, Jacob, 174, 236
Tolley, William P., 208, 217
Toombs, Robert A., 45, 48, 58, 101, 119
Torpedo (C.S. steamer), 47
traditionalism, 12
traitors, 248-250
treason, 219, 225, 229, 243
Treaty of Guadalupe Hidalgo, 131
Trump, Donald J., Sr., 24
Turner, Harry B., 261
Turner, Josiah, 51
Twelve Years in Hell (Seabrook), 11
tyranny, 39
U.C.V., 17, 199, 217
U.D.C., 22
U.S. Constitution, 30, 31, 81
U.S. House of Representatives, 30, 31
U.S. military, 81
U.S.A., 13, 41
Union, 2, 6, 11, 12, 15, 28, 29, 39-42, 44-46, 58, 60, 63, 65, 67-70, 73, 86, 87, 90, 93, 96, 97, 102-106, 108, 111-113, 120, 122, 127, 128, 130, 134, 139, 140, 145, 146, 148-152, 154, 155, 157, 158, 161, 167-169, 174, 176, 181, 186, 193-200, 202, 203, 206, 210, 213, 214, 219, 223-225, 229, 231, 233-235, 238, 239, 241, 242, 244-246, 249-251, 253, 254, 256, 257, 269-271, 274, 275
Union army, 257
Union forces, 128
United Confederate Veterans, 14, 17, 139, 166-168, 217, 218, 243, 271
United States, 2, 6, 9, 12, 20, 23, 40, 47, 57, 63, 68, 71, 80-87, 89-99, 103, 104, 106, 108-110, 114, 119-121, 123, 124, 126, 130, 133, 134, 140, 143, 146-148, 151, 152, 154, 158, 161, 162, 168, 171, 173-176, 179, 180, 182-188, 195, 201, 202, 205-210, 212, 217-223, 225-227, 229, 231, 233, 236-240, 243, 247, 248, 251, 253-255, 263, 269, 271, 272, 274
United States government, 94, 126, 179, 240, 247, 254
United States of America, 2, 6, 23, 81, 87, 130, 271, 274
Vance, Zebulon B., 44, 198
Vaughn, J. C., 260
Vermont, 75
Vest, George G., 99, 157, 187, 231-233
Veterans Association, 225
Vicksburg, MS, 47, 235
Vietnam War, 24
violence, 26, 44, 202
Virginia, 6, 21, 23, 33, 52, 58, 68, 72, 76, 89, 98, 113, 122, 123, 135, 136, 155, 174, 186, 193, 194, 198, 236, 249, 250, 252, 258, 264, 269, 275, 291
Virginia (C.S.S. frigate), 76, 264
Virginia Convention, 250
votes, 69
Wallace, Judge, 224
war, 2, 3, 6, 8, 11-14, 16, 17, 19, 21, 23-25, 27-32, 37, 39-42, 44, 45, 47-51, 54, 56, 58-63, 68, 69, 71-75, 79, 81, 83, 86-88, 90, 92-100, 103-112, 114-116, 119, 121, 122, 124-129, 131, 133, 139, 141-143, 148, 152, 156, 158, 159, 163, 166, 168-170, 172-175, 177, 178, 181, 183-185, 187-189, 193-204, 208, 211, 212, 215, 216, 218-220, 223-228, 231, 233-235, 239-245, 247-249, 251-253, 255-257, 259, 261, 269-275, 291, 293
War Against Northern Aggression, 14
War Between the States, 2, 14, 24,

87, 92, 93, 119, 139, 169, 175, 196, 204, 212, 223, 226, 227, 231, 239, 248, 249, 251, 275
War Department, 8, 62
War for Southern Independence, 6, 12-14, 73
War for the Constitution, 14, 23
war measure, 29, 69, 110-112, 122, 196, 220
War of 1812, 124
Washington, 6, 8, 12, 39, 41, 43, 47, 52, 54, 56, 59-66, 70, 73, 79, 80, 83, 88-90, 94, 103, 104, 107, 117, 130, 132, 133, 141-144, 158, 161, 164, 168, 170, 173-176, 180, 200, 201, 216, 231, 235-237, 240, 242, 245, 252, 253, 262, 269-271, 275
Washington City, 60, 65, 79, 80, 90, 143, 170, 180, 237
Washington Globe, 177
Washington, D.C., 6, 12, 39, 43, 52, 54, 56, 61, 62, 66, 70, 73, 83, 88, 107, 132, 133, 142, 158, 168, 170, 174, 176, 200, 201, 236, 242, 252, 253, 262, 269-271, 275
Washington, George, 12, 41, 43, 52, 195, 231, 235
Washington, Mr., 59
Watie, Stand, 21
Watterson, Henry, 98, 140, 141, 157, 159, 160, 162, 167, 172, 186, 199, 216, 243-247, 249, 251, 257
wealth, 3
Welles, Gideon, 47
West India emancipation, 127
West Virginia, 68, 113, 123, 291
Whig Party, 12, 88
Whigs, 142
whipping, 25
White House, 11, 66
white population, 93, 183
Willich, August von, 15
Wilmington, DE, 116
Wilson, Woodrow, 291
Witherspoon, Reese, 291
Womack, Lee Ann, 291

women, 2, 3, 113, 122, 177, 226, 243, 274
Woods Hole, MA, 261
World War II, 24
Worth, Jonathan, 44
writing, 3, 14, 44, 63, 75, 93, 97, 101, 132, 133, 151, 152, 157, 158, 160, 163, 168, 184, 186, 213, 231, 241, 242, 244, 246, 250, 291
Wyoming, 5, 6, 33, 190
Wyoming (U.S.S. battleship), 190
xenophobia, 26
yacht races, 135
Yankee myth, 2, 273
Yankee slave ships, 169
Yankees, 33
Young, Bennett H., 17

Why the South fought...

MEET THE AUTHOR-EDITOR

NEO-VICTORIAN SCHOLAR LOCHLAINN SEABROOK, a descendant of the families of Alexander Hamilton Stephens, John Singleton Mosby, Edmund Winchester Rucker, and William Giles Harding, is a 7th generation Kentuckian and one of the most prolific and widely read writers in the world today. Known by literary critics as the "new Shelby Foote," the "American Robert Graves," the "Southern Joseph Campbell," and by his fans as the "Voice of the Traditional South," he is a recipient of the United Daughters of the Confederacy's prestigious Jefferson Davis Historical Gold Medal. A lifelong writer, the Sons of Confederate Veterans member has authored and edited books ranging in topics from history, politics, science, religion, spirituality, astronomy, entertainment, military, and biography, to nature, music, humor, gastronomy, etymology, onomastics, alternative health, genealogy, and the paranormal; books that his readers describe as "game changers," "transformative," and "life altering."

One of the world's most popular living historians, he is a 17th generation Southerner of Appalachian heritage who descends from dozens of patriotic Revolutionary War soldiers and Confederate soldiers from Kentucky, Tennessee, North Carolina, and Virginia. Also a history, wildlife, and nature preservationist, the well-respected polymath began life as a child prodigy, later maturing into an archetypal Renaissance Man. Besides being an accomplished and esteemed author, historian, biographer, creative, and Bible authority, the influential litterateur is also a Kentucky Colonel, eagle scout, entrepreneur, screenwriter, nature, wildlife, and landscape photographer and videographer, artist, graphic designer, content creator, genealogist, former history museum docent, and a former ranch hand, zookeeper, and wrangler. A songwriter (of some 3,000 songs in a dozen genres), he is also a film composer, multi-instrument musician, vocalist, session player, and music producer who has worked and performed with some of Nashville's top musicians and singers.

Currently Seabrook is the author and editor of nearly 100 adult and children's books (totaling some 30,000 pages and 15,000,000 words) that have earned him accolades from around the globe. His works, which have sold on every continent except Antarctica, have introduced hundreds of thousands to vital facts that have been left out of our mainstream books. He has been endorsed internationally by leading experts, museum curators, award-winning historians, bestselling authors, celebrities, filmmakers, noted scientists, well regarded educators, TV show hosts and producers, renowned military artists, venerable heritage organizations, and distinguished academicians of all races, creeds, and colors.

Of northern, western, and central European ancestry, he is the 6th great-grandson of the Earl of Oxford and a descendant of European royalty through his Kentucky father and West Virginia mother. His modern day cousins include: Johnny Cash, Elvis Presley, Lisa Marie Presley, Billy Ray and Miley Cyrus, Patty Loveless, Tim McGraw, Lee Ann Womack, Dolly Parton, Pat Boone, Naomi, Wynonna, and Ashley Judd, Ricky Skaggs, the Sunshine Sisters, Martha Carson, Chet Atkins, Patrick J. Buchanan, Cindy Crawford, Bertram Thomas Combs (Kentucky's 50th governor), Edith Bolling (second wife of President Woodrow Wilson), Andy Griffith, Riley Keough, George C. Scott, Robert Duvall, Reese Witherspoon, Lee Marvin, Rebecca Gayheart, and Tom Cruise.

A constitutionalist, avid outdoorsman, and gun rights advocate, Seabrook is the author of the international blockbuster, *Everything You Were Taught About the Civil War is Wrong, Ask a Southerner!* He lives with his wife and family in the magnificent Rocky Mountains, heart of the American West, where you will find him hiking, filming, and writing.

For more information on author Mr. Seabrook visit
LochlainnSeabrook.com

If you enjoyed this book you will be interested in Colonel Seabrook's popular related titles:

☛ ABRAHAM LINCOLN WAS A LIBERAL, JEFFERSON DAVIS WAS A CONSERVATIVE
☛ EVERYTHING YOU WERE TAUGHT ABOUT THE CIVIL WAR IS WRONG, ASK A SOUTHERNER!
☛ ALL WE ASK IS TO BE LET ALONE: THE SOUTHERN SECESSION FACT BOOK
☛ EVERYTHING YOU WERE TAUGHT ABOUT AMERICAN SLAVERY IS WRONG, ASK A SOUTHERNER!
☛ CONFEDERATE FLAG FACTS: WHAT EVERY AMERICAN SHOULD KNOW ABOUT DIXIE'S SOUTHERN CROSS
☛ LINCOLN'S WAR: THE REAL CAUSE, THE REAL WINNER, THE REAL LOSER

Available from Sea Raven Press and wherever fine books are sold

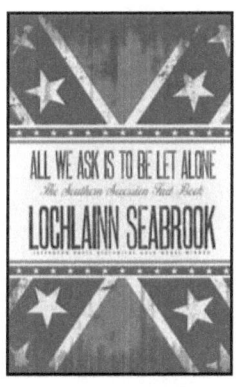

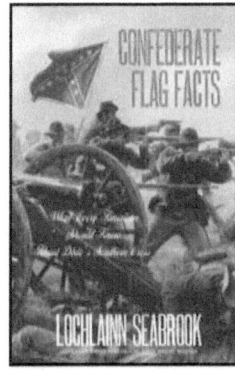

ALL OF OUR BOOK COVERS ARE AVAILABLE AS 11" X 17" COLOR POSTERS, SUITABLE FOR FRAMING

SeaRavenPress.com

www.ingramcontent.com/pod-product-compliance
Lightning Source LLC
Chambersburg PA
CBHW020351170426

43200CB00005B/132